A DOOMSDAY
READER

A DOOMSDAY READER

•

PROPHETS, PREDICTORS, AND HUCKSTERS OF SALVATION

•

Edited by Ted Daniels

NEW YORK UNIVERSITY PRESS
NEW YORK AND LONDON

NEW YORK UNIVERSITY PRESS
New York and London

Library of Congress Cataloging-in-Publication Data
A doomsday reader : prophets, predictors, and hucksters of
salvation / edited by Ted Daniels.
p.   cm.
Includes bibliographical references and index.
ISBN 0-8147-1908-2 (alk. paper)
ISBN 0-8147-1909-0 (pbk. : alk. paper)
1. Survivalism. 2. Millennialism. 3. Millennium. 4. Judgment Day.
5. Militia movements. 6. White supremacy movements.   I. Daniels,
Ted, 1939–
HM866 .D66 1999
301—dc21   99-6337
                    CIP

New York University Press books are printed on acid-free paper,
and their binding materials are chosen for strength and durability.

Manufactured in the United States of America

10 9 8 7 6 5 4 3 2 1

To Carol, Ben, and Isabel

for the long haul

CONTENTS

ACKNOWLEDGMENTS

A number of people helped this book get written. Dave Noble and John J. Reilly read early drafts and helped me find the direction I wound up taking. Hannah M. G. Shapero, Paul de Armond, and Catherine Wessinger provided background information and sources on some of the specialized areas of the book. I owe a special debt of gratitude to Jennifer Hammer, whose patient herding of its rambling author kept the book on its subject and on its schedule. My family's support was essential. Especially as the deadline approached, they absorbed without complaint a lot of my routine chores. I owe them a great deal.

A number of people also generously granted permission to use their own prophetic material. For a variety of reasons most of it didn't get into the book, but I am grateful to everyone who trusted me with their ideas.

INTRODUCTION

At Jonestown, Guyana, in November 1978 the Christian-Socialist movement called the Peoples Temple was in grave trouble. Jim Jones, the charismatic leader of the group, had recently moved most of his following to Guyana from the San Francisco Bay Area upon learning of a forthcoming exposé of his alleged abuse of his flock.

Relatives of members had raised enough concern about their well-being for California congressman Leo Ryan to visit Guyana to investigate. He found a community in disarray struggling to reestablish the life as a "family" it had known. He took some dissident followers with him as he left, but the party got no further than the airport before a Temple hit squad ambushed it and killed five of them, including Ryan. The infamous mass suicide of 922 members of the Temple followed.

"Jonestown" has since become a catchword in American political and religious rhetoric, summoning images of the destructiveness of religious belief carried too far. Its name is evoked at every subsequent occasion of religious violence: In 1993 when David Koresh's Branch Davidians died in Waco, at the deaths of the Solar Temple in 1994, the Montana Freemen siege in 1996, and especially the Heaven's Gate suicides the following year.

Jones belonged to a category of believer known as *millenarian,* that is, one who anticipates and hopes to participate in a sudden and dramatic change in the world order, perhaps with the guidance of supernatural beings. This book examines some of the practices and beliefs that engaged the world's attention near the end of the twentieth century. It includes writings produced by millenarian thinkers and movements, some of which are not readily available elsewhere. These texts are introduced by essays providing some religious and social context for the beliefs they express and the people who produced them.

Apocalypse and Millennium

The literal meaning of *apocalypse* is *unveiling*. Its use as the title of the biblical Book of Revelations gives it a special connotation of uncovering hidden knowledge. More recently it has come to suggest the ultimate battle. The word *millennium* has two meanings. In its most basic sense it refers to a span of a thousand years. But in the years near the turn of the calendar millennium this mundane fact began to carry more symbolic freight. Part of the reason for this is that in Christian belief millennium also refers to the prophesied return of Christ to earth at the end of history. Some Christians believe he will defeat Antichrist at Armageddon and found a kingdom whose capital will be the New Jerusalem. This kingdom will last a thousand years, terminating in the final release of Satan from hell and his ultimate destruction in another global war. This will be followed by the resurrection and last judgment of the dead.

These two meanings are often confused, so that it is easy to suppose a necessary coincidence. Some Christians assumed that the arrival of the year 2000 foretold Christ's return. But there is no necessary relationship between millennium as calendar date and the millennium as theological concept.

There appears to be a general anticipation that momentous events will occur sometime during the next thirty years or so. A generation seems to be the maximum shelf life of viable prophecy. Anything more remote lacks the compelling interest of imminent events. Prophecies are good for the long haul only when the prophet accumulates a good deal of charisma, like Nostradamus or Isaiah.

The millennium narrative begins when someone says the world is about to be changed in every respect, down to its very physical form. Commonly he or she foretells that nearly everyone will die, or at least suffer, in the process. But there is hope for a tiny number of very special people. They will survive the changes, and afterwards they will be (at least) demigods, who will live forever. In most millennial narratives the earth returns to its original condition: paradise.

This kind of prophecy involves a familiar form of belief about the end of human life as we know it. Many religious systems have their own versions of this account, and they all involve destruction of the way things are, a sort of cosmic recycling. Life starts over on a cleansed planet, with all things made new and perfect.

These ideas belong to a theological category called *eschatology*, which means ideas about last things. The word derives from a Greek root *eschaton*, meaning "last" or "farthest." Catherine Keller gives a somewhat more nuanced translation of this root word, saying it is best rendered as "edge." Her definition suggests an important distinction.[1] It is commonplace for prophets and commentators to refer to the millennium as "the end," but their focus ultimately is always on a new beginning. It is never the world that will end, but the world order. There is always something beyond the edge for the millenarian believer.

Many prophets warn of the end of the world, but if we read symbolically their threats of falling stars, massive earthquakes, famine, pestilence, and wars, we see that it is the order of the world, not the world itself, that will end. But these "earth changes," as the New Age movement calls them, serve to manifest the scope and seriousness of the change that is envisioned. Even the fabric of creation becomes a moral player in this titanic and final battle between the forces of good and evil, no matter how those forces are conceived.

What Is Millennialism?

Perhaps the most generally accepted definition of *millennialism* is Norman Cohn's. He calls it a type of salvationism: it must be collective, terrestrial, imminent (i.e., to be expected soon and suddenly), total (embodying perfection, not mere improvement), and brought on by a recognized supernatural agency.[2] There is room to argue with some of these points; many of the movements discussed in this book invoke no supernatural agency, for example, relying instead on conceptions of natural law to legitimize their predictions of change. However, a key point in Cohn's definition, one with which no one I know of has found fault, is that the salvation millennialism invokes is terrestrial: It will involve this world. Millennialism is not, or not only, a matter of finding an individual heavenly home. It promises rescue from evil, perhaps for everyone, but typically for a small community of believers. This salvation will happen in time, that is, in this world, not in a hereafter. However, in religious doctrines of apocalypse, it is placed at time's end: the present is always just on the cusp of dissolution into eternity.

Stephen O'Leary's study of apocalyptic persuasion makes it clear that Christian apocalyptic is a rhetorical drama proposing a solution to the problem of theodicy—that is, how evil can exist in a world created by a beneficent and omnipotent deity.[3] It is rhetorical in that it seeks to convince listeners of the correctness of its point of view, to persuade them that their lives have meaning, despite all the evidence to the contrary produced by the chaotic torments of history. It tells the believer that his or her presence on the planet will turn out to matter, to make an ultimate difference. The believer is promised a pivotal role in the ultimate drama in which the purpose of existence will finally be revealed. In its promise of ultimate eternal life, the apocalypse defeats the true core of evil: death. As O'Leary points out, time and evil are of the same substance, if only in that death is the prime marker of time's passage.[4]

Apocalypse is dramatic in that it presents the solution to the problem of evil in history in terms of a struggle between forces of good and evil. This is a problem that every human society, regardless of what religious tradition it adheres to, must grapple with. Apocalypse, like all myths, attempts to reconcile life's inherent contradictions in an explanatory story whose effect is to promote social order.[5] All societies have an account of creation, attributed to some superhuman, if not supernatural, force. These accounts of how we came to be all serve to provide a charter for society, a set of basic assumptions that, in the ordinary course of events, go unquestioned.[6] Nearly all such cosmologies propose that the earth was perfect at its beginning. Who would worship a god who couldn't make a perfect world?

Yet in every paradise there is a fall. Some event introduces change into paradise and turns it into the imperfect world we know. This change can be brought about by almost anything: sin, a mistake, or mere chance. Whatever it was, the world since has been bad, and life has been hard and painful.

Apocalypse promises the destruction of evil and a return to a perfected world. We, or at least the saints, will live out a blissful existence in Eden.

Paradise

It is an odd fact of apocalyptic literature that its paradises are sketchy. Their most striking attributes are the things they lack. In the once and future paradise there was and will be a complete absence of everything that makes us wretched. Food is free for all, so there is no need to toil. Health is perfect, and there is no death. Joyous sex is available for everyone who wants it; or else no one wants it at all.

Since paradise is perfect, it is incapable of change. Change in perfection can only transform it into something else, and something less. The situation of a dweller in paradise confronting change is like that of someone standing at the North Pole: every direction is south. Perfection can only degrade, and any change in paradise is subversive. Paradise is outside time, but it never lasts for more than a moment as millenarian communities try to enact it. It always fails, and when it does, it changes to its opposite: hell. In myths of perfection there is no middle ground, no compromise. Paradise, like everything else in the millennium, reflects a precarious shifting polarity.

As O'Leary points out, time is a major topic of every apocalypse, for they all propose its end.[7] It is never the geophysical world that is going to end in apocalypse, but its theological counterpart: the temporal, secular (literally, "of the ages"), unholy order of the world. Apocalypse proposes finally to force the world to make sense, to moralize and convert it—and at least some of its human inhabitants—to the holy realm it was originally supposed to be. As we shall see, however, not all millenarians proclaim a retrograde progress back to an original paradise; some propose something quite new: a millennium that undertakes our conversion into a new sort of humanity, free of sin and error and suffering.

Time

Time and change are the enemies of all fantasies of perfection, but time is not a simple notion. Broadly speaking there are two conceptions of time: it is either linear, a movement from a beginning to an end, or it is cyclical, with events repeating themselves over a span ranging from generations to immense eons, more or less as the seasons repeat themselves. There is no sense of finality in a cyclical system, or of any significant change. Things just go around as they always have. Even people are recycled, so to speak: They become ancestors who are then reborn in new generations.

Mircea Eliade classified the world's religions into two main streams: cosmic and historical. In cosmic religions based on agrarian modes of life, the cosmic source is periodically renewed in an endless process stimulated by human fecundity.[8] The cosmic creation is enacted ritually each new year. Since time is endless, religions of this type imagine no eschaton, and no apocalypse; death is simply a recycling, typically in a series of rebirths. African animist traditions are of this kind.

The main Chinese traditions—Confucianism and Taoism—also lack the notion of a decisive end of history. Confucianism is a pragmatic system of political morality that aims to harmonize the state with the will of heaven; accordingly, its aim is to convince the ruler and his or her people to abandon passion and self-interest in the service of harmony. Put another way, it requires conformity above all else. Since apocalypse is inherently revolutionary and therefore subversive, it is remote from the Confucian system, especially after Confucianism was adopted as state policy and made the basis of all Chinese education.

The Chinese pantheon involved a remote high god, accessible only to the spirits of the king's ancestors, who in turn were accessible only to the king.[9] There were other lesser gods as well, who do not figure in the general ordering of the universe. As with the animist systems, the king performed regular sacrifices to ensure the continuity of creation. In Taoism the cyclical view is emphasized. It is a contemplative system, with no concern for Confucianism's decorum, in which *tao* (the way) governs both the order of the universe and (proper) human lives. The basic principle is that everything reverts to its original status in the *tao*. In a partial prefiguring of Hegel's dialectic, it holds that extreme variations impose their own opposites. But Taosim offers a conservative worldview because all reform involves a return to origins, and the *tao* moves through everything, varying being with nonbeing, without end.

Shinto is similar to Confucianism in that, for most of Japanese history, it was considered identical to the state. It has no fixed doctrine and seems to function more as a set of attitudes than a way of devotion. It apparently originated as a system of agricultural rites. It has two distinct cosmologies, one involving a heaven and hell along with this world, the other involving a remote utopia aside from the world. But it imagines no end to things as they are.

The linear view of time is common to Judaism and its monotheistic offshoots. Other traditions were literate but none gave history the same importance, perhaps because few of them suffered so much from it. Few other peoples have such continuos challenge to their existence. In Judaism history itself is holy, a record of God's working on the earth for the benefit of his chosen people. The "people of the book" possessed literacy and made the most of it, turning the written word into an extension of memory that made change evident, history possible, death final, and a millennium necessary.

Revelation

The primary Christian apocalyptic text, the biblical Book of Revelation, is perhaps the most influential surviving instance of eschatological doctrine, certainly in the West. In O'Leary's dramatistic theory of apocalypse, the book combines elements of tragedy and comedy—that is, respectively, either a passage from happiness to misery or vice versa. I see some room for argument with this point, since in my observation apocalyptic texts invariably promise a desirable outcome *for the believer.* Nearly everyone else will suffer hideous torments, and that is either a cause for compassion or for *Schadenfreude,* depending on the purpose and point of view of the text and its reader. The consumers of apocalyptic prophecy may either be believers to be assured, in which case the primary purpose will be consolation (comedy), or outsiders to be converted, for whom the prophecy will issue a warning (tragedy). The balance of tragedy to comedy in any particular instance is going to depend, among other things, on which purpose a particular text is intended to serve.

In the case of the Book of Revelation, its purpose is clear. It was intended to be a quasi-secret testament of its author's vision, to be read in the Christian churches of his day. It carefully avoids any direct reference to Rome and the identity of the "Beast" (666 is a coded reference to the emperor Nero), but in its symbolic encoding and the grotesque monsters that swarm through its pages, it can have left little doubt in its hearers' minds what it referred to.

Ultimately all apocalypse ends in eternal bliss, no matter what use the narrative is put to. The Book of Revelation is no exception. Its audience is invited to identify with the faithful, not the beasts of the pit and the sea and their minions. Yes, we the hearers (the book was originally intended for reading aloud) will shudder at the latter's dreadful fate and resolve to avoid it, but ultimately we rejoice in salvation as prospective saints. As in any other comic narrative, tragedy looms along the way, but the protagonists always win and the antagonists always lose. This is necessary, given apocalypse's nature as a moral reconciliation of evil.

O'Leary demonstrates that Revelation's enduring hold on Christian believers (and others) owes as much to its literary strengths and peculiarities as to its canonical status in Christianity.[10] The book is fragmented and complex, defying critical analysis, but it nevertheless has strong artistic appeal. I suggest that much of its endurance as a source of speculation about the timing of the apocalypse can be attributed to the same symbolic coding that assured its deniability at the time of its writing. Its monsters, demons, and obscure dreamlike references uniquely combine the attributes of vividness and obscurity in a way that leaves them irresistible to believing analysts of every epoch. What can John have meant by the beast with ten horns, and what is the little horn? Who or what is the Whore of Babylon? These questions have no ultimate answer, since they can and have been taken to refer to nearly any conspicuous figure whose power seems mysterious or suspect.

Political Apocalypse

Secular and political millenarianism are just beginning to attract the kind of analytic attention that for years has been paid to their religious counterparts, in part because the conclusion that millenarianism is inherently political is becoming inescapable. To some degree this can be said of religious texts in general. Religion is political to the extent that it attempts to govern access to power and to prescribe its exercise.

Martha F. Lee makes this point in her *Earth First!: Environmental Apocalypse*. Following Clifford Geertz and others, she observes that, their purported origins aside, political ideology and religious dogma share most attributes in common.[11] Both consist of "basic assumptions" about humanity and its place in the world. The two arenas often remain rigidly separated, especially in their own self-presentations, and frequently come into conflict, but at the analytical level the similarities are striking. Religion and politics are competing gladiators in the arena of opinion, where they must also compete with science. Neither politics nor science ordinarily makes any reference to spiritual matters, of course, and ordinarily both reject any attempt to find it in their texts; nevertheless, like religion they attempt to provide and govern a social worldview. Lee observes that it is therefore difficult to classify any given movement with millenarian ideas as either political or religious. I suggest that the attempt be abandoned in recognition that the two are not ultimately distinct.

Philip Lamy observes that strictly secular millenarian ideas propose a human apocalypse.[12] In other words, in the secular apocalypse humans are both the promoters of evil and the agents of salvation. Individual self-salvation is the best we can hope for in most of the movements he discusses, though there are others where salvation will be collective. Lamy notes that many such secular millenarian movements are closely allied with, if not actually part of, nationalist movements, though the latter have "purely political" goals in mind.[13] It is not clear what distinction he intends to draw here, since all apocalypses propose political aims: it is the order of this world that is to be redeemed, and that is a political action, regardless of the nature of the agency that will bring it about. The observation that millennialism has political aims appears in any number of analytical writings on millennialism and apocalypse, but few if any observers have reached the conclusion that seems to me inescapable: that millennialism is inherently political because it arises from the perception of political evil—the abuse of power—which it seeks to remedy.[14]

The failure to observe the inherently political nature of millenarianism may arise from an unspoken assumption that politics necessarily includes direct involvement in political activity—everything from getting out the vote to staging coups to mailing bombs. Millenarian movements frequently (but by no means invariably) withdraw from the world in an effort to protect their purity from contamination by the world's corruption. They oppose and frequently renounce the world's order. But these actions are in fact political. Rejection of politics is political. The act of withdrawing condemns that which will not change. O'Leary's point that millennialism is rhetorical furthers this argument. Apocalypse is an argument about power, and it is not always addressed to its adherents. Apocalyptic movements often make proclamations across the ideological divide, to those on the outside.

Why It Is

In "ordinary" times, if there are such things, fantasies of world salvation are usually the province of the crazed and the desperate, of people on society's fringes. We are tempted to dismiss both the ideas and the people who support them with a shrug and a snicker and go on with life's routine business. Why concern ourselves with such fantasies?

There are several good reasons to do so. First, none of us is ultimately immune to the millennium's strange attractor. It promises to provide the ultimate meaning to our lives—a chance for a starring role in the terminal drama of all creation, the moment when the meaning of everything will finally be revealed. More than that, in times of turmoil and change it promises us certainty, salvation from death and ruin, and a measure of control over chaotic conditions. Finally, a passion for glory lurks somewhere in even the most bovine heart. Few things speak to this passion like the millennium. Ego is rarely remote from apocalyptic drama, though it may not appear overtly. Otto Friedrich, speaking of the *Danse Macabre* that arose in Europe in response to the Black Death of the fourteenth century, quotes Johan Huizinga on the "self-seeking" quality of the vision that inspired it. As with all apocalyptic visions, it was ultimately driven by the fear of personal death.[15]

Hitler was a millenarian. His speeches emphasize the theme of salvation for *das Volk* from their oppressors, tangible and chimerical. Marxism is another secular millennium, with its promise of a superhuman inevitability to history and an apocalyptic dialectic ending in the workers' paradise. It would be well to understand not just the nature of apocalypse, but also the desires that drive it, sometimes, to wrench history out of joint.

The American politics of apocalypse has left and right wings that correspond closely to those of ordinary politics. Right-wing apocalypse focuses on the battle, the final showdown that will, in an ultimate triumph of the conservative impulse, return the earth to the state it occupied at the beginning. We will return to Elysium when the wicked structures of the world are shucked off and burned away. Militia movements, for example, pretend we can restore the pristine Eden of the United States at its beginning—somewhere between the ratification of the Constitution (the creation) and the adoption of the Fourteenth Amendment, which opened citizenship to nonwhites (the fall).

The leftmost wing of the American millennium is the New Age, where there will be no final battle, only a glorious transition to a future of sheer bliss. In this system there is no evil, only the perception of evil; therefore, perception is all that has to change. We need only recognize that the material world is delusion in order to make an "evolutionary leap" into a higher "dimension" of existence, where the Light Workers (those whom Christians call the Saved) will live, eternally disembodied and all-knowing. The difference is just what we would expect: The right wing imagines perfection only in the past, the left in what's to come. This distinction is not absolute, but the relative emphasis a group places on apocalypse in relation to the millennium is a pretty good index of where it falls on the left-to-right scale.[16]

The Prophet and the Following

Every social order's founding myths contain instructions on how to attain, if not actual paradise, at least an earthly approximation of it. But what happens when that paradise, once accessible by certain well-known means, suddenly becomes unavailable? When it becomes impossible to thrive, perhaps even survive, by the familiar commonsense means? A new system, a new way of viewing and making sense of the world and history must be found, or the social form sustained by the old one will perish. The way has to be reopened. Salvation has to become attainable again through a radical and total revision of the world and the rules that govern it. The prophet shows the way.

A few people claim occasionally to touch the ultimate source of power, rarely of their own choice. Some virtuosi of the holy learn to invite this contact, but never to command it. An even smaller number find that it comes to command them. Prophets fall into this last category. These poets of cosmic meaning are probably among us all the time, often unnoticed like stars at noon. It is during the darker periods of social crisis that prophets begin to appear, like stars emerging at dusk. They and their messages address a deep abyss of need. They bring messages from God about the road to salvation. When most of us don't feel any particular need to be saved, prophets can be dismissed as madmen. They only enter the category of divine messenger when the context is right: when the rules of ordinary humanity no longer work. When all our own best efforts fail we must have salvation, and that is what the prophet offers.

It is a commonplace that millennial prophecy always fails. However, this observation assumes that prediction is the essence of prophecy. I would suggest instead that prediction is a relatively minor part of the prophetic mission. Prophecy's real task is to warn the world of God's anger and tell it what God will do if it does not mend its ways. If the prophecy is well constructed, its warnings will be conditional. The terrible dangers it describes are what will happen *unless* the people heed the prophetic warning. If the people reform, or the prophet's followers pray with enough devotion, then God will withhold his wrath for the time being; the prophet's movement will have saved the world. But God will lose patience eventually, even if not at the predicted moment. So the prophecy as such does not fail where believers are concerned, even though a particular prediction goes unfulfilled. The only real prophetic failure is in cases like Noah's, where no one outside his own family listened, and the world was destroyed.[17]

Conversion and Apocalypse

True conversion is one of the marks of a prophet. Conversion effects radical, literally soul-shaking change to the person who undergoes it. It is personal apocalypse, just as apocalypse is a planetary conversion, and both are a final healing from which there will be no looking back. The therapeutic value of conversion has been noted at least since William James's *The Varieties of Religious Experience.* The prophet finds a new unity in the self, a new happiness definitive of the process of conversion.[18]

Prophets are outsiders. They generally come from the margins of their societies, or at any rate spend a good deal of time there, possibly following a severe crisis. Where they are visionaries, the vision typically comes upon them following a personal crisis, often involving what is popularly known as a "near-death experience."

A case in point is provided by the career of Handsome Lake.[19] At the time of Handsome Lake's vision (1799) the Seneca Nation had gone from one of the three major powers in northern North America to a rural proletariat in extreme deprivation and hardship in the course of a single generation. Alcoholism was rampant, and Handsome Lake suffered heavily from it and other miseries typical of his people, among whom he was a chief, albeit a despised one.

Handsome Lake's alcoholism and other troubles had made him so ill that he was bedridden, and that is when he had his vision. It seems to have been a near-death experience; Anthony Wallace reports that Handsome Lake's relatives were preparing to bury him when he revived. The gist of the vision was that in order to survive the Seneca had to adopt white agricultural practices, but otherwise stick to their old ways as much as possible. Following this vision and others, Handsome Lake became a widely known and well-respected prophet. He quickly recovered from his ailments, giving up alcohol for the rest of his life and leading his people to do likewise. This vision did in fact save the people, and Handsome Lake is revered among them today.

The prophet's personal conversion conveys charisma. It lends the prophet unshakable confidence and complete dedication. In profound conversion there is no room for doubt. This confidence is a powerful attractor. It suggests to those drawn by it that a person—frequently but not necessarily a leader—has unusual or even sacred powers. Such a person can do the impossible—defeat Satan's allies, bring salvation to the faithful—because he or she is God's chosen messenger. Charisma is frequently accompanied by powerful sexual attraction.[20]

Not everyone is susceptible to this appeal. Charisma also has a powerful negative component, and prophets' enemies loathe them as sincerely as their followers love them.

It is crucial to understanding charisma that it is negotiated.[21] It does not exist without recognition, just as there is no prophecy without believers. Charisma has to be seen to be believed. This places a terrible stress upon the prophet, who must produce a daily stream of miracles to keep the faithful as fully committed to the mission as she or he is.[22] The production of miracles is not as arduous as it sounds, however, for in a milieu ruled by charisma, every desirable outcome takes on the luster of the miraculous. For example, in an online forum devoted to prophesy one young man related the story of a "miracle" that occurred following his mother's loss of a special rosary at a prayer meeting. The writer's father's "stubbornness"—he refused to go back and look for it—proved to be a means of God's glory, since the writer asked God to bring it back. "Miraculously the rosary reappeared in our car several days after. God made it reappear on the ledge behind the back seat under the back window to show it was a miracle because my mother doesn't place her rosaries back there."[23]

But charisma exists only in the moment of its creation; it must constantly be refreshed.[24] This helps account for the odd anomaly that many prophets break their own rules. David Koresh indulged in promiscuous sex with his female followers while imposing chastity on the men. In the Davidians' terms this was legitimate because Koresh was God's anointed, and therefore he was free from the rules that bind lesser men. His "sin" proved the point, because it did not damage his holiness, whereas in his own terms it would have corrupted his followers.

Who are these followers? What sort of person chooses to devote life itself to bringing about the climax of humanity's story? A small but significant number of people fervently believe in the drama of apocalypse and the prophets who propose it; they sacrifice everything for it. It is a drama that is repeated over and over, nearly everywhere at some time or another, and it always has the same conclusion in the world's perception: failure. But the world is the millennium's eternal opponent, and the believer's perception is necessarily contrary to the world's.

The world order does change gradually across the centuries, though with little improvement where justice and peace are concerned. But this commonsense view of history is not at all what believers typically perceive. Much of the rest of this book will examine the ways believers find to overrule the world and its common sense. The faithful continue to believe in the millennium, commit themselves to it, and reenact it.

At least in Western societies, these believers frequently belong to a type sociologists call "seekers:" people whose lives are chiefly devoted to a career of self-improvement.[25] They are "spiritual shoppers" who move from one promise of a more or less ultimate fulfillment to another, searching for an undefinable goal. They frequently are educated in the occult milieu, where mysterious forces are seen to be at work on human affairs, guiding and thwarting them. Knowledge of the sources of these powers is deemed useful in controlling and improving one's destiny.

This quest cannot succeed but it is a striking fact that it also cannot fail. In the seeker's worldview, everything that happens contributes to the goal.

Failure simply does not exist: no ideal pursued, no spiritual exercise attempted, can fail to add to spiritual growth. All stages of the process have equal value, and no part of the quest is rejected.

A seeker is a spiritual consumer. In exact parallel to the consumer of material goods, there is no goal, no final achievement. The grail eternally retreats and there is always more to buy. And what the seeker ultimately seeks is meaning. Often this is a meaning that will put the seeker at the center of creation and give him or her a high seat at its climax in the millennium.

Why This Book?

This book grows out of a collection of the literature of twentieth-century chiliastic belief.[26] The collection is meant for scholars, journalists, and others interested in understanding beliefs in the end of the world and what they mean in context. These ideas have important historical effects; the collection is their archive. This book aims to provide readers with material drawn from a wide variety of sources, though I certainly make no claim to inclusiveness. The book contains no material from the Nation of Islam, for instance, or from Native American sources, due to space constraints.

The texts in this book support, in a variety of ways, my major claim about apocalypticism: that it is inherently political and that we might come to understand it better by taking that aspect of it fully into account. Some of the texts included here make that point explicitly; in others, it is not so obvious. Some texts are standards known to everyone, at least by reputation, although their millenarian content may not be so apparent. Some are highly obscure but find a place here either because they present an odd twist on old ideas, or because they demonstrate a commonplace point especially vividly.

It is my hope that this book will prove useful in that original sources of apocalyptic material are generally scarce. They frequently burn with the bodies of those who promote them, in confrontations with the powers of the earth; or, they appear in scholarly literature only through an interpreter's paraphrase. Almost never do the prophets who proclaim the millennium have an opportunity to be heard by anyone outside their own circle. This book aims to remedy that defect.

Notes

1. Catherine Keller, *Apocalypse Now and Then: A Feminist Guide to the End of the World* (Boston: Beacon Press, 1996), 20.

2. Norman Cohn, "Medieval Millenarism: Its Bearing on the Comparative Study of Millenarian Movements," in *Millennial Dreams in Action,* ed. Sylvia L. Thrupp (The Hague: Mouton, 1962), 31–43.

3. Stephen O'Leary, *Arguing the Apocalypse: A Theory of Millennial Rhetoric* (New York: Oxford University Press, 1994).

4. Ibid., p. 32.

5. Paul Ricoeur, quoted in ibid., p.21.

6. O'Leary, *Arguing the Apocalypse,* 25.

7. Ibid., 31.

8. Mircea Eliade, *A History of Religious Ideas,* vol. 1, *From the Stone Age to the Eleusinian Mysteries,* trans. Willard R. Trask (Chicago: University of Chicago Press, 1978), 41.

9. Mircea Eliade, *A History of Religious Ideas,* vol. 2, *From Gautama Buddha to the Triumph of Christianity,* trans. Willard R. Trask (Chicago: University of Chicago Press, 1978), 8.

10. O'Leary, *Arguing the Apocalypse,* 64–68.

11. Martha F. Lee, *Earth First!: Environmental Apocalypse* (Syracuse, N.Y.: Syracuse University Press, 1995), 14–15.

12. Philip Lamy, "Secularizing the Millennium: Survivalists, Militias, and the New World Order," in *Millennium, Messiahs, and Mayhem: Contemporary Apocalyptic Movements,* ed. Thomas Robbins and Susan J. Palmer (New York: Routledge, 1997), 93–118.

13. Ibid., 113.

14. Peter Worsley observes that a religious movement "must always, objectively, be *politico-religious,*" if only in defining its members' relations with the rest of the world (*The Trumpet Shall Sound: A Study of "Cargo" Cults in Melanesia* [New York: Schocken Books, 1968], xxxvi). See also Patricia R. Pessar, "Millenarian Movements in Rural Brazil: Prophecy and Protest," *Religion* 12, no. 2 (1982): 187–213; Michael Walzer, *The Revolution of the Saints: A Study in the Origins of Radical Politics* (Cambridge: Harvard University Press, 1965); Theodore E. Long, "Prophecy, Charisma and Politics: Reinterpreting the Weberian Hypothesis," in *Prophetic Religions and Politics: Religion and the Political Order,* ed. Jeffrey K. Hadden and Anson D. Shupe (New York: Paragon House, 1986), 3–17; Vittorio Lanternari, *The Religions of the Oppressed: A Study of Modern Messianic Movements* (New York: Alfred A. Knopf, 1963); William Lamont, *Godly Rule: Politics and Religion, 1603–60* (London: Macmillan, 1969); Robert C. Tucker, "The Theory of Charismatic Leadership," *Daedalus* 97 (1968): 731–56; Yonina Talmon notes that millenarianism is often strongly related to po-

litical movements and often becomes itself such a movement ("Millenarianism," in *International Encyclopedia of the Social Sciences* [New York: Macmillan/Free Press, 1968]: 10:349–62). More contemporary sources include Lamy, "Secularizing the Millennium's"; O'Leary, *Arguing the Apocalypse* ("The apocalypse is [among other things] a mythic narrative about power and authority" [55]).

15. Otto Friedrich, *The End of the World: A History* (New York: Fromm International, 1986), 137.

16. This classification of millenarian movements places them on a scale relative to one another rather than attempting to fit them into disjunctive types. All attempts in that direction have failed, since the movements and the ideas they propagate are, like the millennium itself, relentlessly protean. Movements and their ideas change in accordance with their social contexts. This schema replaces the failed classification of movements as pre- or postmillennial, which draws no useful distinctions. It follows closely Lee's proposal (*Earth First!* 18–19) that groups can be compared on the basis of their emphasis on apocalypse (the struggle between good and evil) on the one hand, and millennium (the final paradisiacal state) on the other. Nearly all movements contain at least traces of both, but it is clear that most also emphasize one over the other, though the extent to which they do so may change in the course of their history. This is the thrust of Lee's study of the environmentalist group Earth First!

17. One of the few detailed studies of prophets who failed in this sense that I am aware of can be found in Harold B. Barclay, "Muslim 'Prophets' in the Modern Sudan," *Muslim World* 54 (1964): 250–55.

18. William James, *The Varieties of Religious Experience: A Study in Human Nature* (New York: Collier, 1961), 160.

19. Anthony F. C. Wallace, "Mazeway Resynthesis: A Bio-Cultural Theory of Religious Inspiration." *Transactions of the New York Academy of Science,* 2 ser., 18, no. 2 (1956): 626–38.

20. The attributes of charisma are ably summarized in Douglas F. Barnes, "Charisma and Religious Leadership: An Historical Analysis," *Journal for the Scientific Study of Religion* 17 (1978): 1–17.

21. An early source on this point is William H. Friedland, "For a Sociological Concept of Charisma," *Social Forces* 43, no. 1 (1964): 23–24. It is generally accepted in current scholarship.

22. Paul Doyle Johnson, "Dilemmas of Charismatic Leadership: The Case of the People's Temple," *Sociological Analysis* 40, no. 4 (1979): 315–23.

23. Posted by Name@withheld.com to: marian@mail.catholicity.com, Subject: Miraculous Rosary (July 19, 1998).

24. Robin Theobald, "The Role of Charisma in the Development of Social Movements: Ellen White and the Emergence of Seventh-Day Adventism," *Archives des Sciences Sociales*

des Religions 49, no. 1 (1980): 83–100. Charisma exists "only in the process of originating" (quoting Max Weber, p. 84).

25. Robert Balch and David Taylor, "Seekers and Saucers: The Role of the Cultic Milieu in Joining a UFO Cult," *American Behavioral Scientist* 20, no. 6 (1977): 839–60.

26. *Chiliasm* comes from the Greek word for "thousand" and is exactly equivalent to its Latin cognate *millenarism.*

CHAPTER 1

MILLENNIALISM IN WORLD RELIGIONS

This book will deal with political millenarianism and the ideas that inform it. However, all millenarianism ultimately derives from a religious original. Before moving on to the primary texts, it is therefore worthwhile to discuss some of the forms that millennialism has taken in the major world religions. This chapter provides brief historical sketches of the main streams of apocalyptic and millenarian ideas and texts, focusing on those that have had the most influence on later ideas and movements.

Hinduism

Hinduism is probably the oldest, most diverse, and most tolerant major religion practiced today. It is largely confined to India, but in recent years it has embarked on the process of becoming a world religion. However, it is doubtful that any system so diverse and decentralized—it has no central authority, nothing resembling a Pope or hierarchical organization—can be said to act with single purpose.

Hinduism recognizes no founder and has no single body of teachings that all must adhere to. Two major streams of Hindu belief and practice can be identified: a sophisticated, urbane, and philosophical Hinduism; and a village-based folk version. These streams remain distinct, though they have influenced each other and may continue to do so.

However, there are certain core beliefs that every Hindu recognizes. The primary belief is in Brahman, personified as Brahma, the god of creation. Brahman is an abiding, unchanging spirit behind the world's constant flux. It is conceived as a trinity; its aspects are Brahma the creator, Vishnu the preserver, and Shiva the destroyer.

Every being, including the gods, partakes of the spirit of Brahman in its *atman*, or soul. This spirit is reborn after death to reincarnation in another life, where its standing and destiny reflect its karma, the accumulated balance of positive and negative actions of its past lives. One may reincarnate as a god, a human, or even an insect.

Correct behavior is called *dharma*, and in Hinduism it is strictly regulated according to one's caste, among other attributes. These hereditary and rigidly hierarchical groups are themselves a reflection of the proper observance of *dharma*.

The karmic system fails to satisfy some Hindus, who find it pointless and even frightening. For them there is the concept of *moksha*, or final release from the cycle, comparable to the Buddhist notion of nirvana. Attainment of this state usually requires some withdrawal from ordinary human life, a measure of austerity, and meditation.

In Hindu cosmology the course of the universe through time is cyclical. Every event has occurred before and will occur again. This applies at every level, from the individual life to the cosmos. The cycle passes through four *yugas* (world ages), which get shorter and nastier as they progress. Each represents a loss of cosmic *dharma*, reflected in increasing moral disorder. The last of these epochs, the *kali yuga*, where *dharma* is only one-quarter of its beginning level, is blessedly the shortest, only 432,000 years long.

When the *kali yuga* ends there is a breakdown of social class and an end to religion, as well as loss of respect for holy people, writings, and ideas: a secularization of society. When this situation is beyond all recovery, the world order will end in general catastrophe and the cycle will begin again with a new *mahayuga* lasting 4,320,000 years.

One thousand of these cycles (4,320,000,000 years) is a *kalpa*, a day in Brahma's life. When the day ends, all the cosmos's matter rejoins the cosmic spirit for a *kalpa*-long Brahmanic night, during which it exists only in potential. At dawn, Brahma reappears out of a lotus growing from Vishnu's navel and creation begins once again. We are at present in the first day of Brahma's fifty-first year; he will live to be a hundred, with each year made up of 360 of these immense days and nights. When he dies the universe dissolves. Nothing exists for a divine century, until he is reborn and everything starts anew, for another 311,040,000,000,000 years.

In this system only Brahman is real. It alone is stable and eternal. All else is an emanation of Brahman, mere illusion: *maya.*

We live in the era called *kali yuga,* which began in 3012 B.C.E.[1] Near the end of its course there will arise the Kalki or White Horse Avatar, Vishnu's last incarnation for Hindus. (For Buddhists Maitreya, the last Buddha, will appear. This figure is comparable to Saoshyant in Zoroastrianism and the figure called "Faithful and True" in Revelation 19:11, as well as the Muslim Mahdi.) This tenth avatar will arrive when the heavens open and Vishnu appears on his white horse, his sword "blazing like a comet, for the final destruction of the wicked, the renovation of 'creation' and the 'restoration of purity.'" The end of every *yuga* is called the world's destruction, since it involves a change in the fabric of the planet, when familiar continents sink, new ones arise, and the karmic cycle begins anew.

Despite the enormous span of time left until the end of the current *kali yuga,* there are several people claiming to be the last avatar among us now, and there have been others in the recent past. Hinduism has an eschato-logical text called the *Divya Maha Kala Jñana.* Literally this means *The Divine Knowledge of Time,* though "Gnosis" might be a better word than "knowledge" to translate *Jñana.* This scripture is said to have been composed about a thousand years ago by Jagad Guru Srimad Virat Potaluru Veera Brahmendra Maha Swami, who lived in what is now Andhra Pradesh, India. Brahmendra recited his text to a number of people, who later recorded what he said. He also wrote poetic versions of the story himself. In traditional belief these *Kala Jñana Patrikas* (*patrika* is a general term meaning "writing" or "manuscript") appear from time to time as Brahmendra ordained they should. The *Jñana* describes conditions and events anticipated at the end of the terrible *kali yuga,* just before the arrival of Kali Purusha (Kalki Avatara: a new incarnation of Kali, the destructive/procreative aspect of Brahma) as Sree Sree Sree (thrice great) Veera Bhoga Vasantaraya Maha Swami by the year Kali 5101 (1999 C.E.).

The *Kala Jñana* is a Hindu counterpart to Christian prophecies of an end-time.[2] According to Hindu scholar Narayana Rao, the claim that it is a thousand years old is highly suspect.[3] It is an item of Telugu folklore, though a Sanskrit version is attributed to Vidyaranya, the royal guru of the Vijayanagara dynasty (ca. 1350-1650 C.E.). Like other revelations of the end of the age, it describes past events in the future tense, thereby gaining an unimpeachable authority as correct prediction among believers. There is a tradition that the *Kala Jñana* was composed by an avatar of Shiva, who commits an inadvertent sin (shooting a cow while trying to protect it from a tiger) that causes him to be reborn as a Muslim. Even so, he remembers Brahman and rules his people accordingly.

The *Kala Jñana* describes freakish and chaotic changes in the world and in society: males become females and odd behavior predominates amid terrible disasters, until Krishna—Vishnu's eighth incarnation and a supreme Hindu deity—returns to earth in a new incarnation, to restore the planet to its pristine condition. His followers will have earthly rewards, not heavenly ones. There is no notion of a supernatural afterlife in this system.

Buddhism

Buddhist teachings derive in some respects from Hindu precepts. The ultimate aim of all the many schools of Buddhism is the attainment of a state of enlightenment, in which the devotee sees through all the illusions of this world to the ultimate core of being and meaning. This state is called nirvana. However, the greatest Buddhas (enlightened beings; there are many of them, reincarnations of the founder Gautama) renounce nirvana in favor of helping the rest of us attain it.

Buddhism is predicated on compassion for all suffering beings: humans, animals, and some tormented spirits in parallel universes as hellish as our own. Humanity is a special blessing because it confers the ability to recognize and choose the good. It is a special opportunity to acquire good karma by seeking the happiness of other beings.

Eschatology is, strictly speaking, absent from Buddhism, since it has no doctrine of ultimate ends, no hope of ultimate reward or fear of eternal punishment. Salvation is nirvana, the extinction of the desires that keep us chained to the endless cycle of rebirth. It is desirable, but attainable only by a very few, and then only after eons of suffering in existence. It amounts to a blessed and compassionate indifference to the things that stir up our passions. However, the texts are unclear as to whether or not nirvana is extinction of the human essence.

Though Buddhism derives from the Hindu devotion to Brahma, that supreme god is not present in Buddhist doctrine. Buddhism acknowledges gods, but it gives them no place in individual salvation, which is a matter of the exercise of will. The gods, in fact, are in need of nirvana just as much as we are, with the exception of the perfected Buddha.

The Buddhist concept of time involves the Kalachakra, or wheel of time, which describes the interaction of dualistic cosmic energies that cause evolution to occur and influence its function. An unfortunate side-effect of this intermingling of macrocosmic with microcosmic energies is a strengthening of our "negative" propensities: ego, hatred, and self-delusion. However, through the intervention of a third force, the transcendent Kalachakra, an initiate may transform these negative energies into pure enlightenment.[4]

The dogma of Kalachakra leads believers to a paradoxical state of perfection even while they still inhabit the material world of imperfection. This may be accomplished through cultivating purity in habits of thought, diet, and speech. This course leads to inner peace, from which point it finally becomes possible to attain nirvana's bliss.

The Buddha of the end of the cycle of time is Lord Maitreya. A good deal of Buddhist devotion is centered on him, since he has not yet entered nirvana, as Gautama eventually did. This gives him special merit, because he has renounced his own bliss in favor of the world's, and because he is thought to be aware of those who worship him. In Buddhist teachings he is revered as a savior who will emerge on earth to start the wheel of the law moving once again.

In the *Maitreyavyankarna* (Prophecy of Maitreya), the world is already almost paradise at the time of his coming. There will have been "earth changes," involving a leveling of mountains and a partial emptying of the seas, so a world ruler will be able to walk between his continents. Food will be plentiful, tasty, and available without labor. Trees will produce fabrics directly, with no work of processing. People will be free of blemishes and immoral actions; everyone will be joyous and free, though they will continue to age.

This world ruler will enforce *dharma*. Then Maitreya will descend from the heaven where he waits, to be born to the wife of the ruler's Brahmin adviser. He will clearly be a superman. He will walk from the moment of his birth, and lotuses will bloom in his footprints. His enlightenment will take no more than a day. But ultimate salvation for the rest of us, the perfection of our natures, must await his moment of nirvana and his teaching. Worshipers of Shakyamuni (the Buddha) will attain paradise. The gods will adore him, and all will be freed from their desires.

The *Maitreyavyankarna* is one of the literally thousands of canonical Buddhist sutras. These oral teachings were not written down until sometime around 100 C.E.; their authorship is essentially communal up until that point. The name Maitreya derives from the root *mitra*, meaning "friend," and that is a prominent attribute of this next avatar of Buddha. It is a strong desire of many northern Buddhists to enter rebirth during Maitreya's time on earth, and there are numerous Tibetan inscriptions urging "Come, Maitreya, come," just as some Christians sign their notes "Maranatha" (Come O Lord).[5]

Ancient Near Eastern Religions

The ancient peoples of the Near East imagined that the gods were involved in a struggle like their own, to maintain a degree of predictable order in the face of encroaching primal chaos.[6] Order was always in danger and required godly, or more accurately, heroic support. In these belief systems heaven and earth were exact parallels, and whatever happened in one realm was reflected in the other. Chaos erupted in the form of natural disasters and, above all, invasions. At the same time, war reflected the force of order, but only as long as one's own side won. Warrior gods led these warrior cultures. The structure of these primal pantheons was essentially the same as that of a royal court. Order was decreed by a remote high god, always identified with the sun, and enforced by subordinate warriors: a king and his generals. All these gods were national: the cosmos was supremely ethnocentric.

The people in general and their kings and priests in particular were partners with the gods in this struggle. They held at bay the forces of collapse by their own moral behavior and the proper performance of ritual. In Babylon, Marduk not only made the world out of Tiamat's female body, he eternally defended the very shape of his creation against her unending attacks. The Canaanites believed that their high god, El, commissioned Ba'al to fight Yam, who was, like Tiamat, a female sea monster and the source of chaos. Egyptian cosmology told of a demiurge who created a multitude of beings from the primal chaotic unity. Thoth, god of wisdom, "lord of laws," enforced order (*ma'at*), under the supervision of Ra. All the gods gained strength from human devotion.

In each of these systems there is no vision of an eternal paradise. Instead, the world simply continues as it always has, in permanent battle to maintain order. All these religions are charters of royalty. Their purpose is to account for and rationalize a system that presents the king as a quasi-divine intermediary between the gods and humanity. People serve the king as he and the priests serve the gods. Politics is divine, a part of the created order of the world. Theirs was a steady-state cosmos, locked in an eternal and essentially unchanging battle. Zoroaster changed that for good.

Zoroastrianism

Zoroastrianism is perhaps the oldest living religion, aside from the Oriental pantheisms. It seems to represent a bridge between them and the later, more aggressively monotheistic systems of Judaism and Christianity. Its texts, the Avestas, closely resemble aspects of Hindu and Buddhist texts, on the one hand, and of the Jewish and Christian scriptures, on the other. It is quasi-monotheistic, since it posits a single supreme deity called Ahura-Mazda. There are other, lesser gods in this system, as well, created by Ahura-Mazda as needed.

Zoroastrianism arose in Persia sometime around the seventh century B.C.E. (Some commentators give Zoroaster's dates as c. 1500–1000 B.C.E.; there was a lapse of time before his system was accepted as the state religion in Iran.) It is fundamentally dualistic in nature, portraying life as a continuous struggle between forces of good and evil that will only be resolved at the end-point. This notion of an end-point was a new departure in cosmology. Zoroaster (Zarathustra in his native Persian; the better-known version of his name is Greek) is the first prophet on record to imagine a final conclusion to the otherwise ceaseless battle. He was also the first to imagine a single primal deity. Though Ahura-Mazda was the first god, he was not a solitary being, for his opponent Angra Mainyu, the proponent of *druj* ("the Lie"), already opposed him. Although these opposing forces are closely matched, the supreme good god Ahura-Mazda will eventually win the struggle against Angra Mainyu.[7]

The primal creation occurred in seven stages, as Ahura-Mazda arranged and organized all things in a static, lifeless, and timeless array. Life began with struggle, when Angra attacked Ahura. Ahura won this first battle, leaving Angra comatose for three thousand years. The primal woman, a prostitute, revived him. He then sacrificed the first bull, whose marrow gave rise to plants, and from whose semen (purified on the moon) arose animals.

Angra next killed the first man, whose bones became metal ore and whose semen (purified in the sun) produced the first rhubarb, from which sprang the first human couple.[8] Angra corrupted them and ruled the planet for another three thousand years. Zoroastrianism, perhaps borrowing from Babylonian ideas of cyclical time, came to reckon a twelve-thousand-year cosmic cycle (nine thousand years in some variants). This great cycle is divided into three-thousand-year lesser epochs. At present we inhabit the second of these, called the "Time of Mixture" (of good and evil).

After Zoroaster's death his semen was miraculously preserved in an Iranian lake called Kansaoya. At the opportune moment it will impregnate a young girl swimming in the lake and she will give birth to the first Saoshyant (savior). There will be three of these spiritual sons of Zoroaster. The first, called "Ukhshyat-ereta" ("He who makes righteousness grow") will later be known as "Hoshedarmah." A millennium later the second will appear as "Ukhshyat-nemah" ("He who makes reverence grow"). The third Saoshyant will appear in the last part of the cycle. He will be called "Astvat-ereta," ("Righteous world") and will bring on the end of time.

There is difficulty with this prophecy because Zoroaster died about three thousand years ago, and there has been no Saoshyant. Many contemporary Zoroastrians therefore hope for an intervening fourth Saoshyant.

The Saoshyant shares some attributes with the Davidic messiah of Judaism and with Jesus, but perhaps is closest to the Islamic Imam Mahdi. He is a miraculous son, not of God, but of the human founder of his religion. While he is a human with extraordinary attributes, like Maitreya, he undergoes no reincarnation. He is a distinct individual in a set role each time he comes. The idea of return is implied in this series of miraculous births, but it is not made explicit. Much less is the Saoshyant the scion of an ancient kingly house, or a divine king himself. He probably fits best in the category of "culture hero," which also can accommodate all these messianic figures, their other attributes notwithstanding.

Like the Eastern avatars, the Saoshyant arrives at a time when the earth, though waning, seems to be improving rather than falling into chaos. Angra's evil reign is long over at the time he appears. The idea of cosmic relapse into chaos seems to emerge only in the later traditions.[9]

The *Bundahishn* ("Creation," also known as *Zand-agahih*: "Knowledge from the Zand") is a Pahlavi text with a number of versions dating from some time following the Arabic conquest (636 c.e.) to its final version in 1178.[10] It is a compilation of earlier texts of unknown authorship. It combines material from the Zend-Avesta, or Zand, as commentaries on those canonical scriptures. The Avesta known today is said to be a fraction of a much larger work, itself a compilation attributed to Zoroaster, which was destroyed in Alexander the Great's conquest of Persia.

Its apocalyptic chapter, number 30 of the *Bundahishn*, sets the tone for much writing to come about saviors and their arrival at the end of an epoch of the world. There is no known documentary connection between these writings and the Bible, but the similarity of theme and motifs is striking. The creation account in the *Bundahishn* is structurally close to that in Genesis; even the order of creation is the same, culminating in humanity. The *Bundahisn's* apocalyptic chapter begins with a reversed recapitulation of the world's ages in the life of each human. As the first couple fed upon water, then plants, then milk, and finally meat, so do we reverse that dietary order as we fail and life departs from us. And in this fashion our appetites will wane "in the millennium of Hoshedarmah," the first Saoshyant and savior. (Similar recapitulation occurs throughout both the Hebrew and Christian Testaments, and it has been observed that the Book of Revelation recapitulates the whole Bible.) The people will eventually cease to eat altogether, and will live ten years in that fashion before the Saoshyant comes. During the Saoshyant's lifetime, Ahura-Mazda will resurrect the dead, beginning with the first humans. This recapitulation of the first creation will continue for fifty-seven years (presumably the Saoshyant's life span).

With the help of the sun's light, the newly resurrected will recognize their friends and kin. When all are gathered "they will form the assembly of the Sadvastaran, where all mankind will stand at this time [the Sadvastaran are "righteous judges"; this is a last judgment]; in that assembly every one sees his own good deeds and his own evil deeds; and then, in that assembly, a wicked man becomes as conspicuous as a white sheep among those which are black." Anyone who has not spoken of his good deeds will be shamed.

Then the righteous and the wicked will be separated. The good will go to heaven, but the wicked will suffer three days in hell, where they will be allowed to see the righteous in heaven. Both groups grieve for the wicked, or at least for their friends among them. Then a great comet will fall to the earth, and the fire and halo it produces will "melt the metal of Shahrewar." Shahrewar (approximately "chosen power") is a being akin to an archangel with special powers over metals, especially ritual tools. This molten metal will become another test of virtue, for all will be forced to walk in it. To the righteous it will feel like "warm milk," but the wicked will feel its torment. All will be purified by it and reunited afterward. A ritual will follow in which everyone is given an elixir of immortality. This forgiveness of the wicked is rare in apocalyptic literature, which typically condemns them to eternal torment.

In the combat that follows, Ahura-Mazda will defeat the forces of evil with the help of his *kusti*, a ritual sash apparently similar to the Jewish *tallis*.

Judaism

Yahweh seems to have begun as a tribal god for the Hebrews, their defender against supernatural and human enemies. Like Ba'al, however, Yahweh was subordinate to El, the local high god. Psalm 74 describes Yahweh as a conqueror of sea monsters, like Marduk and Ba'al, and Isaiah foretells Yahweh coming again to punish the monster Leviathan.

The earliest belief in the region seems to have been that each people had its own guardian god under the supreme El Elyon, who divided up the earth like an inheritance among his sons. In time Yahweh absorbed El, so to speak, and became the single supreme God. Worship in his temple was probably not much different from what could be found anywhere in the Middle East. Its purpose was to help Yahweh in his constant battle against chaos.

Norman Cohn's major point in his history of apocalypse is that monotheism, and various forms of apocalypticism, arose from a singular

Jewish response to a history that was typical of those times.[11] From about 1000 to 925 B.C.E. the Hebrew kingdom enjoyed a golden age under David and Solomon. A chain of disasters followed: division of the nation, defeat, and destitution. It appeared that Yahweh himself had failed and suffered defeat by foreign gods. It seemed logical that they ought to be worshiped and served instead.

The solution proposed by the prophet Hosea and others was a radically new theology. Yahweh must become the only god the Jews acknowledged in any way. The Hebrews insisted on Yahweh's singularity. The first commandment is "thou shalt have no other gods before me." In this scheme the people suffered, not because their god was weak, but because they had failed in their loyalty to him. They had become idolaters, and Yahweh, contrary to all common sense, was actually all-powerful and was exacting punishment for their disloyalty. By defeating Israel, its enemies carried out Yahweh's plan. There was no possibility that they had defeated Yahweh.

Not only did the Israelites convert their god to a singular being, they transformed history into a record of his doings.[12] All failures of the Israelites to thrive were the result, never of Yahweh's failure, but of royal idolatry, especially in the past. For example, Solomon let his wives introduce "heathen" worship to his palace. That was why Israel fell to the Assyrians. This mode of explanation alone could account for the sufferings endured by a people who were the Elect of the Most High God, in fact, the only God. Arguably that this single innovation has been largely responsible for the survival of Judaism ever since.

But the Israelites' troubles had only begun. The Babylonian captivity and especially their destruction of the Temple strained even this ingenious account of suffering. Chaos had finally won. "Life had ceased to make sense."[13] This is the situation in which millennialism is most likely to arise.

The response to this total defeat began with Ezekiel. He proclaimed that this utter debacle really reflected an astounding victory that was on the verge of occurring. It would be nothing less than the complete destruction of all of Israel's enemies and, perhaps especially, of those Jews who failed to keep faith. Babylon had to be destroyed as a horrible example of what happens to those who cross Yahweh.

Isaiah invokes Yahweh as a dragon-slayer, like Ba'al, but this time Yahweh is absolutely omnipotent. There are no more contests with other gods, and not only Israel but all of humanity and the rest of creation will be transformed in the final victory. This is the beginning of familiar apocalyptic imagery and the entry of the idea of a return to paradise in a transformed world.

Cyrus the Persian (Koresh in Hebrew) fulfilled the prophecies. He defeated Babylon and freed the Jews again. But even then, things did not go quite according to prediction. Some Jews refused to return to Israel, becoming the pioneers of the Diaspora. Israel was still weak and the House of David was definitely extinct. Divine grace was in the future.

Yahweh was going to intercede directly in history. Every other country, especially the enemies of Israel, would either serve Yahweh or face destruction. They would "bow themselves down at the soles of thy feet," but the devout would get their reward. Isaiah's words have echoed across the ages: God would give them "new heavens and a new earth" (65:17) where there would be no suffering, no tears, and perfect justice—a new paradise.

Following Cyrus's overthrow of Babylon and liberation of the Jews, Persia itself was overthrown by Alexander's conquest and the imposition of Greek rule and culture over the eastern Mediterranean. During this time, the second and third centuries B.C.E., Jews began to compose a new kind of literature called *apocalyptic*. The name means "unveiling," and that is appropriate, for every apocalypse undertakes to reveal to humanity sources of hitherto unknown divine wisdom. Usually this is knowledge of earth's future, which is closely parallel to what happens in heaven.

These apocalyptic writings are usually pseudonymous, attributed to ancient holy men. Among them are the Apocalypse of Baruch, the Book of the Secrets of Enoch, and II Esdras. The major reason for this was to establish the authority of the text. It was usually said to have been written by the sage and then secreted away until the time was right for humanity to learn its secrets, which concerned the real meaning of biblical prophecy. Even the original prophets had not fully understood the meaning of what they recorded. These new revelations were to be revealed only to believers, if only because of their subversive nature.

Unlike earlier prophecies, apocalypses present a determinate future, one that human action cannot change. It is already written in a heavenly book. The events they describe are also quite different from those foretold in classical prophecy. Apocalypse tells of final judgment and an afterlife in which the living and the resurrected dead will get what they deserve: eternal punishment or everlasting bliss.

According to Cohn these writings revive ancient Canaanite and Mesopotamian myths, especially in the struggle between the forces of good and evil that they portray.[14] They reflect some influence from Zoroastrian sources as well. Cohn's view is that the apocalypses were a response to the attacks of Antiochus IV Epiphanes—the Seleucid ruler of the province of Palestine—against Judaism in general and the Temple in particular. He robbed the Temple of its treasures in 169 B.C.E. Two years later he returned to Jerusalem, laid it waste, then rebuilt it, and garrisoned it with his own troops. He prohibited all Jewish observances, but his worst offense was to replace Yahweh in the Temple with the cult of the Phoenecian god Baal Shamen, to whom pigs were sacrificed. The revolt led by Judas Maccabeus succeeded in driving the Seleucids out in 164 B.C.E., after which Jewish observance was reinstated and the Temple cleansed.

The next Jewish millenarian movement of any scope was the one that formed around the anti-Roman rebellion of Simeon Bar Kochba (d. 135 C.E.). Bar Kochba ("Son of the Star") was proclaimed the messiah by that era's most respected rabbi. However, Bar Kochba was defeated by the Emperor Hadrian, and Jews were banned from Jerusalem after his revolt was crushed.

For nearly sixteen hundred years after Bar Kochba there were no significant millenarian movements within Judaism, due to rabbinical opposition, until political events in Europe led certain Jews once again to radically revive their sacred cosmology, paving the way for a messianic movement that swept Europe and the Middle East.[15] This in turn led to radical breaks within both Judaism and secular culture.

In fourteenth- and fifteenth-century Spain, rabid Christian anti-Semitism led to massive pogroms. Many Jews were executed for their faith, while others converted. Some of the converts, contemptuously called Marranos by their Christian neighbors, continued to practice Judaism in secret. They passed their faith on to their children. However, their conversion allowed them to attain high ranks in Spanish society within a short period of time.

The victims of the Inquisition and the pogroms were considered martyrs by the rest of Jewry, which had maintained close contact with them.

Most Spanish Jews went into exile rather than convert, but some of the original 100,000 Marranos hung on until their complete expulsion in 1492. Jews everywhere regarded this displacement as a catastrophe. It seemed as though redemption was needed as seldom before.

In Judaism in general, messianic salvation is seen as a public event. It will involve the entire nation and can in no way be taken as solely a spiritual happening. This world emphatically must be saved for Jews. According to Gershom Scholem, the idea finds almost its only expression, aside from the biblical prophecies, in exile.[16]

In striking contrast to the work of the prophets, which was to be given the widest possible publicity, apocalypses were secret. They are strongly aligned with Jewish mystic literature, called Kabbalah. Nearly every kabbalistic book contains an apocalyptic chapter along with its visions of Merkabah and Shekinah (respectively, the throne or chariot of God, and God's presence in the world.)

By the time of the expulsion from Spain there was an extensive body of this literature. The masterpiece of kabbalistic literature is the *Zohar*, written in Spain late in the thirteenth century. Its title translates as "Splendor," which can be understood as a halo or divine radiance.[17] The *Zohar* looks to divine redemption as a miracle, unrelated to earthly conditions. This salvation will come about gradually, like the dawn, a slow increase in light until the messiah is finally revealed and Israel is made whole and healed. The Gentiles will suffer the reverse, as the light they received all at once gradually recedes until Israel destroys them.

Especially important for later messianism was the *Ra'ya Mehemma*, a late addition to the *Zohar*. Prominent in the *Ra'ya Mehemma* are the two trees of Eden, the tree of life and the tree of knowledge of good and evil, also called the tree of death.[18] The two trees control the state of the world—respectively the divine world of unbridled power of the holy, which connects all things to the divine source; and the fallen world of Torah. The tree of knowledge, which now governs the world, contains a mixture of good and evil, while the tree of life is purely holy.

In the world as it is, Torah must be interpreted in many ways, according to the world's mixed conditions. Everything is according to law (*halakhah*) and is categorized by opposition: pure and impure, sacred and profane, and so on. When the tree of life rules the world once again, Torah will be whole and have but one perfect meaning. *Halakhah* will still exist, but our understanding of it will be completely new—it will prohibit nothing because its meaning will have changed.

Following the expulsion from Spain it became necessary to rewrite Kabbalah to account for catastrophic new conditions, in which a main part of Judaism was uprooted. It was not just history that needed new understanding; ideas about the entire cosmos had to be revised to account for this disaster. At first many thought that the messiah must be on his way; in Jewish belief the world must either be entirely evil or perfectly good when he comes, and it seemed to Jews everywhere to be going rapidly downhill. They awaited his arrival breathlessly for about forty years. This was, they felt sure, the "birth pangs of the messiah," the upheavals that must precede his coming.

It was only after these expectations were frustrated that it became necessary to revamp creation in a new cosmology that would permit such disasters in a meaningful (that is, moral) world. In Scholem's view, this took place in a merging of messianism with Kabbalah carried on by a community of "saints, devotees, priests and reformers" in the Palestinian city of Sefed.[19] The answer to the problem they contrived in the span of forty years (1540–1580) swept across all of Judaism in the years that followed.

The preeminent doctrine in this community was that of Rabbi Isaac Luria Ashkenazi (1534–1572). Instead of denying *galut* (the Diaspora), as one might be tempted to do, Luria expanded it. He made it the condition, not just of the Jews, but of the entire world, cosmos, and even God himself. Simply put, Lurianic Kabbalah rewrote creation. In Luria's cosmology, God concealed himself at the creation so that he might permit it to exist on its own. He withdrew, confining his limitless infinity so that there would be room for creation outside himself. This effected an exile from his own nature; God was in *galut*.

When God withdrew, he fashioned "emanations" of light from his own being, to infuse the planets and build the world we know. It was necessary that he form "vessels" to contain these emanations, to prevent their reversion to infinity. But God, it seems, miscalculated, for the vessels could not contain the emanations. They broke, and God's light dispersed throughout all of his creation. Some of it returned to its source, but bits of it, called sparks of the Shekhinah, fell downward into evil places. Thus the divine light is now, like the Jews, out of place. In the world, as well as in the whole cosmos, the light is in *galut*. Rabbi Hayyim Vital (1543–1620), Luria's chief disciple and scribe, said the sparks are "bound in fetters of steel in the depths of the shells [i.e., the forces of evil] and yearningly aspire to rise to their source, but they cannot avail to do so until they have support."[20]

This situation required amendment; and though God began the process, he left it to us to finish it. This is where the Genesis account of creation enters the picture, for had Adam not sinned, redemption would have followed his creation on the next Sabbath. There would have been no history. As it is, the world is as bad as it was before God began to mend it. The fall, like the creation, is double. Both happened twice: once with God, once with man.

In order to arrive at the restoration (*tikkun*) of the world's perfection, it is up to the Jews to observe Torah as strictly as possible. The very best of them should also devote themselves to contemplation of the divine. Once they have perfected their own souls (and, by transmigration, their neighbors') redemption will happen by itself. The messiah's arrival will symbolize the completion of the process.

In this way Luria and his followers repeated Hosea's feat of elevating God to a new, unique level, but to some extent the kabbalists threw the elevation into reverse, by having God partake of the world's fallen condition.

Luria's ideas were generally accepted shortly after Vital compiled and published them in his *Etz Hayyim* (Tree of Life).[21] They provided a powerful source of renewed dignity and hope for Jews, who found in the idea that their plight reached even God a powerful assertion of their worth, which had been badly damaged in the course of recent history. Their pain, finally, made holy sense. This amounted to a powerful, but so far potential, test of the value of tradition in Jewish life. In biblical times Torah was fixed and unchanging. The new doctrine of a second Torah in times of redemption, once put into practice, promised to challenge the Torah's fixed status.

This challenge appeared in the next century, when the recognized prophet Nathan of Gaza declared that he had received a vision telling him that a wandering holy man named Sabbatai Zvi (1626–1676) was the messiah. Despite Zvi's apparent instability—he was given to what in our era we call "mood swings" of an extreme nature—and his uncertainty about his own calling, he was widely and almost immediately accepted as the messiah throughout world Jewry, despite opposition from certain rabbis. Even Christians applauded this apparent sign of the imminence of the Second Coming. This sudden change in the apparent course of history created what Scholem calls "the crisis of tradition," for in Sabbatai and his movement the tradition met its first serious internal challenge in well over a millennium. Lurianic Kabbalah was rife with messianic fervor and had been widely accepted; it was a bomb waiting to explode, and Sabbatai lit the fuse. There was an immediate and intense revival of Jewish devotion throughout Europe and the Middle East.

In Scholem's account, Zvi made his way from his native city of Smyrna (now Izmir) to Jerusalem, where he was a conspicuous figure. He had a sound rabbinic education but was given to ecstatic moments in which he would perform bizarre and quite unlawful acts. He professed to find deep religious meaning in these performances, which is what they seem to have been, for he claimed ritual significance for some of them.[22] He was a type utterly unknown to Judaism, the holy sinner. From the moment he first became known in Smyrna in 1648 until Nathan had his vision and proclaimed him the messiah in 1665, there was literally no one who would have acknowledged him as such. In fact Nathan had to convince Sabbatai of the authenticity of his mission, for the messiah had grave doubts.

As noted, he was accepted with great enthusiasm everywhere, but his career was meteoric. In 1666 he went on a mission to Adrianople, the sultan's seat, with the mission of dethroning him and taking over the Ottoman Empire. The sultan had him arrested and offered him a choice between conversion and martyrdom. Sabbatai took the path of least resistance and became a Muslim.

In his mind the choice confirmed his mission, and his supporters were not long in reaching the same conclusion. Sabbatai, they said, had to become an apostate for the very purpose of bringing on the restoration of the lost sparks of divinity from among the Muslims. He penetrated evil in order to rescue and elevate the divine within it.

This was a break with tradition that no one could have anticipated. There was simply no suggestion of anything like it anywhere in either the Talmud or the Torah. But to the believers (as Sabbatai's followers called themselves) it now appeared that literally everything in the ancient writings foretold and led up to this moment. This was the new Torah of redemption, or rather the old one seen through redemption's new eyes and with its deeper wisdom.

Acceptance of this view was far from unanimous, and a good many believers fell away and returned to traditional practice. But for the many who stayed, there was an uncanny glamour to Zvi and his acts. His movement persisted until the first decades of the twentieth century in quasi-underground heretical sects of voluntary Marranos. Some of them decided that full holiness was only to be found in copying the messiah. They converted, or gave that impression, to whichever was the dominant religion of the country where they lived: Roman Catholicism in the case of the Frankists of Poland; Islam in the case of the Turkish Dönmeh. There was in this new dogma an implicit but quite logical antinomianism—that is, a justification for acts that, in the traditional system, were condemned as sins. We shall meet this tendency again.

Baruchya Russo succeeded Sabbatai as leader of the movement in Turkey, and the followers there eventually became the Dönmeh. Jacob Frank succeeded Sabbatai in leading a movement in Poland that converted en masse to Catholicism, a move the Church saw as the opening wedge in its final conversion of all the Jews. The Church's conversion failed to materialize and Frank's followers eventually drifted away, for the most part, some of them to work for the French Revolution, others to found the Reform movement in Judaism. None, apparently, returned to orthodoxy. A few Frankists retained their identity in secret as late as the end of the nineteenth century.

Early Christianity

Christianity began as a messianic movement. Its primary message to the world was that God's anointed king had arrived. When he was arrested and executed, this claim became difficult to sustain. The prophecies on which the first Christians had relied to support their claims before the crucifixion were unanimous: The messiah's career would be one of unalloyed triumph until he ruled the Jews. It was only at Jesus' Second Coming to his disciples on the first Easter (1 Cor. 15:3 ff.) that he announced the doctrine of the resurrection.

It is not at all clear that Jesus actually claimed to be the messiah. However, his *followers* certainly gave him the title ("Christos," hence Christ, in

Greek) and the authors of the gospels traced his ancestry back to David to try to legitimize that claim. In the gospels Jesus calls himself "Son of Man," which carries equally heavy eschatological portent but clearly is not a messianic alias.

Jesus' sect was eschatological and dualistic from the outset. His numerous acts of healing represented defeats for the forces of evil; even more explicit was his casting out of demons.[23] His mission was precisely to prepare the way for the Kingdom when God's will would enter history free from Satanic interference and divine order would be restored.

Once the Gentile churches accepted the title "Christ," all the Jewish messianic implications of national salvation and political redemption vanished into a neutral, spiritual meaning of "messiah." Prior to that Jesus was seen as he had seen himself: a new prophet to the Jews alone, and specifically to the poorest and least regarded among them. Jesus' essential divinity came later, with the adoption of the dogmas of his being the Son of God, a member of the trinity, and the Word incarnate.

The general acceptance of Jesus' divinity, the cornerstone of Christian faith, kept believers watching for signs of his return in the flesh for several years. Along with the burden of spreading the news and avoiding persecution from Romans and Jews alike (for the latter, Jesus' sect was a heresy), the faithful had to keep watch for the signs Jesus himself had announced (Matt. 24).

When he failed to return as he had promised in Matthew 24:34 ("Verily I say unto you, this generation shall not pass, till all these things be fulfilled") believers faced a problem similar to the one they had dealt with in the resurrection. The world was just as bad as it had always been—perhaps worse, in view of the persecutions that had forced the church underground in its first century of existence. They solved the problem in the doctrine of the Second Coming: The true nature of his new epoch would not be revealed until he appeared again.

It was about this time that the Book of Revelation was composed, in clear and direct response to those persecutions. There is little doubt that the figure of Antichrist was composed with Nero in mind. Jesus appears as the king on a white horse, with flaming eyes and a sword protruding from his mouth, to strike the nations with his word.

The Book of Revelation is clearly derived from the Jewish apocalyptic tradition. Like others in the genre, it contains standard elements and motifs. Among them are a break with tradition, both in language and in content.[24] Amos Wilder calls all apocalypses "postcultural," in that by the time of the crisis to which they respond the culture from which they emerge is already defunct. It would be closer to the mark to say that the culture is perceived to be defunct, and modern apocalyptic visions frequently respond to a perceived demise of certain elements of a culture taken to be crucial to its nature. Some contemporary Christian writers, though they rarely compose original apocalyptic visions, fervently foretell the fulfillment of the biblical apocalypse based on the perception that legal abortion, for example, has brought morality to an end.

The motifs of apocalyptic writing are archaic (this certainly applies to the monstrous images of John's revelation) and the language is that of archetypes. Categories are dissolved in this perceived new order of the world, and the future comes to depend on miracles as the only available means for averting disaster.

The author of the Book of Revelation is unknown, though tradition ascribes the book to St. John the Evangelist. It is generally thought to have been written on the Island of Patmos in the Aegean, where its author had been banished by Roman authority "on account of the word of God and the testimony of Jesus" (Rev. 1:9). Sometime between the years 69 and 96 C.E., by the best estimates, the author says he heard "a loud voice like a trumpet" telling him to "write what you see in a book and send it to the seven churches, to Ephesus and to Smyrna and to Pergamum and to Thyatira and to Sardis and to Philadelphia and to Laodicea" (1:10–11). The book's purpose was to prepare those churches for the Second Coming and the end of history, which Christians still expected momentarily. Emperor Domitian's reign (81–96) renewed the persecution of Christians, which persuaded them that the time was at hand. The author's aim was to provide encouragement for his brothers and sisters in their time of need.

The author deliberately used an obscure and coded array of symbols to conceal his anti-Roman polemic intent from the authorities. It was intended for use in its time, and many of its symbolic referents are no longer understood. Contemporary interpretations vary widely, and none is generally accepted. But given its claim to prophetic authenticity, interpreters continue to try to find contemporary applications of its vivid but obscure symbols.

As Christianity made Roman converts in large numbers, some of this antagonism to Rome waned, especially in those periods when persecution abated. Still, many of the most eminent Church fathers confidently expected the quick arrival of a time when the earth would bear fruit without labor.[25]

The first recorded Christian heresy arose in the second century, among the followers of Montanus. Like thousands of interpreters who have come after him, Montanus was intrigued with the idea of making calculations of prophetic fulfillment. According to an antiheretical writer whose polemic provides the only surviving record (most prophetic literature is destroyed when it is judged heretical, as most of it is), Montanus proclaimed himself the prophet of another testament and an age of the spirit that was about to begin. He and his followers claimed to have ecstatic visions and proclaimed the imminent Second Coming. This idea of a third age of mankind, a third dispensation, recurs throughout the history of Christian apocalyptic, sometimes in response to the doctrine of the trinity. The end of Montanus's sect also set a precedent: His Phrygian followers, upon hearing the emperor had proscribed them, shut themselves in their churches and burned them down.[26]

St. Augustine's *Civitas Dei* (City of God) put an end to apocalyptic speculations within the Roman Church. Augustine (354–430), responding to this and other heresies in the early Church, composed a Christian view of history in which the world was permanently divided between the City of the World and the City of God. Everyone must choose whether to ally himself or herself with God or Satan. The Church represents God's City; the world is Satan's. The apocalyptic tinge to these ideas is unmistakable, especially in their dualism and their pessimism about the ultimate fate of the world and its servants. Augustine's asceticism, however, led him to reject even the hope of an eventually perfected world that drives all apocalyptic. Millenarians do not ordinarily reject the world as such, only its control by forces of evil.

Augustine interpreted apocalyptic imagery allegorically. In his system, the world will eventually end but the millennium is already present. The Church entered the millennium at Pentecost, and it is available to any Christian who contemplates God. Augustine surrendered the world to evil. There would be no intervention in history. His eschatology was "realized," in that it took the millennium's presence in the Church to represent the completion of salvation. This became the Church's official position, and Christian millenarianism went underground until the Reformation.

The next important apocalyptic movements were those inspired by Joachimism. These ideas came from a branch of the Franciscan order that insisted on maintaining its founder's ideal of poverty and humility in the face of an increasingly wealthy and arrogant Church hierarchy. The Spirituals, as they were called, promoted ideas they attributed to their founder, the Abbott Joachim of Fiore (c. 1130–c. 1201). The chief element in his doctrine was a third dispensation, that is, a new covenant between God and his people. There had already been one dispensation of God and another of Jesus; the third would be a millennial age of the Holy Spirit, inaugurated by the Spirituals, when everyone would become perfected monks and the world a domain of purity and contemplation. It is ironic that this idea seems to have influenced Hegel's theory of the dialectic of history, and thus the great atheist Marx.

According to Cohn most of these prophecies and others attributed to Joachim were forgeries. The Church's opposition to the Spirituals led them to condemn the Church as the Whore of Babylon mentioned in Revelation, and the Pope as Antichrist, an idea that reappears repeatedly since, especially in Protestant but also in conservative Catholic teachings.

Gnosticism

Images of enlightenment dot the history of Western millenarianism. Gnostic illumination is a prime metaphor of the light that symbolized the divine even in the oldest religious texts, and Gnosticism is a religion of revelation: It always concerns holy hidden knowledge that, in the hands of the adepts who are permitted to know it, has properties of salvation. Gnosticism, like millennialism, is profoundly subversive to state religions, which claim a monopoly on the divine and its wisdom, and is suppressed wherever possible.

The Egyptian god of wisdom (and confusion) Thoth seems to be at the root of the first legendary Gnostic magus, Hermes Trismegistus, an apocryphal source for this wisdom.[27] Writings attributed to Hermes aroused a great deal of interest upon their rediscovery in the Renaissance, that millennial return to a past golden age, when the appeal of reason and human-ism over faith and divinity opened the way for the Enlightenment.[28]

The Church fathers were already concerned about Gnosticism, for even in their times it was a multifaceted movement, or rather set of diverse movements sharing a particular set of ideas; Gnosticism had no central the-ology or doctrine, nor did any particular group claim exclusive access to wisdom.[29] Gnostic elements popped up in apocryphal gospels, like the one ascribed to Thomas. As fragmentary manuscripts were discovered and translated, the tradition came to have an important influence on the Re-naissance as well as later movements, as we shall see.

Gnosis is the Greek word for knowledge or understanding. Practitioners of Gnosticism were concerned, not with intellectual or theoretical knowl-edge, but with knowledge that would liberate and redeem the believer. The content of such knowledge is basically religious, in that its main concern is God, and it rests, not on investigation, but on meditation. It is exclusive and esoteric, in that it is given only to an elect by revelation. Its possession makes the knower superior to others, as a partaker of the sacred.

Gnosticism is like Buddhism in that it concerns knowledge higher and deeper than ordinary sense awareness can convey. It shares with later kab-balism the notion of divine sparks emitted by God, which fell into the dense matter of humanity. It requires reawakening in order to ascend back to the divine (*pleroma*). Each human carries a bit of divine illumination, which can be increased through the acquisition of knowledge. Salvation from the world is essentially individual, but there is a Gnostic eschatology as well, for the ultimate liberation is death. Gnostic thought includes con-cepts of hell for unbelievers and sinners and the notion that the attainment of knowledge amounts to a resurrection.

In Gnosticism time is linear, and follows an inevitable process to its ul-timate conclusion. This process is helped along by the successive return of particles of light to the godhead, until the conditions of origin are once again attained. The division of light and darkness is restored and the other basic categories of existence—sacred/profane, spirit/body, good/bad, above/below—are once again distinct and separate.

As everywhere in Middle Eastern thought, evil conditions arise from the mixing of categories. Gnostic salvation involves individual souls as well as the collective of all souls. However, it proposes neither an apocalyptic final struggle nor an eventual redemption of the planet. The earth and life on it are irredeemably evil, and separation from earthly life is precisely salvation.

Gnosticism's alliance with millennialism is profound, for, like all apocalyptic thought, it is dualist: It proposes, in its earliest embodiments, a double creation, akin to that proposed by Luria. The Gnostic view is that this world was the creation of an evil spirit. Matter itself is chaos; it is the baser half of their dualistic universe.

Gnosticism's pretense to exclusive divine knowledge is also implicitly millenarian, for prophetic knowledge is often exactly of this kind: suitable only for the awareness of a select few who can comprehend it. Its specially privileged view of the world and its destiny makes Gnosticism, or Gnostic forms at any rate, especially prone either to become involved with millenarianism or to arouse suspicions of millenarianism in its opponents. Gnostic forms often appear to outsiders to be the most evil of conspiracies, aimed at nothing less than the total domination of the world. They can be apocalyptic, and it can inspire anti-apocalyptic in others. This book will look in some detail at texts from both sides of the divide.

Protestantism

The earliest Protestant churches adhered to Augustine's views for a while. It is worth mentioning that Lutherans, Calvinists, and Anglicans all had state sanction, which put them in the same relationship to the powers of the world as the Catholics had enjoyed, and still did in Southern Europe. They would scarcely care to rock the worldly boat in which they were important passengers.

They followed Augustine's doctrine, albeit with one reversal: The Catholic Church was now Satan's abode, the Pope his Antichrist. Protestantism soon began confronting its own internal reform movements, however, most notably in the form of Puritanism and Pietism. Pietism was in essence the Continental counterpart to English Puritanism. Both arose in response to the perceived failure of the Protestant Reformation to act quickly or thoroughly enough, and both arose in a context of religious warfare: Pietism emerged during the thirty years' war on the continent and Puritanism in the English civil war. Both have had enduring effects on the countries where they emerged. Both movements focused their energies heavily on a quasi-millenarian renewal of a faith thought to have been corrupted by power and hierarchy. Both relied on direct individual experience of the divine.

The American strain of Puritanism was especially prone to revival. There were a series of "great awakenings" through the eighteenth and nineteenth centuries. The Puritan experiment in America was inherently millenarian in its purpose, which was to found there the New Jerusalem, God's millennial city on Earth, as a shining example to the rest of the world. Pietism has had important influence on American evangelism and other strains of Protestant thought, though it gets no credit for the founding impact of Puritanism on the nation's culture.

In the 1830s and 1840s there arose in America an important millenarian movement among Protestants. It appears to have arisen in reaction to perceived threats to the Protestant establishment in the form of labor agitation, immigration, and an increased Roman Catholic population. The movement called for strict adherence to the Bible and acceptance of its literal inerrancy, as well as strict adherence to the main doctrines of Christianity.

Out of this millenarian strain arose the fundamentalist movement, which remains preoccupied with ideas of the Second Coming and devotes a good deal of energy to searching for signs of its fulfillment. It underwent a revival of its own at the turn of the twentieth century when a new wave of immigration accompanied by new ideas in science, especially Darwinism, seemed to threaten the nation's moral fabric. Fundamentalism remained a powerful religious and political force at the century's end, as conditions continued to change rapidly. Unlike earlier millenarian movements, fundamentalism seems prohibited from undertaking radical revisions of cosmology by its doctrinal commitment to the original word of the Bible. Its believers are interpreters rather then visionaries; they scan the news for events that seem to fulfill the Bible's prophecies.

Progressive Millennialism

Augustine's establishment millenarianism did not survive the Enlightenment. The Enlightenment restored nature as a worthy object of human attention, rather than the abode of the devil. People began to see the world as manipulable by human effort and accessible to our understanding. Measurement became more interesting than allegory as a means of knowing; lenses opened new vistas into nature, and dogma about it began to appear simply wrong.

In accordance with this new spirit Bible study took on a literalist approach, and a new form of progressive religious millenarianism also arose. It was in many respects closely allied with progressivism in general—the belief that society tends toward perfection—except that it still relied on divine guidance, if not intervention. The main figure in this movement was Joseph Mede (1586–1638), whose study of Revelation convinced him that it promised a literal Kingdom of God on earth, and that redemption would happen in history. The book revealed to him a record of the Kingdom's progress. Where Mede departed sharply from earlier understanding of Revelation was in his sense that the millennium would not be a reversal of history or an undoing of the world's work; it would not even involve a Second Coming. For him and other thinkers of his school, the past revealed, not a record of Satan's victories, but of his progressive defeat. With the Enlightenment and its enthronement of reason, Satan was losing ground and would soon be defeated. There would be no miraculous rescue, since humanity would arrive at the millennium by its own efforts.

These views came to dominate Protestant thought on history during the eighteenth century. Jonathan Edwards (1703–1758) advocated the idea in America and anticipated Christ's return around the end of the twentieth century. Edwards and other Protestant ministers promoted the notion of America's "special election" later formulated in the political doctrine of manifest destiny. America was to be the site of the millennial kingdom. The Social Gospel movement of the late nineteenth and early twentieth centuries continued this progressive tradition, aiming to establish the Kingdom here through its own reformist efforts.

Though these optimistic believers were convinced they would eventually win, they still foresaw that there would be destruction and suffering in the course of the millennium's arrival. These ideas animated Abolitionism and Union propaganda during the Civil War, which was seen as a grand purgation of the "Redeemer Nation."[30] In "The Battle Hymn of the Republic," Julia Ward Howe wrote, "I have seen Him in the watchfires of a hundred circling camps / They have builded Him an altar in the evening dews and damps / I can read His righteous sentence by the dim and flaring lamps / His day is marching on." Woodrow Wilson was not immune in his progressive millenarian promise to make the world safe for democracy.

With progressivism millenarian ideas and rhetoric begin to spread from religious systems into specifically secular ones. The most conspicuous of our era's millenarian beliefs have been the two with the greatest impact on our history: Marxism and Nazism. It may be an essential component of their power that both these movements aroused near-religious devotion in their most fanatical followers, making it problematic to insist that they are really and fundamentally secular. Certainly both movements denied in their own writings any religious element in their doctrines or programs. However, it seems that every secular millennium needs a replacement for God to legitimize its project. There must be some unquestionable prime principle whose force is taken for granted. In all the secular cases examined in this book, that principle is natural law, however it is defined.

Islam

In Arabic *Islam* literally means "submission" or "surrender." This indicates the prevailing attitude among Muslims ("those who submit," approximately) toward the will of God, which is made known through the religion's holy book, the Qur'an.[31] It was revealed to the prophet Abu al-Qasim Muhammad ibn 'Abd Allah ibn 'Abd al-Muttalib ibn Hasim (Muhammad), Allah's messenger, during the seventh century c.e. According to Islam, Muhammad was the last of God's prophets, among whom are Adam, Noah, and Jesus, among others. The *shahadah*, or confession of faith, sums up the primary tenets: "There is no god but God; Muhammad is the prophet of God." Other core beliefs include angels; the revealed biblical scriptures; a Day of Judgment; and the necessity of daily prayer, paying a welfare tax, fasting during Ramadan, and a pilgrimage to Mecca.

God dictated the Qur'an to Muhammad through the angel Gabriel (Jibreel in Arabic). According to tradition, Muhammad would go into trance on these occasions. He was born in Mecca, where he may have been influenced by contact with Christian and Jewish visitors. Like most prophets,

Muhammad was persecuted in his own country, and after recording the Qur'an he moved to Medina, where his religion began to spread.

In Islamic cosmology everything is governed by a cosmic pattern under God's unity, but everything is limited by this order. There is no real autonomy in Islam's cosmos. It is inhabited by human beings and by spirits called *jinn,* which seem to be parallel races, although the Qur'an says little about the *jinn.*

Islam has its own conception of apocalypse. At the end of time, Islamic tradition tells, monstrous beings called Yajuj and Majuj (borrowed from the biblical Gog and Magog) will lay the earth to waste. They were loose in the world, wreaking havoc, until Alexander the Great took pity on a tribe they terrorized and imprisoned them between two mountainous walls. Every night they try to dig their way out, and every morning God rebuilds the wall.

When their time arrives, Yajuj and Majuj will begin their apocalyptic course from somewhere in the northeast and move southwest toward Israel. On the way, they will drink the Tigris and Euphrates dry and kill everyone they meet. When they have killed all the people they will shoot their arrows at the sky, but God will destroy them, either by stopping their breathing with worms or by sending birds to drown them in the sea.

On the last day there will be resurrection and judgment of the dead and living alike. Each will be treated according to his or her actions. In some verses this is an individual matter, though there are other passages in the Qur'an that mention communal resurrection and judgment, according to each community's "book." Though Allah may forgive some sinners, there was originally no intercession for them. The unforgiven will burn in hell, while the saved enjoy an especially sensuous paradise. The afterlife is both physical and spiritual, and reward and punishment are experienced in both ways.

In Islam millennialism appears to be most fervent and common among adherents of the Shi'ah sect, who make up about 10 or 15 percent of believers.[32] The sect originated in a dispute over who was the proper Caliph (Muhammad's successor as head of Islam), a question that remains central to Shi'ites' belief. For years they were a despised and often persecuted minority in Islam. At the same time the sect has traditionally been an important center of ferment and unrest within the religion. Shi'ah was declared the state religion of Iran in the sixteenth century, since which time the sect has enjoyed a measure of stability.

Shi'ites use the term *Imam* (spiritual leader; the Caliph is a governor) only to refer to descendants of Ali, their favored Caliph. The Imam is a special and potent presence, reflecting and embodying God's presence in the world. Most importantly, he is the source of special hidden knowledge of creation and mystic knowledge of God.[33]

Shi'ites are divided between those who recognize twelve Imams and those who acknowledge seven or four. The "Twelvers" are of most interest here, for they believe that a twelfth Imam called the Mahdi ("divinely guided one"), who has been in hiding since the tenth century, will emerge at the end of history to cause a great revival and purification throughout Islam. This is a world-savior of the sleeping-hero type, who returns at the hour of worst need to restore justice and peace to his people. The Mahdi, it is said, will bring a brief golden age of seven years or so. Sunni (orthodox) Muslims question this belief, since it appears neither in the Qur'an nor in Hadiths (traditions) of the prophet.

Twelvers place special emphasis on the Mahdi. He is a mysterious figure, the son of Hasan al-Askari, the eleventh and last legitimate Caliph, in Twelver belief. He was born to a slave in 868 C.E., and his father kept the birth a secret to protect the boy from persecution. Hasan was killed in a faction fight in 871, and the Mahdi appeared at the age of six to claim his birthright. Since the factions had not abated their anger, he disappeared down a well to avoid murder and has been in hiding ever since. One of his hiding places is said to be a cave beneath a mosque in Samarra, a pilgrimage site for the Shi'ite faithful.

For some seventy years, a period called the "lesser occultation," he maintained contact with the rest of the world by means of letters entrusted to agents (called "Bab," or gate) for delivery. Since then he has withdrawn completely from human contact and will not rejoin us until his moment arrives. This peculiar history is in some sense supported by fact. The tenth and eleventh Imams both spent much of their lives under house arrest, communicating with their followers only through messengers, so the idea of an absent leader had solid precedent.[34]

In both Sunni and Shi'ite traditions, the story of the Mahdi eventually merges with the Christian story of Jesus' return.[35] They expect Jesus to return to Israel at a place called Afiq, carrying a spear with which he will destroy al-Dajjal (literally "the deceiver"; an Islamic Antichrist). Then he will go to Jerusalem, arriving at the time of morning prayer. The Imam will offer Jesus his place, but he will refuse it, praying behind the Imam according to Islamic law (Sharia).

After worshiping, Jesus will kill pigs (forbidden meat in Islam, as in Judaism), break the cross, and destroy all Christians who do not accept him. All Jews and Christians, apparently convinced by his victory over al-Dajjal, will accept Christ and form a single *umma* (community). Jesus will rule for sixty years of perfect justice, then die and be buried in Medina next to Muhammad.

Both Jesus and the Mahdi will take part in the resurrection; Jesus' arrival during the Mahdi's reign will be a sign of its approach. In Shi'ite tradition Jesus is distinct from the Mahdi (the two often seem much alike) because the latter's descent from Muhammad and the Imam is emphasized, as is the fact that Jesus' name follows his in prayer. In some versions of Sunni tradition, Muhammad is supposed to have said, "There is no Mahdi save Jesus, son of Mary." This seems to have been a polemical device to undercut Shi'ite chiliasm and the Mahdi's role.

Some Shi'ite traditions reserve for the Mahdi the task of killing al-Dajjal, who is described as having one eye and a single ear on his forehead and being radiant "like the morning star." Everyone, whether they can read or not, will understand the words on his forehead proclaiming him the *kafir* (unbeliever). He will appear, riding on a donkey, after a time of suffering, proclaiming himself to the entire world as its creator and savior. His followers will be enemies of God, marked by wearing green on their heads. God will bring about his destruction at the hands of the Mahdi; after this there will be a great revolution, led by the returned twelfth Imam. The time for repentance will then have run out.

Al-Dajjal behaves much like Satan in traditional sources, bringing food and water to tempt a starving people. His temptation will separate God's sheep from Satan's goats.

Apocalyptic Renewal

The Western religious traditions are especially prone to highly creative responses to historical adversity, but they tend to stagnate and become corrupt when the living is easy, so to speak. Established churches have a lot to protect from apocalyptic radicals, and they tend to move against them without mercy. The striking exception to this rule is Judaism, which now undergoes an extraordinary degree of millenarian, or better messianic, ferment. The foundation of the state of Israel has given Judaism its first self-governed home in almost two millennia, and the country is abuzz with groups making plans to rebuild the Temple and to train a priestly caste to administer sacrifices there and to make the equipment required to conduct them. These and others expect the messiah momentarily. Some members of the Hasidic (literally, "pious") sect of Lubavitchers expect their recently deceased rebbe Menachem M. Schneersohn to be resurrected as the messiah. It is the return of Judaism to Israel that sparks these messianic expectations, which represent, not the overthrow of the traditional order, but its glorious fulfillment in a new order for the world.

Against this fervor Islamic Palestine fights a holding action to retain control over its own holy sites, some of which coincide with those of Judaism and Christianity, while its own fundamentalist movements gear up for jihad against the West in general and Israel in particular, agitating for the return of true Islamic law to the nations of Islam.

Christian millenarians also are not idle either, for the return of the Jews to their ancestral lands is one of the prophesied signs of the end-times. Dispensationalists, who believe in a series of covenants, each offering a different way to salvation, await the fulfillment of the Second Coming.[36]

There is material here for another book, if a book is the right form to contain such an expanding ferment. It seems to call instead for the Internet's instant transmission, since developments are instantaneous. But these religions are the background of the main subject of this book: apocalypse in the West and its effects on our politics and our lives.

Notes

1. Kenneth Crim, ed., *The Perennial Dictionary of World Religions* (San Francisco: Harper, 1981), 398.

2. The text of the *Kala Jñana* is available on the web (as of September 1998) at http://www.wp.com/KalaJñana/. I have been unable to find a print version in English.

3. Personal communication, October 1998.

4. Takpo Tashi Namgyal, *Mahamudra: The Quintessence of Mind and Meditation,* trans. Lobsang P. Lhalungpa (Boston: Shambhala, 1986).

5. An English version of this text is available in Edward Conze, ed., *Buddhist Scriptures* (New York: Penguin, 1959), 238–42.

6. Norman Cohn, *Cosmos, Chaos, and the World to Come* (New Haven: Yale University Press, 1993).

7. Some scholars think these ideas are later Pahlavi accretions to the original doctrine contained in Zoroaster's own hymns (Gathas). In their view, his original doctrine was much simpler and more refined than this.

8. I have been able to find no account of this odd-seeming origin. Perhaps rhubarb's blood-red color has something to do with it.

9. Mary Boyce, *Zoroastrians: Their Religious Beliefs and Practices* (London: Routledge and Kegan Paul, 1987). Thanks to Hannah M. G. Shapero for leading me to this reference, and for sharing a wealth of information about this tradition.

10. *The Bundahishn, or Knowledge from the Zand,* trans. by E. W. West, vol. 5 of *Sacred Books of the East* (Oxford: Oxford University Press, 1897).

11. The main source of this history is Cohn, *Cosmos, Chaos, and the World to Come.*

12. The ancient Hebrews became known as Israelites after their conquest of Canaan. Their descendants began to be called Jews after their return from the Babylonian captivity.

13. The quotation is from Jasper Griffin, "New Heaven, New Earth," review of *Cosmos, Chaos, and the World to Come* by Norman Cohn, *New York Review of Books,* December 22, 1994, 23–28.

14. Cohn, *Cosmos, Chaos, and the World to Come,* 166.

15. The *halakic* (legal) view on messianism was formulated by the great Moses Maimonides (1135–1204), who codified the position for rabbinical Jews in his *Hilchos Melachim* ("Laws of Kings and Their Wars"). Briefly stated, they concern the eventual coming of the messiah, an earthly but divinely anointed (the meaning of the word *Mashiach,* from which "messiah" derives) king of Israel who will rule in perfect justice and wisdom and offer a shining example for the rest of the world. This is one of the thirteen fundamental beliefs of Judaism. An English version of the text is available in Raymond L. Weiss and Charles Butterworth, eds., *Ethical Writings of Maimonides* (New York: Dover Publications, 1975).

16. In this and most of what follows on Judaism, I am following Gershom Scholem's *The Messianic Idea in Judaism and Other Essays in Jewish Spirituality* (New York: Schocken, 1971).

17. Gershom G. Scholem, *Zohar: The Book of Splendor—Basic Readings from the Kabbalah* (New York: Shocken, 1949).

18. Scholem, *The Messianic Idea,* 22.

19. Ibid., 43.

20. Ibid., 45.

21. An introduction to Luria's writings can be found in Yehuda Ashlag and Philip S. Berg, *An Entrance to the Tree of Life* (New York: Research Center of Kabbalah, 1977).

22. Scholem, *The Messianic Idea,* 60.

23. Cohn, *Cosmos, Chaos, and the World to Come,* 196.

24. Amos N. Wilder, "The Rhetoric of Ancient and Modern Apocalypse," *Interpretations* 25 (1971): 436–53.

25. Norman Cohn, "Medieval Millenarianism: Its Bearing on the Comparative Study of Millenarian Movements," in *The Year 2000: Essays on the End,* ed. Charles B. Strozier and Michael Flynn (New York: New York University Press, 1997), 32.

26. Dick J. Reavis, *The Ashes of Waco: An Investigation* (Syracuse, N.Y.: Syracuse University Press, 1995), 89.

27. Kurt Rudolph, *Gnosis: The Nature and History of Gnosticism* (New York: Harper and Row, 1987), 26.

28. On the influence of Hermetic writing, see Frances A. Yates, *Giordano Bruno and the Hermetic Tradition* (Chicago: University of Chicago Press, 1964).

29. Ibid., 53.

30. Charles B. Strozier, "God, Lincoln, and the Civil War," in *The Year 2000: Essays on the End,* ed. Charles B. Strozier and Michael Flynn (New York: New York University Press, 1997), 63.

31. There are a number of Islamic apocalyptic texts. English versions of some them can be found in James Morris's translation of Mulla Sadra' (Sadr al-Din al-Shirazi), *The Wisdom of the Throne: An Introduction to the Philosophy of Mulla Sadra* (Princeton: Princeton University Press, 1981); al-Ghazali, *The Remembrance of Death and the Afterlife,* Book 40 of *The Revival of the Religious Sciences,* trans. T. J. Winter (Cambridge: Islamic Texts Society, 1989); and Morris's translations of eschatological texts from Muhyiddin Ibn 'Arabi, in *Les Illuminations de la Mecque/The Meccan Illuminations,* ed. Michel Chodkiewicz (Paris: Sindbad, 1989), forthcoming in English from Pir Publications, New York.

32. D. Josiah Negabahn, "Sh'i" in *Encyclopedia of the Orient, 1997,* http://i-cias.com/e.o/ (March 18, 1998).

33. Richard Hooker, "Imam," World Cultures Home Page, http://www.wsu.edu:8000/~dee/GLOSSARY/IMAM.HTM (March 18, 1998).

34 D. Josiah Negabahn, "Muhammad al-Mahdi," World Cultures Home Page, http://www.wsu.edu:8000/~dee/GLOSSARY/IMAM.HTM (March 18, 1998).

35. Abdulazziz Abdulhussein Sachedina, *Islamic Messanism* (Albany: State University of New York Press, 1981).

36. Paul Boyer, *When Time Shall Be No More: Prophecy Belief in Modern American Culture* (Cambridge: Belknap Press, 1992).

PART I

Enlightenment and Secular Millenarianism

WE CAN ALREADY see in Gnosticism the emphasis on individual thought that was to come into its fullest expression in the views of the secular Enlightenment, and eventually in modernism. Gnosticism's reliance on individual effort and exploration, rather than acceptance of dogma and submission to authority, also appears forcefully in Enlightenment rhetoric. Enlightenment ideals included a version of the Gnostic emphasis on salvation through knowledge, although Enlightenment thinkers saw salvation as collective rather than individual. They promoted the belief that the increase of knowledge would lead the world to perfection through a slow but inevitable progress, which is a basic principle of Gnosticism. In fact, Enlightenment thinkers proclaimed the battle already half won. With their superior insight it was already possible, they thought, for humanity to begin to control nature, that is, ultimately, to moralize it. The Golden Age of a rational, ordered society was at hand.

However, the Enlightenment's reliance on reason was quite alien to Gnosticism. That thread first entered Western thought in Greek philosophy and was taken up by the Church in its theological disputations, though here it was always subordinate to Scripture. This created a degree of tension in the system, because a good deal of Scripture does not accord with observed reality.

Columbus's discovery of America was a crucial precursor to the Enlightenment. Colonialism provided an outlet and a field of play for the enormous new energies fueled by the emerging capitalist system. Catherine Keller notes of apocalyptic colonialism (a pun, she points out, on Columbus's name: Colón in Spanish) in general and Columbus's in particular that it was an explosion of patriarchal organization into a new and paradisal field of operation, where the conquerors, by virtue of their military domination over the indigenes, did no work. Eden's curse was lifted, and a New World was presented for Europe's rape: conquest was womanless.[1]

It is significant that the first major successes of Enlightenment thought appeared in cosmology. Isaac Newton's work in particular demonstrated the human capacity to understand the order of the universe; at the same time, it seriously subverted ideas of a personal God and individual redemption. Parallel discoveries in other areas, especially Charles Lyell's in geology and, above all, Charles Darwin's *On the Origin of Species* and *The Descent of Man,* seemed to condemn religious cosmology to defeat. Naturally there was serious and widespread opposition to Darwin's ideas from theologians and other believers, but Rationalists proclaimed, much too soon, the death of religions and faith.

Rationalist thought about the nature of humanity and society led to reformist and revolutionary movements throughout Europe and America. A prime source of this thought was the French philosopher and Christian communist Auguste Comte (1798–1857). His positivist system of thought proclaimed that society obeyed precise and knowable laws, exactly as Johannes Kepler, Newton, and Galileo had shown the planets and stars to do.

Comte's thought had a profound and enduring influence, especially on Karl Marx and G. W. F. Hegel. He based his theories of inevitable progress on a scientific trinitarianism that owed a lot to Joachim of Fiore (see chapter 1). Like Joachim, Comte supposed there would be three world ages, the last of which, a Golden Age, was about to dawn.[2] In the process he secularized Joachim's millenarian struggle. What had been a churchly and mystically peaceful progression of the ages became under Comte's system a secular class war. Comte believed that the acquisition of knowledge would inevitably transform society into a "perfectly ordered [and] egalitarian" organization.[3]

Hegel followed Comte by proposing that the "spirit" of an age determined its political structure. Hegel's system also included historical ages, each with its own spirit or "archetype." These ages progressed through a dialectical process: harmony would be disrupted by contradictions inherent in the system, giving rise to an *antithesis*. The struggle between antithesis and the first principle or *thesis* would lead to a *synthesis,* which resolved the conflict at a new and higher level. This new ideal of progressivism reversed the ancient historical process whereby the world, in an organic model, inevitably decayed from its original Golden Age into corruption, metaphorical illness, and eventual moral decrepitude, requiring a divine regeneration and rebirth.

Positivism's core belief in the inevitability of progress bracketed the eighteenth century with optimism. Bernard de Fontenelle, who popularized the discoveries that fueled this optimism, wrote in 1702 of "a century which will become more enlightened day by day, so that all previous centuries will be lost in darkness by comparison."[4] Kant supported this judgment in 1784, despite the fact that the French Revolution, supposedly the herald of a new age of reason, had ended in a bloodbath, a state despotism, and eventually in a restored monarchy.

Progressivism shrugged off the attacks of nineteenth-century Romanticism with its emphasis on the individual, on emotion, and the irrational. Progressivism retained its rationist bent. Natural law remained the primary source of authority for emerging systems of thought about the nature of humanity and society. Especially in the writings of Karl Marx and his successors, progress toward a shining Elysium became a necessary outcome of history's inevitable progress.

Notes

1. Catherine Keller, "The Breast, the Apocalypse, and the Colonial Journey," in *The Year 2000: Essays on the End,* ed. Charles B. Strozier and Michael Flynn (New York, New York University Press, 1997), 42–58.

2. Nicholas Campion, *The Great Year: Astrology, Millenarism, and History in the Western Tradition* (New York: Penguin, 1994), 428.

3. Ibid., 412.

4. Quoted in "European History and Culture: The Great Age of Monarchy, 1648–1789: The Enlightenment," Britannica Online, http://www.eb.com:180/cgi-bin/g?DocF=macro/5002/20/136.html (20 September 1998).

CHAPTER 2

MARXISM

Marxism arose out of a reaction to and critique of the conditions of early capitalism. Karl Marx amassed statistics to support not only his critique, but the principles behind his revolutionary response. The statistics performed admirably in his critique of the early capitalist system, because Marx was observing actual conditions. Where his system went awry was in its predictions of the inevitable rise of a dictatorship of the proletariat out of the class struggle inherent in capitalism.

Marx's system is based on "natural law"—in this case, the supposedly inevitable working-out of the dialectic of history. This process was progressive in that it would inevitably lead to a better and more just society with fairer distribution of wealth, and a humanity that was no longer alienated by its enslavement to labor. Marx's history was cyclical—society had begun in communism, to which it would return, albeit in a much more "advanced" form, at the end of history.

Like earlier apocalyptic ideologies, Marxism is dualistic. The interaction of opposing forces—in this case, labor and capital—drives events in the world. Marx's colleague, Friedrich Engels, described the coming workers' paradise: "And what a wonderful constitution it is, this gentle constitution, in all its childlike simplicity! No soldiers, no gendarmes, no police, no nobles, kings, regents, no prison, or lawsuits—and everything takes its orderly course."[1] History would finally lift us beyond the grasp of necessity and evade the spell of time. In Engels's words, we would finally be the "lords of nature."

That Marx's "scientific" socialism ultimately rested on faith is clear. His commitment to Enlightenment principles led him to perceive the ultimate goal of history as the ability of humankind to master both nature and society and mold them to suit its needs.[2] In this Marx followed Ludwig

Feuerbach, who had said that the properties ascribed to God actually reflect this exalted human potential.[3]

The socialism which Marx codified and systematized arose out of the disappointments brought on by the French Revolution, which claimed to liberate all men but had in fact merely liberated capital. There remained in Europe a strong current of social discontent and resentment of the conditions industrialism imposed on workers. Abortive revolutions in 1848 and after only fueled this disappointed radicalism, to which Marx and Engels's *Communist Manifesto* eventually gave new resilience and a clear programmatic direction.

This little pamphlet shares many attributes with other apocalyptic texts. First, it offers hope and consolation to believers. It foretells the perfection of the world in a cataclysmic overthrow of the existing order: the revolution and dictatorship of the proletariat. The Communist League, in which Marx and Engels held leadership positions, commissioned the manifesto in 1847. It appeared just before the 1848 uprisings, but seems to have had little effect on them.

When the *Communist Manifesto*'s promised fulfillment failed to materialize as quickly as some adherents hoped, apologetic texts appeared accounting for this failure in terms familiar from religious contexts. According to Eduard Bernstein, for example, the revolution's time had not yet come because capitalism needed to expand to its fullest potential, which it certainly appeared to be doing at the time he wrote, in 1899.[4] Marx had expressed a similar logic—that is, that capitalism's power and scope would have to increase before it would become vulnerable to its own internal contradictions and fall to the class struggle. With this in mind, he urged socialists to support moves in the direction of free trade, despite its apparent incompatibility with their goals.[5] This is a clear example of the tendency of extremes in general, and of millenarian ones in particular, to reverse themselves to account for unexpected developments. We saw this with Sabbatai Zvi (see chapter 1), where the Jewish prophet's conversion to Islam became another sign of his divine election.

Perhaps this process of reversal reveals the workings of the dialectic. It is of the essence of Hegel's dialectic that it involves "Aufhebung."[6] He uses the word to mean abolition, transcendence, and preservation. All these processes are carried out in the dialectic, where a structure is dissolved and transcended at the same time that its essence is preserved in the new state to which the dialectic has elevated it. With this in mind, the apocalyptic necessity of entering fully into evil in order to transform, eliminate, and transcend it finally becomes clear.

Like other apocalyptists, Marx gave his own generation an eschatological significance that failed to materialize. It was not until 1917 that anyone put some of Marx's ideals into practice. Like all millennial systems, the Bolshevik Revolution quickly fell away from its early high purpose into compromise and, under Stalin, corruption into a cult of personality. Shlomo Avineri observes that it was the vulgarization of Marx's thought and the apotheosis of his person that dug Marxism's grave.[7]

It has been observed that Marx's critique of capitalism is still valid, though Marxism's power as a movement seems to have died out for a time. In subsequent chapters, we will find some of its ideas resurfacing in a new guise and a quite unexpected context.

In this passage from the *Communist Manifesto,* notice in particular the "inevitability" that Marx supposed must drive history toward his desired conclusion. It was, he thought, a determinate process, an ineluctable synthesis of force and its own contradiction concluding in a classless workers' paradise. Notice also those points about bourgeois society that Marx made a century and a half ago and that we can still observe all around us at the turn of the millennium, when capitalism appears to reign triumphant. His critique is powerful, even if his prophecy leaves something to be desired.

• • •

The Communist Manifesto

Chapter I

The proletariat goes through various stages of development. With its birth begins its struggle with the bourgeoisie. At first the contest is carried on by individual labourers, then by the workpeople of a factory, then by the operatives of one trade, in one locality, against the individual

From Karl Marx, *The Communist Manifesto,* ed. Frederic L. Bender (New York: W. W. Norton, 1988), 62–66.

bourgeois who directly exploits them. They direct their attacks not against the bourgeois conditions of production, but against the instruments of production themselves; they destroy imported wares that compete with their labour, they smash machinery to pieces, they set factories ablaze, they seek to restore by force the vanished status of the workman of the Middle Ages.

At this stage the labourers still form an incoherent mass scattered over the whole country, and broken up by their mutual competition. If anywhere they unite to form more compact bodies, this is not yet the consequence of their own active union, but of the union of the bourgeoisie, which class, in order to attain its own political ends, is compelled to set the whole proletariat in motion, and is, moreover, still able to do so for a time. At this stage, therefore, the proletarians do not fight their enemies, but the enemies of their enemies, the remnants of absolute monarchy, the landowners, the non-industrial bourgeois, the petty bourgeoisie. Thus the whole historical movement is concentrated in the hands of the bourgeoisie; every victory so obtained is a victory for the bourgeoisie.

But with the development of industry the proletariat not only increases in number; it becomes concentrated in greater masses, its strength grows, and it feels that strength more. The various interests, and conditions of life within the ranks of the proletariat are more and more equalized, in proportion as machinery obliterates all distinctions of labour and nearly everywhere reduces wages to the same low level. The growing competition among the bourgeois and the resulting commercial crises make the wages of the workers ever more fluctuating. The unceasing improvement of machinery, ever more rapidly developing, makes their livelihood more and more precarious; the collisions between individual workmen and individual bourgeois take more and more the character of collisions between two classes. Thereupon the workers begin to form combinations (trade unions) against the bourgeoisie; they club together in order to keep up the rate of wages; they found permanent associations in order to make provision beforehand for these occasional revolts. Here and there the contest breaks out into riots.

Now and then the workers are victorious, but only for a time. The real fruit of their battles lies not in the immediate result but in the ever expanding union of the workers. This union is furthered by the improved means of communication which are created by modern industry, and which place the workers of different localities in contact with one another. It was just this contact that was needed to centralize the numerous local struggles, all of the same character, into one national struggle between classes. But every class struggle is a political struggle. And that union, which the burghers of the Middle Ages, with their miserable highways, required centuries to attain, the modern proletarians, thanks to railways achieve in a few years.

This organization of the proletarians into a class, and consequently into a political party, is continually being upset again by the competition between the workers themselves. But it ever rises up again, stronger, firmer, mightier. It compels legislative recognition of particular interests of the workers by taking advantage of the divisions among the bourgeoisie itself. Thus the Ten Hour bill in England was carried.*

Altogether, collisions between the classes of the old society further the course of development of the proletariat in many ways. The bourgeoisie finds itself involved in a constant battle—at first with the aristocracy; later on, with those portions of the bourgeoisie itself whose interests have become antagonistic to the progress of industry; at all times with the bourgeoisie of foreign countries. In all these battles it sees itself compelled to appeal to the proletariat, to ask for its help, and thus to drag it into the political arena. The bourgeoisie itself, therefore, supplies the proletariat with its own elements of political and general education; in other words, it furnishes the proletariat with weapons for fighting the bourgeoisie.

Further, as we have already seen, entire sections of the ruling classes are, by the advance of industry, precipitated into the proletariat, or are at least threatened in their conditions of existence. These also supply the proletariat with fresh elements of enlightenment and progress.

Finally, in times when the class struggle nears the decisive hour, the process of dissolution going on within the ruling class, in fact within the whole range of old society, assumes such a violent, glaring character that

*This bill set a limit to working hours.—*Ed.*

a small section of the ruling class cuts itself adrift and joins the revolutionary class, the class that holds the future in its hands. Just as, therefore, at an earlier period a section of the nobility went over to the bourgeoisie, so now a portion of the bourgeoisie goes over to the proletariat, and in particular, a portion of the bourgeois ideologists who have raised themselves to the level of comprehending theoretically the historical movement as a whole.

Of all the classes that stand face to face with the bourgeoisie today, the proletariat alone is a really revolutionary class. The other classes decay and finally disappear in the face of modern industry; the proletariat is its special and essential product. The lower middle class, the small manufacturer, the shopkeeper, the artisan, the peasant—all these fight against the bourgeoisie, to save from extinction their existence as fractions of the middle class. They are, therefore, not revolutionary but conservative. Nay more, they are reactionary, for they try to roll back the wheel of history. If by chance they are revolutionary they are so only in view of their impending transfer into the proletariat; they thus defend not their present but their future interests; they desert their own standpoint to place themselves at that of the proletariat.

The "dangerous class," the social scum *[Lumpenproletariat]*, that passively rotting mass thrown off by the lowest layers of old society, may here and there be swept into the movement by a proletarian revolution; its conditions of life, however, prepare it far more for the part of a bribed tool of reactionary intrigue.

In the conditions of the proletariat, those of the old society at large are already virtually swamped. The proletarian is without property; his relation to his wife and children has no longer anything in common with the bourgeois family relations; modern industrial labour, modern subjection to capital, the same in England as in France, in America as in Germany, has stripped him of every trace of national character. Law, morality, religion are to him so many bourgeois prejudices, behind which lurk in ambush just as many bourgeois interests.

All the preceding classes that got the upper hand sought to fortify their already acquired status by subjecting society at large to their conditions of appropriation. The proletarians cannot become masters of the productive forces of society except by abolishing their own previous mode of appropriation,* and thereby also every other previous mode of appropriation. They have nothing of their own to secure and to fortify; their mission is to destroy all previous securities for, and insurances of, individual property.

All previous historical movements were movements of minorities, or in the interest of minorities. The proletarian movement is the self-conscious, independent movement of the immense majority, in the interest of the immense majority. The proletariat, the lowest stratum of our present society, cannot stir, cannot raise itself up, without the whole superincumbent strata of official society being sprung into the air.

Though not in substance, yet in form, the struggle of the proletariat with the bourgeoisie is at first a national struggle. The proletariat of each country must, of course, first of all settle matters with its own bourgeoisie.

In depicting the most general phases of the development of the proletariat we traced the more or less veiled civil war raging within existing society, up to the point where that war breaks out into open revolution, and where the violent overthrow of the bourgeoisie lays the foundation for the sway of the proletariat.

Hitherto, every form of society has been based, as we have already seen, on the antagonism of oppressing and oppressed classes. But in order to oppress a class certain conditions must be assured to it under which it can, at least, continue its slavish existence. The serf, in the period of serfdom, raised himself to membership in the commune, just as the petty bourgeois, under the yoke of feudal absolutism, managed to develop into a bourgeois. The modern laborer, on the contrary, instead of rising with the progress of industry, sinks deeper and deeper below the conditions of existence of his own class. He becomes a pauper, and pauperism develops more rapidly than population and wealth. And here it becomes evident that the bourgeoisie is unfit any longer to be the ruling class in society and to impose its conditions of existence upon society as an overriding law. It is unfit to rule because it is incompetent to assure an existence to its slave within his slavery, because it cannot help letting him sink into such a state that it has to feed him, instead of being fed by

*Private ownership of the means of production and wage labor—*Ed.*

him. Society can no longer live under this bourgeoisie, in other words, its
existence is no longer compatible with society.

The essential condition for the existence and sway of the bourgeois
class is the formation and augmentation of capital; the condition for capital is wage labour. Wage labour rests exclusively on competition between
the labourers. The advance of industry, whose involuntary promoter is
the bourgeoisie, replaces the isolation of the labourers, due to competition, by their revolutionary combination, due to association. The development of modern industry, therefore, cuts from under its feet the very
foundation on which the bourgeoisie produces and appropriates products. What the bourgeoisie, therefore, produces above all are its own
grave-diggers. Its fall and the victory of the proletariat are equally inevitable.

Notes

1. Friedrich Engels, *The Origins of the Family,* quoted in Nicholas Campion, *The Great Year: Astrology, Millenarism, and History in the Western Tradition* (New York: Penguin, 1994), 443.

2. Eugene Kamenka, introduction to *The Portable Karl Marx,* ed. Eugene Kamenka (New York: Penguin, 1983), xxxiii.

3. Ibid., xxxvii.

4. Edward Bernstein, *Evolutionary Socialism* (New York: B. W. Heubsch, 1909), quoted in Karl Marx, *The Communist Manifesto,* ed. Frederic L. Bender (New York: W. W. Norton, 1988), 126–28.

5. Shlomo Avineri, *The Social and Political Thought of Karl Marx* (Cambridge: Cambridge University Press, 1996), 253.

6. Ibid., 37.

7. Ibid., 251.

CHAPTER 3

NAZISM

Adolf Hitler and Mein Kampf

Despite literally tons of biography and analysis of his life and career, Adolf Hitler remains one of the twentieth century's most emblematic, and enigmatic, figures. His image continues to exercise a fascination that time cannot abrade. One writer says it is the best-known face ever; its appearance on a book or magazine cover is "known to increase sales by 25 to 50 percent," a figure rivaled only by the late Princess Diana.[1] Both his character and his appeal are mysteries to most responsible writers about his career, though some lesser figures claim to have knowledge of these matters. There is an element that claims to have found esoteric and magical influences on him.

Trevor Ravenscroft wrote a book called *Spear of Destiny* in which he claims that Hitler was obsessed with "the spear of Longinus," supposedly the one that wounded Christ.[2] This was no ordinary weapon, but nothing less than the talisman of divine power, the same spear the prophet Phineas caused to be made as a symbol of the power of God's chosen people. It had been used by Joshua at Jericho, and Saul once threw it at David; it was present at Golgotha as a symbol of Herod's authority over the proceedings there.

It is safe to dismiss this work out of hand, but Hitler does indeed seem to have come under the influence of exactly such dangerous nonsense. He steeped himself in quasi-mystical and pseudo-mythical racist beliefs sponsored by Jörg Lanz von Liebenfels in his magazine *Ostara* and the banker-financed castle where, as early as 1907, he held forth these notions under a swastika flag.[3] Hitler came into contact with Lanz sometime during his prewar stay in Vienna.

Lanz called for a program of racial extermination against a subhuman race he called *Äfflings,* or ape-men. This effort, like Hitler's program, was conceived as a counterattack on Marxist class warfare. As Joachim Fest points out, these ideas were a minor aspect of a more general fin-de-siècle atmosphere of amok Romanticism and endemic European anti-Semitism, which Hitler made uniquely his own.

It is not often mentioned that in Germany and elsewhere in Europe, the principles of "scientific racism" had the support of the very highest level of academic scientists. The history of racism is long and complicated, but it is striking that no notion of the existence of biologically differentiated subgroupings of humanity with distinct and identifiable behavioral characteristics existed until the Enlightenment. Of course there is a long and dismal record of bloody opposition between nations and states, but there never existed a theory distinguishing them on these grounds until the emergence of scientific anthropology. Even then the process was a long and slow one.[4]

Exploration and colonialism brought Europeans into contact with a wide array of peoples and patterns of behavior. It was necessary to account for them all, and an intrinsic part of rendering an account was and is classification. The process of constructing racist theories developed over the centuries and continues even today. Here I will mention only some of the more important points that influenced the development of Hitler's ideology of race.

A crucial step in developing a theory of race was the work of Johann Gottfried von Herder (1744–1803), who is credited with the concept of the *Volk* (plural *Völker*). Herder asserted that culture is an organizing principle among humans of different groups. In his thinking the *Volk* is a quasi-mystical spiritual union of people sharing language, poetry, education, and tradition. It has nothing to do with the idea of the state and everything to do with this commonality of form. In Herder's thought, each *Volk* is unique, but all humans still belong to one species.

The next major step in the notion that history is the record of the interaction of races was the work of Count Arthur de Gobineau (1816–1882), usually cited as an important influence on Hitler's thought. For Gobineau, who published his *Essays on the Inequality of the Human Races* in 1853–1855, race was the definitive key to history. The mixing of unequal races was the determining factor in the destiny of a people. History in his scheme had nothing to do with greatness of intellect or other talents, but only with natural laws and their violation. It was the failure to obey nature's law that caused the defeat of every people.

In Gobineau's thought, shifting fortunes in the lives of peoples were entirely due to degeneration in their (literal and figurative) blood. The adulterative admixture of the blood of other peoples polluted their heritage. Efforts to "civilize" peoples such as American Blacks and Indians were futile, barring generations of work and patience. They were simply too brutish to benefit from the influence of civilization. Slavery thus was justified and natural, according to Gobineau.

The next major step in racist theory came with Charles Darwin. Though he was not a racist himself, his theory of evolution was almost immediately applied to social matters by authors influenced by Herbert Spencer's laissez-faire politics, wherein everything had its own laws and ought to be left alone to follow them. Darwin's *Evolution of Species* (1859) seemed once and for all to establish that life was progressive. Life clearly followed a path from simpler organisms to more complex ones, and since the most complex of all was the summit of creation—humanity—it was also clear that increasing complexity was synonymous with improvement. At the same time, the "backward" races of humankind, and the poor among the "higher civilizations," deserved their fate. They were, *ipso facto,* unfit.

A German follower of Darwin named Ernst Haeckel (1834–1919) may have had an important influence on Hitler, and clearly reached most of educated Europe with his ideas.[5] Haeckel was an academic superstar of his day, recognized as one of Germany's great thinkers. He read Darwin early in his career and was immediately captivated. In 1877 he called for a radical reform of education to rely entirely on evolution as the grand universal theory of life at the level of both biology and society. He also proposed a political policy to unite Germans as one race. True Germanism required the rejection of everything foreign, including the "sickly degeneracy" of Christianity. Haeckel adopted from Gobineau the notion that the Germans were Aryans. Following Augustin Thierry, he believed that the Aryans were the original pure source from which degenerate lesser races had sprung by means of intermarriage, and he identified the Aryans with modern Germans, the *Volk*. By the 1870s Haeckel "was perfectly positioned to effect a radical overhaul of the German educational system."[6] The time was ripe for his ideas. Otto von Bismarck was in the process of consolidating his military gains and was using anti-Semitism to consolidate his hold over the reactionary German public. According to historian of science Daniel Gasman, Haeckel's hold over Germans was akin to Hitler's.[7] Germans thought him godlike, a prophet, a genius speaking holy words. His book *Die Welträthsel* (The World Riddle), which Gasman describes as a statement of a modern scientific faith, sold half a million copies in Germany.

Haeckel defined a race as a group that differed *culturally* from others; genetics was now out of the picture. These culturally defined races were ordered in a strict hierarchy of advancement, with the lower orders having quite a different value assigned to their lives. It thus became of utmost importance to Haeckel and his followers that Germany establish, or reestablish, its racial purity. Like Marxists, these racial mystagogues perceived society's progress toward their favored goals as inevitable. Also like the Marxists, they proclaimed the necessity for activism. Though the outcome was not in doubt, the pace at which it might be attained was variable; quick success depended on the dedication and activism of believers. This is millenarian thought already.

Another scientist named Rudolf Virchow, a staunch opponent of Haeckel's mystical evolutionism but with nothing like his influence, conducted a survey of German schoolchildren in 1876, aimed at determining their "racial characteristics." Virchow's project, in which children were "measured" at school, immediately started a series of chillingly prophetic rumors: blue-eyed Catholics with black hair were going to be deported, said some, while others insisted that the King of Prussia had bet forty thousand Aryans in a card game with the Sultan of Turkey. He had lost, and Moors would soon be coming to collect the debt. State racism entered the emotional world of Germans well before its actual arrival.

Haeckel and his followers had "established" that Germans were the master race. The identity of those at the lowest end of the scale had long been known. They were, unquestionably, Jews. Throughout the medieval era, long before any "scientific" basis of race or even before the concept had entered European thought, Europeans had looked on Jews as loathsome contaminants of Christian purity. What goes unmentioned in many histories of racism is its emotional component.

An important element of the complex of emotions underlying racism is suggested and elaborated in William Ian Miller's *The Anatomy of Disgust.*[8] The gist of Miller's analysis of disgust is that it is a visceral and quite uncontrollable emotional reaction to the perceived presence of pollutants. It is frequently though not necessarily an aspect of social life, used in marking boundaries between the pure and the unclean. Those experiencing such disgust are unfailingly vivid in their portrayal of what inspires it. And, most tellingly for our purposes, the roots of disgust lie ultimately in human nature. It is reflexive; we disgust ourselves.

What is more, pollution has an uncanny power. It overwhelms the pure in defilement. Only the very holiest contact can redeem it, as we saw in the case of Sabbatai Zvi's conversion. St. Anselm's wash water was a cure for leprosy, the most dreaded disease of his epoch, one of a number of cases of holiness secured and made plain through polluting contact.[9]

According to Miller, Jews were the medieval era's equivalent to today's disease germs. Approximately on a par with lepers in their defiling potential, they were yet lower than lepers, whom Christians should pity for God's judgment working on them. Jews were reviled, not just for their refusal of Christ and their alleged guilt in his death,[10] but for their ascribed physical loathsomeness. Miller quotes medieval sources on their leper-like stench, their association with filth, "exceptional sexual voracity . . . and in the menace they presented . . . to the wives and children of honest Christians."[11] Some devoted ascetics even prayed to become lepers, but no Christian prayed to become a Jew. Christian polemics justified Jews' suffering by their stiff-necked refusal to convert. Few things excite as much fury as the refusal of salvation, as we shall see. The horror of Jews was based, like conspiracy theory, on an elaborate structure of fear built upon a flimsy undercarriage of observed fact. Europeans thought that Jewish men menstruated, for example. This feminization was thought to be contagious, apparently, though it was based on nothing more than ritual circumcision.

As Hannah Arendt points out, European Jews were in a precarious state in the nineteenth century.[12] In most countries they had certain well-defined rights as servants of the state, but they did not participate in politics and in general kept themselves apart from Christians. Their "privileges," especially their financial power, aroused suspicion, and people accused them of depriving honest *Volk* of their rightful opportunities. However, it was not until the 1870s, after the Franco-Prussian War, that rationalized and organized anti-Semitism arose as pseudo-scientific ideas of social evolution replaced older ideas of the nature of the state.

The point has often been made that Hitler brought nothing original to his ideology or its program. He claimed much the contrary, of course, and his primary ideological statement, *Mein Kampf* (My Struggle), repeatedly claims that all his ideas are the result of his unique genius working in grand isolation. Later he came to acknowledge influence from Houston Stewart Chamberlain and Haeckel, but Fest makes a clear case that Hitler got most of his ideas from his time's counterpart to our own *National Enquirer:* periodicals like Lanz's anti-Semitic *Ostara.*

Hitler received additional support for these notions from army demobilization classes he took in Munich after his release from military hospital in 1919. They featured heavily right-wing political indoctrination into anti-Semitic, nationalist, and antisocialist ideas.[13] Hitler took to this training with such speed and enthusiasm that he was hired as a propagandist and spy by the Reichswehr (German army) News and Enlightenment Department. In that capacity he was assigned by his supervisor to respond to a query about these ideas, which had entered political discourse only after the suppression of revolutionary movements in 1918 and 1919.

Hitler was just beginning to feel his political oats at this moment; his work in the classes had displayed a talent for rhetoric, and he had made his first undercover visit to the German Workers' Party (soon to become under his leadership the National Socialist German Workers' Party: NSDAP, or Nazis). On September 16, 1919, he wrote what his translator describes as his first anti-Semitic writing. This example of "rational" anti-Semitism is tame compared to his later rabble-rousing, but it already calls for the "irrevocable removal" [*Entfernung*] of Jews from German life. The letter does not spell out specifically how this ought to be done, so it cannot be taken as a forecast of the holocaust.[14]

In the letter he notes a widespread aversion to Jews among Germans, attributing it to personal distaste rather than any political awareness of their supposed evil plots against Aryans. This was exactly the process his own anti-Semitism took. According to his account in *Mein Kampf*, he was repelled and disoriented by his first sight of exotic, caftan-wearing Jews in Vienna. "Is this a Jew?" he wondered. Later, he thought, "Is this a German?"[15] He was moved to buy pamphlets to learn more about the "Jewish problem." As his "education" progressed he became ever more aware of the Jews around him and began to notice their personal attributes with a measure of disgust. "By their very existence you could tell that these were no lovers of water, and, to your distress, you often knew it with your eyes closed."[16]

He felt a similar distaste for the Marxists he met working construction jobs. He bought more pamphlets to learn to dispute them. The arguments continued until his supervisor threatened to throw him off a scaffold. He learned an impressive lesson in the dialectic of violence, but went home "filled with disgust," wondering, "Are these people human, worthy to belong to a great nation?"[17]

What Hitler really learned was the power of disgust arrayed against a friendless population. About this time he also witnessed a mass demonstration that made a strong impression on him. Hitler learned that people will respond to emotion with an energy that mere reason can never evoke. His innovative and enormously successful propaganda program was based on evoking such emotions.

There are hints of his emotional appeal in an odd collection of letters from German women found in the Chancellery after the end of the war. These women wrote to Hitler to express their deluded passion. "'Sweetest love, favorite of my heart, my one and only, my dearest, my truest and hottest beloved,' one of the letters begins. 'I could kiss you a thousand times and still not be satisfied. My love for you is endless, so tender, so hot and so complete.'"[18] One woman imagined she was already having an affair with Hitler, saying she was sending him keys to her parents' house, so they could meet and spend the whole night together.

Hitler's program combined two related elements common to many apocalyptic movements: revenge and purity. In *Mein Kampf* Hitler blames Jews for all of Germany's social, political, and economic woes, real and imagined, especially her humiliating defeat in World War I and the suffering imposed by the punitive Treaty of Versailles. All this, he argues, was the work of the international Jewish cabal bent on world domination.

His image of the Jews is one of disgusting infectious matter attacking the weakened and corrupted body of the German State:

> Was there any form of filth or profligacy, particularly in cultural life, without at least one Jew involved in it? If you cut even cautiously into such an abcess, you found, like a maggot in a rotting body, often dazzled by the sudden light—a kike![19]

The images of insect life carried over into the holocaust as well. Rudolph Hoess, commandant at Auschwitz, described the executions in these words: "The door would now be quickly screwed up and the gas discharged by the waiting *disinfectors*."[20]

Hitler's program, the Final Solution, was his millennium, his racial paradise for Aryans: *lebensraum* (living space) free of polluting subhuman races and their corruption, populated by a resurrected German people. Specifically and above all, subhumans races referred to Jews. But, as the holocaust showed, others were to be eliminated as well: Gypsies, Communists, and homosexuals, among others. And this was no mere local utopia he had in mind. In his office was a globe he annotated with his own comments. On Russia he wrote, "I am coming," and on North America, "I will be there soon."[21] More telling is the coda to *Mein Kampf*: "A State which, in an epoch of racial adulteration, devotes itself to the duty of preserving the best elements of its racial stock must one day become ruler of the Earth. The adherents of our Movements must always remember this, whenever they may have misgivings lest the greatness of the sacrifices demanded of them may not be justified by the possibilities of success."

Hitler shares with other prophets an absolute and unshakable conviction of the truth of his perceptions. In at least one respect, however, he is also like Marx: None of Hitler's ideology rests on any appeal to higher authority, except to his perceptions of natural law. As Marx relied on a supposed inevitable dialectic of history, Hitler relies on a pseudo-Darwinism where the strong always dominate, the weak always give in, and races mix only at their peril. But the authority for his ideas is never anyone other than Hitler himself. Fest makes it clear that Hitler subscribed to a Wagnerian notion of sublime individual genius, a role in which he saw himself and no one else.[22]

Hitler was, for himself and shortly for most Germans, completely sui generis. There can be little doubt that he did possess certain talents to an unusual degree. Perhaps the most important of these was audacity. He was utterly fearless in trying new things and going for high stakes. This was the source of his astonishing early success, but it also ultimately caused his defeat.

His charisma was immense, though it remains obscure to most outside commentators. Like all charismatic figures, his effect was polar. As much as most Germans adored him, many others despised him from the very beginning. Like most charismatic figures, he kept his own council, never letting even his closest associates in on the workings of his mind. He was especially reticent about his early life and quickly arranged the removal of inconvenient witnesses to it, when he had the power to do so.

It is small wonder that fantastic tales like Ravenscroft's have gathered around this enigmatic figure. Scarcely was his body cold in the Reichstag bunker before the rumors of his escape and survival began to circulate. He became the salvation/terror of the conspiracist world, a sleeping hero, like Charlemagne, Jesus, Frederick Barbarossa, destined to rise from the dead and save his people at their hour of greatest need.

His *Mein Kampf* is unusual. It is both an anti-apocalypse in its opposition to the fantasy of Jewish world domination and an apocalypse in its own right, though the full scope of Hitler's ambitions is muted in *Mein Kampf.* Hitler knew what his priorities had to be: first Germany, then the world. He still had to win a national following. And he saw that destruction has to precede creation.

The following passage from *Mein Kampf* reflects the character of his rhetoric and the millenarian nature of his aims: to achieve a new order. As a nationalist he focuses on German and Germans, but his greater ambitions are not difficult to find. He also clearly understood the nature of ideology: it has to be taken as fervently as a faith and fought for with the same consuming devotion. No compromise is permissible when you want to change the world.

• • •

Mein Kampf, Volume 2

Chapter 5. Weltanschauung and Organization

The trend of development which we are now experiencing would, if allowed to go on unhampered, lead to the realization of the Pan-Jewish prophecy that the Jews will one day devour the other nations and become lords of the earth.

In contrast to the millions of "bourgeois" and "proletarian" Germans, who are stumbling to their ruin, mostly through timidity, indolence and stupidity, the Jew pursues his way persistently and keeps his eye always fixed on his future goal. Any party that is led by him can fight for no other interests than his, and his interests certainly have nothing in common with those of the Aryan nations.

If we would transform our ideal picture of the People's State into a reality we shall have to keep independent of the forces that now control public life and seek for new forces that will be ready and capable of taking up the fight for such an ideal. For a fight it will have to be, since the first objective will not be to build up the idea of the People's State but rather to wipe out the Jewish State which is now in existence. As so often happens in the course of history, the main difficulty is not to establish a new order of things but to clear the ground for its establishment. Prejudices and egotistic interests join together in forming a common front against the new idea and in trying by every means to prevent its triumph, because it is disagreeable to them or threatens their existence.

That is why the protagonist of the new idea is unfortunately, in spite of his desire for constructive work, compelled to wage a destructive battle first, in order to abolish the existing state of affairs. . . .

An existing order of things is not abolished by merely proclaiming and insisting on a new one. It must not be hoped that those who are the partisans of the existing order and have their interests bound up with it will be converted and won over to the new movement simply by being shown that something new is necessary. On the contrary, what may easily happen is that two different situations will exist side by side and that a

From Adolf Hitler, *Mein Kampf,* trans. James Murphy (http://www.crusader.net/texts/mk/mkvxch05.html July 10, 1997).

Weltanschauung [worldview] is transformed into a party, above which level it will not be able to raise itself afterwards. For a *Weltanschauung* is intolerant and cannot permit another to exist side by side with it. It imperiously demands its own recognition as unique and exclusive and a complete transformation in accordance with its views throughout all the branches of public life. It can never allow the previous state of affairs to continue in existence by its side.

And the same holds true of religions.

Christianity was not content with erecting an altar of its own. It had first to destroy the pagan altars. It was only in virtue of this passionate intolerance that an apodictic faith could grow up. And intolerance is an indispensable condition for the growth of such a faith.

It may be objected here that in these phenomena which we find throughout the history of the world we have to recognize mostly a specifically Jewish mode of thought and that such fanaticism and intolerance are typical symptoms of Jewish mentality. That may be a thousandfold true; and it is a fact deeply to be regretted. The appearance of intolerance and fanaticism in the history of mankind may be deeply regrettable, and it may be looked upon as foreign to human nature, but the fact does not change conditions as they exist today.

The men who wish to liberate our German nation from the conditions in which it now exists cannot cudgel their brains with thinking how excellent it would be if this or that had never arisen. They must strive to find ways and means of abolishing what actually exists. A philosophy of life which is inspired by an infernal spirit of intolerance can only be set aside by a doctrine that is advanced in an equally ardent spirit and fought for with as determined a will and which is itself a new idea, pure and absolutely true.

Each one of us today may regret the fact that the advent of Christianity was the first occasion on which spiritual terror was introduced into the much freer ancient world, but the fact cannot be denied that ever since then the world is pervaded and dominated by this kind of coercion and that violence is broken only by violence and terror by terror. Only then can a new regime be created by means of constructive work. Political parties are prone to enter compromises; but a *Weltanschauung* never does this. A political party is inclined to adjust its teachings with a view to meeting those of its opponents, but a *Weltanschauung* proclaims its own infallibility. . . .

But a general *Weltanschauung* will never share its place with something else. Therefore it can never agree to collaborate in any order of things that it condemns. On the contrary it feels obliged to employ every means in fighting against the old order and the whole world of ideas belonging to that order and prepare the way for its destruction.

These purely destructive tactics, the danger of which is so readily perceived by the enemy that he forms a united front against them for his common defense, and also the constructive tactics, which must be aggressive in order to carry the new world of ideas to success–both these phases of the struggle call for a body of resolute fighters. Any new philosophy of life will bring its ideas to victory only if the most courageous and active elements of its epoch and its people are enrolled under its standards and grouped firmly together in a powerful fighting organization.

To achieve this purpose it is absolutely necessary to select from the general system of doctrine a certain number of ideas which will appeal to such individuals and which, once they are expressed in a precise and clear-cut form, will serve as articles of faith for a new association of men. While the program of the ordinary political party is nothing but the recipe for cooking up favorable results out of the next general elections, the program of a *Weltanschauung* represents a declaration of war against an existing order of things, against present conditions, in short, against the established *Weltanschauung*.

It is not necessary, however, that every individual fighter for such a new doctrine need have a full grasp of the ultimate ideas and plans of those who are the leaders of the movement. It is only necessary that each should have a clear notion of the fundamental ideas and that he should thoroughly assimilate a few of the most fundamental principles, so that he will be convinced of the necessity of carrying the movement and its doctrines to success. The individual soldier is not initiated in the knowledge of high strategical plans. But he is trained to submit to a rigid discipline, to be passionately convinced of the justice and inner worth of his cause and that he must devote himself to it without reserve. So, too, the individual follower of a movement must be made acquainted with its far-reaching purpose, how it is inspired by a powerful will and has a great future before it.

Supposing that each soldier in an army were a general, and had the training and capacity for generalship, that army would not be an efficient fighting instrument. Similarly a political movement would not be very efficient in fighting for a *Weltanschauung* if it were made up exclusively of intellectuals. No, we need the simple soldier also. Without him no discipline can be established.

By its very nature, an organization can exist only if leaders of high intellectual ability are served by a large mass of men who are emotionally devoted to the cause. To maintain discipline in a company of two hundred men who are equally intelligent and capable would turn out more difficult in the long run than in a company of one hundred and ninety less gifted men and ten who have had a higher education.

The Social-Democrats have profited very much by recognizing this truth. They took the broad masses of our people who had just completed military service and learned to submit to discipline, and they subjected this mass of men to the discipline of the Social-Democratic organization, which was no less rigid than the discipline through which the young men had passed in their military training. The Social-Democratic organization consisted of an army divided into officers and men. The German worker who had passed through his military service became the private soldier in that army, and the Jewish intellectual was the officer.

The German trade union functionaries may be compared to the non-commissioned officers. The fact, which was always looked upon with indifference by our middle-classes, that only the so-called uneducated classes joined Marxism was the very ground on which this party achieved its success. For while the bourgeois parties, because they mostly consisted of intellectuals, were only a feckless band of undisciplined individuals, out of much less intelligent human material the Marxist leaders formed an army of party combatants who obey their Jewish masters just as blindly as they formerly obeyed their German officers.

The German middle-classes, who never bothered their heads about psychological problems because they felt themselves superior to such matters, did not think it necessary to reflect on the profound significance of this fact and the secret danger involved in it. Indeed they believed that a political movement which draws its followers exclusively from intellectual circles must, for that very reason, be of greater importance and have better grounds for its chances of success, and even a greater probability of taking over the government of the country than a party made up of the ignorant masses. They completely failed to realize the fact that the strength of a political party never consists in the intelligence and independent spirit of the rank-and-file of its members but rather in the spirit of willing obedience with which they follow their intellectual leaders.

What is of decisive importance is the leadership itself. When two bodies of troops are arrayed in mutual combat victory will not fall to that side in which every soldier has an expert knowledge of the rules of strategy, but rather to that side which has the best leaders and at the same time the best disciplined, most blindly obedient and best drilled troops.

That is a fundamental piece of knowledge which we must always bear in mind when we examine the possibility of transforming a *Weltanschauung* into a practical reality.

Notes

1. The History Channel, "Hitler," http://www.thehistorychannel.co.uk/classroom/frames/hitlerbf.htm (May 5, 1998).

2. Trevor Ravenscroft, *Spear of Destiny* (New York: Samuel Weiser, 1987).

3. Joachim Fest, *Hitler* (San Diego: Harcourt Brace Jovanovich, 1974), 36.

4. Ivan Hannaford, *Race: The History of an Idea in the West* (Washington, D.C., and Baltimore: Woodrow Wilson Center Press and Johns Hopkins University Press, 1996), is my authority here.

5. Pat Shipman, *The Evolution of Racism: Human Differences and the Use and Abuse of Science* (New York: Simon and Schuster, 1994).

6. Ibid., 95.

7. Daniel Gasman, *The Scientific Origins of National Socialism: Social Darwinism in Ernst Haeckel and the German Monist League* (London: McDonald, 1971), quoted in Shipman, *Evolution of Racism,* 101.

8. William Ian Miller, *The Anatomy of Disgust* (Cambridge: Harvard University Press, 1997).

9. Ibid., 150.

10. Yet if Christ had lived to a ripe old age and died in his era's equivalent of Miami Beach (Capri?), what would we know of him or his sect today? Judas, instead of being

Christianity's first scapegoat, ought to be its first saint. Without the sacrifice inherent in his "betrayal," what would have become of the Passion?

11. Miller, *Anatomy of Disgust,* 155.

12. Cited in Hannaford, *Race,* 315–16.

13. Richard S. Levy, Adolf Hitler's First Antisemitic Writing, September 16, 1919. http://h-net2.msu.edu/~german/gtext/kaiserreich/hitler2.html (May 5, 1998).

14. Adolf Hitler, *Sämtliche Aufzeichnungen 1905–1924,* ed. Eberhard Jäckel, trans. Richard S. Levy (Stuttgart: Deutsche Verlags-Amstalt 1980), 88–90.

15. Adolf Hitler, *Mein Kampf,* trans. Ralph Manheim (Boston: Houghton Mifflin, 1971), 56.

16. Ibid., 57.

17. Ibid., 40–41.

18. Stephen Kinzer, "'Love Letters' to Hitler, a Book and Play Shocking to Germans," *New York Times,* May 25, 1995, A6.

19. Hitler, *Mein Kampf,* 57.

20. Cited in Otto Friedrich, *The End of the World: A History* (New York: Fromm International, 1986), 296 (my emphasis).

21. Associated Press, "Exhibition Features Führer's World View," August 6, 1998.

22. Fest, *Hitler,* 56.

CHAPTER 4

ENVIRONMENTALISM, POLITICS, AND PROGRESS

Old political alignments, the familiar progressive left-wing versus conservative right-wing battles, sometimes converge, blur and ultimately get lost in modern apocalypticism. This is especially true in the environmentalist movements that have emerged since the writings of Rachel Carson and Aldo Leopold—notably *Silent Spring* (1962) and *Sand County Almanac* (1949), respectively—gave new life to an older conservationist tradition.

Many observers date the contemporary American environmental movement from the first "Earth Day," April 22, 1970. In fact, the movement's roots are much deeper. A newfound appreciation for nature was part of the Romantic movement, and starting at least in the 1850s there was a fashion for essays on nature. Environmentalism also found a place in social Darwinism, where enjoyment of healthy outdoor exercise was deemed integral to fitness and, therefore, to survival.

In America, the conservationist tradition seems to have begun with U.S. Congressman George Perkins Marsh's 1847 speech to an agricultural society in his native Vermont. It was almost prescient in the list of its concerns, most of which are now taken as givens in the environmentalist movement. The gist of the speech is that human activity damages our environment. That point seems incontrovertible, but biologists disagree about the extent of the damage and its consequences for human and other life.

Twentieth-century American environmentalism actually began as a moral reform movement among elites who could be viewed as interested in preserving their own more or less exclusive recreation grounds.[1] This approach only gradually gave way to a more scientific and democratic view. Conservationists, who had been largely Republican, left the party in large numbers to join the breakaway Progressive Party (founded in 1912.) As Democrats adopted reform in 1933 and after, conservationists changed their affiliations once again. Conservationism has been firmly Democratic and reform-minded ever since.

Since the 1970s, for Americans at least, the movement has had an apparently unshakable alliance with left-wing politics and political correctness. It is taken for granted that the environmental movement is progressive in nature, in its close alliance with ideas like racial diversity, anti-capitalism, feminism, and a spiritual politics. In fact, all the progressive strains of thought we have examined so far meet and merge in environmentalism, at least in its more radical expressions.

But the movement has a distinctly right-wing appeal as well. Environmentalist notions of natural purity accorded well with Nazism's pseudo-Darwinism and the special value it placed on *Heimat*, homeland, for which Hitler professed a quasi-mystical devotion. The position was succinctly stated by a Nazi botanist named Ernst Lehmann, who wrote:

> We recognize that separating humanity from nature, from the whole of life, leads to humankind's own destruction and to the death of nations. Only through a re-integration of humanity into the whole of nature can our people be made stronger. That is the fundamental point of the biological tasks of our age. Humankind alone is no longer the focus of thought, but rather life as a whole. . . . This striving toward connectedness with the totality of life, with nature itself, a nature into which we are born, this is the deepest meaning and the true essence of National Socialist thought.[2]

As early as 1934 environmentalism was distinctly apocalyptic, but the ultimate aim of all environmentalism is preservation: keeping the earth in a condition that will continue to sustain life. For environmentalism, progress in the material economic sense is inherently hostile, except in the hope that advanced technology will somehow solve our ecological problems for us. But for now technology's immense hunger for energy and resources makes it a major evil, the prime destructive force and the ruin of habitats. Whereas progressivism usually encourages increased economic activity, a main purpose of environmentalism is to forestall such activity, and in extreme versions to reverse it.

The most radical environmentalist movement on the American scene is Earth First!, and its history embodies the convergence and clash of these modern apocalyptic ideas. Like most prophets, its chief founder and long-time advocate Dave Foreman underwent a conversion experience after a sojourn in the wilderness.[3] He and four other social and environmental activists conceived the idea for Earth First! while hiking in a southwestern wilderness area in 1979. On returning to his friends Foreman, like many another prophet, found himself an outsider among them; they rejected his new environmental absolutism.

Foreman had grown up in a strongly conservative milieu—he was New Mexico State chairman of Young Americans for Freedom and a Goldwater supporter—but his conversion began in the Marine Corps. His hitch lasted some sixty days, half of them in the brig. This experience taught him the nature of the "military state," and he abandoned Republicanism. By 1976 he was a Carter activist and a member of the Sierra Club, and later became the Wilderness Society's chief Washington lobbyist. The pro-business leanings of the Reagan administration were too much for him to stomach; he declared President Reagan "King George III."[4]

Foreman shared the common environmentalist perception that industrialism and the unchecked "progress" of the capitalist system were leading the world into ruin. "World" meant not only the social world of humanity, but more importantly the geological and biological basis of all life, which environmentalists believed to be headed for an imminent and catastrophic collapse: an apocalypse for all life, not just "our way of life."

Earth First! aimed to make wilderness the primary value. Its name meant exactly what it said—no concern could take precedence over the environment. But the group's concern was not for an environment of farms, ranches, logging grounds, and parks. The environment meant wilderness in the true sense, land without human activity. That was the primary moral and social value the group espoused.

The philosophical background of this school is the set of doctrines called "deep ecology." The fundamental idea and the name were coined in 1973 by a Norwegian philosopher named Arne Naess.[5] His revolutionary approach was to abandon the primary value placed on human beings in nature in favor of a higher moral priority placed on life itself. This "biocentrism" removes humanity from the summit and center of creation and makes of us only one species among many, of no more intrinsic merit than, say, a virus, or even a river or mountain. Ecosystems as well as species are part of life's web.

Some adherents of deep ecology advocate a quite millenarian backtracking from modern life, to an edenic pastoral age when the planet comfortably supported ten million humans and there was virgin forest everywhere. For Foreman, paradise was even earlier, in the Pleistocene age. Deep ecologists encourage conversion to a new/old spirituality where consumerism is anathema and we all should live in tiny shamanic communities guided by "ancient wisdom." Perfect peace and racial tolerance would flourish in an ambiance of "feminine energies"; patriarchy would no longer exist.

Foreman distrusted all intellectualism and largely banned it from his movement and its publications, but the implications of deep ecology were not lost on him. His only mainstream publication listed protection of the environment as a first priority over human welfare if necessary.[6] Despite later internal conflicts over this point within Earth First!, Foreman retained and in fact hardened his biocentrist views. The group eventually split, and Foreman left, over an emphasis on Marxist views of social justice espoused by an increasing number of Earth First! members. The Marxist faction held that it was possible and necessary to raise the consciousness of those "enslaved" by the capitalist system and promote social justice, which would enable the masses to attend to the earth and its needs. Martha Lee categorizes these beliefs as millenarian, in that they hold out the hope for a human presence on earth, whereas Foreman's apocalypticism does not.

Foreman came to abandon hope for humanity, though not for life as a whole. It is arguable that Foreman's biocentrism was a form of millenarianism from the point of view he espoused: that of life minus humanity. At a later point, however, his ideas of the world after the great biological meltdown he foretold (and even the social-justice wing of the movement agreed on the inevitability of this catastrophe) included a surviving tiny elite of Earth First! believers whose survival skills and "genetic environmentalism" would see them through to found a new race. These believers, who need not actually belong to the movement, constitute an elect, a biologically determined super species, though not quite a master race. They are "Anti-bodies against the Humanpox" as Foreman called them.[7]

In a reprise of the eugenic beliefs that accompanied theories of Aryanism, Earth First! became embroiled in a debate over reproduction.[8] Was it incumbent upon members to sterilize themselves in order to contribute to the population decline they saw as a necessary part of saving the planet? Or should they breed as much as possible, in order to provide future "saviors" for the planet? Lee is at pains to point out that this idea never became an item of movement dogma—Earth First! was and is remarkably democratic—but it was the subject of long-term debate.

Earth First! publications featured debates about population policy for the rest of the world as well. Some members proposed that governments—the U.S. government in particular—should promote birth control, withhold welfare from parents of more than two children, execute those convicted of violent crimes, and, most controversially, prohibit all immigration. Others felt that the rate of population growth should not be interfered with, on the grounds that the sooner it reached the "inevitable" crash point, the better. This is not unusual logic among millenarians. In order to perfect the world, you first have to ruin it. The longer the crash was delayed, the less wilderness there would be to regenerate later.

The debate over population reached a head in 1986 in three Earth First! articles by a movement ideologue named Christopher Manes, who wrote under the pseudonym Miss Ann Thropy. In each of the articles Manes addresses the contribution of overpopulation to the "inevitable" environmental meltdown and what policies should be adopted to rectify the situation. He dismisses technological solutions such as birth control out of hand, since technology is largely a source of the problem, and since its use would do nothing to change the fundamentally evil system.

He notes that through most of human history population was held in check by a sort of Darwinism: high infant mortality rates. He recommends extending the group's sabotage tactics, used against industrial targets, to include medical facilities, in hopes of promoting higher mortality rates. Trying to change American attitudes toward population, consumption, and the environment would be fruitless, according to Manes.

This is already controversial, but Manes breaks new ground in his other proposals: AIDS, he submits, is actually a benign force that ought to be cultivated. First, it only infects humans, leaving the rest of the natural world untouched; it goes right to the heart of the problem. Second, its long incubation period allows for its rapid spread and the indefinite survival of the virus. Finally, its spread through sexual activity ("*the* most difficult human behavior to control") makes it nearly invulnerable.[9] Its "success" might be expected to duplicate that of the Black Death in killing about a third of those living in areas where it occurs. This not only would have an immediately beneficial effect on wilderness, but would eliminate most future threats by shutting down the industrial system. Manes ends the article with a pious expression of his awareness of the suffering AIDS causes, but notes that vast numbers of people would die as a result of overpopulation in any case, so AIDS could be seen as part of the solution.

This antihumanist stance may represent the farthest limit to which the logic of deep ecology can be taken. Removing humanity from the center of creation is an intellectual step with apocalyptic implications. It proposes a new ordering of the world quite unprecedented in history, so far as we can tell. It may eventually amount to another dialectical leap, like those we have seen in the cases of the monotheistic Yahweh, the Christian resurrection, the Lurianic Kabbalah, and the apostasy of Sabbatai Zvi. It is still too soon to tell.

Manes's articles took biocentrism to lengths that Earth First! as a movement could not sustain. The next yearly gathering of the group witnessed severe faction disputes among the biocentrists and the supporters of social justice. Foreman left his jobs in Earth First! and eventually quit the movement altogether. The biocentrist apocalypticists eventually split off and left the movement in the hands of the social-justice faction.

As Earth First! demonstrates, environmental radicalism rests on the perception that life on the planet is in serious danger from human activity. This belief is itself apocalyptic, since it implies a dramatic and irreversible change in the nature of life in general, and thus of human life. Millenarianism always has humanity at its core, whether the concern is with saving humanity or a remnant of it, or with saving a greater purpose from the interference of humanity. The environmental crisis, as in all apocalypses, is all but inevitable, a necessary consequence of human imperfection. Our fate is sealed, unless we can undergo a heroic last-minute change. In a word, we must convert.

Our ideas about impending environmental collapse come wrapped in the highest degree of credibility: They are scientific. One of the founding documents of that belief in our era appears below. The Union of Concerned Scientists (UCS) was founded in 1969 by a group of faculty and students at MIT. It began by drafting a statement whose terms of discourse were as grandiose and universalist as any we will encounter here: "Misuse of scientific and technical knowledge presents a major threat to the existence of mankind. Through its actions in Vietnam our government has shaken our confidence in its ability to make wise and humane decisions. There is also disquieting evidence of an intention to enlarge further our immense destructive capability."[10] This language clearly arises in part out of the peace movement of that time, and it seems to reflect the era's (accurate) sense of impending seismic social change. The world was being reborn in those days, and global concern was on everyone's mind.

Unlike many other such projects floated at the time, this one seems to have thrived. In 1992 the UCS issued a "Warning to Humanity" that called for complete change in almost every area of life, from ethics to economy. This document is a rather complete jeremiad against society's sins of consumerism, belligerence, and greed. Most of the themes common to environmentalism are included, in condensed form. Though these scholars do not carry their attack on the status quo to the extent that Earth First! or other deep ecologists do, their manifesto rests on the same premises.

It is also significant that these Nobelists—ninety-nine laureates appear on the short "prominent" list culled from 1,700 signatories—do not invite our participation in their project, nor do they urge it. Rather, they *require* everyone to join them.

Like all apocalypses, this one calls on the very highest authority for its legitimacy. Like few others, it combines liberal appeals to social justice in the service of a fundamentally conservative purpose. The melding of these streams of progressive thought is by no means complete, and may never be, but it has begun.

• • •

WORLD SCIENTISTS' WARNING TO HUMANITY

Some 1,700 of the world's leading scientists, including the majority of Nobel laureates in the sciences, issued this appeal in November 1992. . . .

Human beings and the natural world are on a collision course. Human activities inflict harsh and often irreversible damage on the environment and on critical resources. If not checked, many of our current practices put at serious risk the future that we wish for human society and the plant and animal kingdoms, and may so alter the living world that it will be unable to sustain life in the manner that we know. Fundamental changes are urgent if we are to avoid the collision our present course will bring about.

The Environment

The environment is suffering critical stress:

The Atmosphere

Stratospheric ozone depletion threatens us with enhanced ultraviolet radiation at the earth's surface, which can be damaging or lethal to many life forms.[*] Air pollution near ground level, and acid precipitation, are already causing widespread injury to humans, forests and crops.

Water Resources

Heedless exploitation of depletable ground water supplies endangers food production and other essential human systems. Heavy demands on the world's surface waters have resulted in serious shortages in some 80 countries, containing 40% of the world's population. Pollution of rivers, lakes and ground water further limits the supply.

Henry Kendall, "Warning Issued on November 18, 1992," http://deoxy.org/sciwarn.htm, March 13, 1998.
*See Union of Concerned Scientists. http://www.ucsusa.org/global/ozone.html

Oceans

Destructive pressure on the oceans is severe, particularly in the coastal regions which produce most of the world's food fish. The total marine catch is now at or above the estimated maximum sustainable yield. Some fisheries have already shown signs of collapse. Rivers carrying heavy burdens of eroded soil into the seas also carry industrial, municipal, agricultural, and livestock waste—some of it toxic.

Soil

Loss of soil productivity, which is causing extensive Land abandonment, is a widespread byproduct of current practices in agriculture and animal husbandry. Since 1945, 11% of the earth's vegetated surface has been degraded—an area larger than India and China combined—and per capita food production in many parts of the world is decreasing.

Forests

Tropical rain forests, as well as tropical and temperate dry forests, are being destroyed rapidly. At present rates, some critical forest types will be gone in a few years and most of the tropical rain forest will be gone before the end of the next century. With them will go large numbers of plant and animal species.

Living Species

The irreversible loss of species, which by 2100 may reach one third of all species now living, is especially serious.* We are losing the potential they hold for providing medicinal and other benefits, and the contribution that genetic diversity of life forms gives to the robustness of the world's biological systems and to the astonishing beauty of the earth itself.

Much of this damage is irreversible on a scale of centuries or permanent. Other processes appear to pose additional threats. Increasing levels

*See http://www.ucsusa.org/global/biodiversity.html

of gases in the atmosphere from human activities, including carbon dioxide released from fossil fuel burning and from deforestation, may alter climate on a global scale.*

Predictions of global warming are still uncertain—with projected effects ranging from tolerable to very severe—but the potential risks are very great.

Our massive tampering with the world's interdependent web of life—coupled with the environmental damage inflicted by deforestation, species loss, and climate change—could trigger widespread adverse effects, including unpredictable collapses of critical biological systems whose interactions and dynamics we only imperfectly understand.

Uncertainty over the extent of these effects cannot excuse complacency or delay in facing the threat.

Population

The earth is finite. Its ability to absorb wastes and destructive effluent is finite. Its ability to provide food and energy is finite. Its ability to provide for growing numbers of people is finite. And we are fast approaching many of the earth's limits. Current economic practices which damage the environment, in both developed and underdeveloped nations, cannot be continued without the risk that vital global systems will be damaged beyond repair.

Pressures resulting from unrestrained population growth put demands on the natural world that can overwhelm any efforts to achieve a sustainable future.** If we are to halt the destruction of our environment, we must accept limits to that growth. A World Bank estimate indicates that world population will not stabilize at less than 12.4 billion, while the United Nations concludes that the eventual total could reach 14 billion, a near tripling of today's 5.4 billion. But, even at this moment, one person in five lives in absolute poverty without enough to eat, and one in ten suffers serious malnutrition.

*See http://www.ucsusa.org/global/climate.html
**See http://www.ucsusa.org/global/population.html

No more than one or a few decades remain before the chance to avert the threats we now confront will be lost and the prospects for humanity immeasurably diminished.

Warning

We the undersigned, senior members of the world's scientific community, hereby warn all humanity of what lies ahead. A great change in our stewardship of the earth and the life on it, is required, if vast human misery is to be avoided and our global home on this planet is not to be irretrievably mutilated.

What We Must Do

Five inextricably linked areas must be addressed *simultaneously*:

1. We must bring environmentally damaging activities under control to restore and protect the integrity of the earth's systems we depend on. We must, for example, move away from fossil fuels to more benign, inexhaustible energy sources to cut greenhouse gas emissions and the pollution of our air and water. Priority must be given to the development of energy sources matched to third world needs—small scale and relatively easy to implement. We must halt deforestation, injury to and loss of agricultural land, and the loss of terrestrial and marine plant and animal species.
2. We must manage resources crucial to human welfare more effectively. We must give high priority to efficient use of energy, water, and other materials, including expansion of conservation and recycling.
3. We must stabilize population. This will be possible only if all nations recognize that it requires improved social and economic conditions, and the adoption of effective, voluntary family planning.
4. We must reduce and eventually eliminate poverty.
5. We must ensure sexual equality, and guarantee women control over their own reproductive decisions.

The developed nations are the largest polluters in the world today. They must greatly reduce their over-consumption, if we are to reduce pressures on resources and the global environment. The developed nations have the obligation to provide aid and support to developing nations, because only the developed nations have the financial resources and the technical skills for these tasks.

Acting on this recognition is not altruism, but enlightened self-interest: whether industrialized or not, we all have but one lifeboat. No nation can escape from injury when global biological systems are damaged. No nation can escape from conflicts over increasingly scarce resources. In addition, environmental and economic instabilities will cause mass migrations with incalculable consequences for developed and undeveloped nations alike.

Developing nations must realize that environmental damage is one of the gravest threats they face, and that attempts to blunt it will be overwhelmed if their populations go unchecked. The greatest peril is to become trapped in spirals of environmental decline, poverty, and unrest, leading to social, economic and environmental collapse.

Success in this global endeavor will require a great reduction in violence and war. Resources now devoted to the preparation and conduct of war—amounting to over $1 trillion annually—will be badly needed in the new tasks and should be diverted to the new challenges.

A new ethic is required—a new attitude towards discharging our responsibility for caring for ourselves and for the earth. We must recognize the earth's limited capacity to provide for us. We must recognize its fragility. We must no longer allow it to be ravaged. This ethic must motivate a great movement, convince reluctant leaders and reluctant governments and reluctant peoples themselves to effect the needed changes.

The scientists issuing this warning hope that our message will reach and affect people everywhere. We need the help of many.

We require the help of the world community of scientists—natural, social, economic, political;
We require the help of the world's business and industrial leaders;
We require the help of the worlds religious leaders; and
We require the help of the world's peoples.
We call on all to join us in this task.

Notes

1. "The Evolution of the Conservation Movement 1850–1920," http://lcweb2.loc.gov/ammem/amrvhtml/conshome.html (September 30, 1998).

2. Ernst Lehmann, *Biologischer Wille: Wege und Ziele biologischer Arbeit im neuen Reich* (Munich, 1934), 10–11, quoted in Peter Staudenmaier, "Fascist Ideology: The Green Wing of the Nazi Party and Its Historical Antecedents," http://au.spunk.org/texts/places/germany/sp001630/peter.htm (May 6, 1998).

3. Martha F. Lee, *Earth First!: Environmental Apocalypse* (Syracuse, N.Y.: Syracuse University Press, 1995). I rely on Lee for the history of the movement. Dave Foreman's and Earth First!'s early careers are described on pp. 27–33.

4. Ibid., 29.

5. Arne Naess, "The Shallow and the Deep, Long-Range Ecology Movement: A Summary," *Inquiry* 16 (1973): 95.

6. Dave Foreman, *Confessions of an Eco-Warrior* (New York: Harmony, 1991).

7. Lee, *Earth First!,* 61.

8. Eugenics was widely popular among an elite of European thinkers between the wars. A logical offshoot of social Darwinism, it held that those deemed the fittest had a duty to reproduce one with another. Its supporters argued that this program should be encouraged by government subsidy and like measures. It was also thought to be essential that those deemed unfit should be prevented from reproducing, forcibly if necessary. Ultimately this led to the Nazi program of exterminating the insane, handicapped, mentally unfit, and others—a precursor to the holocaust.

9. Quoted in Lee, *Earth First!,* 103.

10. Union of Concerned Scientists, "About UCS," http://www.ucsusa.org/about/faculty.html (June 10, 1998).

PART II

Millennial Evil

AN APOCALYPTIC RHETORIC drove the Manhattan Project. Its director, General Leslie Groves, said of the project that it was an accomplishment to equal Columbus's millennial discovery of America.[1] The comparison with Columbus is apt, in view of the Admiral's own apocalyptic agenda: Columbus declared himself "the messenger" of the New Jerusalem, guided by God to find it.[2]

Groves and President Harry Truman alike regarded the bomb "as a gift of God, confirming a symbolic mandate that would make the United States the leader among nations."[3]

Almost since its first discovery, nuclear radiation seems to have held for scientists a millennial hope. Michael Ortiz Hill quotes Frederick Soddy, codiscoverer of a particular form of nuclear decay, on his dreams of this philosopher's stone: "A race that would transmute matter would have little need to earn its bread by the sweat of its brow."[4] The curse of Eden would lift; we would be on our way to Paradise. Soddy could not have foreseen that the road would take us to hell first.

Modern apocalyptic rhetoric is influenced to a great extent by fiction. Hill informs us that H. G. Wells gave us the name "atomic bomb," and wrote the first nuclear holocaust, in his *The World Set Free.*[5] Nuclear physicist Leo Szilard, who cowrote the Einstein letter to President Franklin Roosevelt urging him to undertake the Manhattan Project, professed himself deeply affected by Wells's writings, and "wanted to save the world."[6]

After the first atomic test, called Trinity, which took place near a spot called Jornada del Muerto, or "death trip," most witnesses described the experience in tones reminiscent of apocalypse. They all spoke of the bomb's light; some likened it to the ascension of Jesus or the Second Coming. J. Robert Oppenheimer, the technical head of the Manhattan

Project, recalled the Hindu god Vishnu in the Bhavagad Gita, who, appearing to the hero Arjuna in his full and terrible divinity, with a bomb-like "radiance of a thousand suns," says, "Now I am become death, who conquers worlds."[7]

The creators of the bomb vied with one another for the title of its "father." This was an odd procreation, though, for there was no mother. Hill likens their imagery to the masculine birth of Athene, the war goddess. Modernity opened in Columbus's masculine apocalypse at San Salvador in 1492. It began in subjection and slavery, characterized as rape, and ended at Trinity in another masculine apocalypse of horror and hope whose direction and boundaries we still can barely glimpse. Promise expands with each new epoch, as does the corresponding terror.

Every prophecy is, in a sense, unreal. That is, the events it describes are not actual but potential. This is prophecy's great secret, an admission it can never afford to make. It is of the essence of prophecy that it must be believed—taken to describe events that really will happen. This is why writers of prophecy go to great lengths to garner authenticity for their predictions. As Stephen O'Leary points out, authority is one of the great topics of all apocalypses, the cornerstone of their persuasion.[8] Lacking authority, all of them are viewed as mere nonsense. But even if we accept their authority at full and face value, sooner or later we must come to terms with the fact that what apocalypse describes is not (yet) history.

One of the more interesting developments in the contemporary apocalyptic literature is the extent to which it has come to rely, even overtly on occasion, on material expressly composed as fiction. But before moving directly to consideration of some texts of this kind, it is necessary to introduce in more detail the figure of the great antagonist, the dramatistically necessary and morally essential human force of absolute evil whose competition with Christ drives the drama of apocalypse.

Briefly, Antichrist's story goes as follows: According to prophecy he will appear only when the gospel has been preached to the entire world and the Jews are gathered once again in Israel.[9] There will be a great "falling away" of Christians before he is revealed, which some commentators take to refer to the rapture, the snatching up into heaven of the elect to preserve them from the terrors of the tribulation.[10] Antichrist will convince even many believers that he is the Second Coming and reign over the entire world for a period of three and a half years, during which there will be unprecedented peace and harmony everywhere. He will unite all the world's religions into one, in a philosophy based on monism.

All who follow him and accept his mark (666) on their foreheads and hands (paralleling the *tfillin* orthodox Jews wear at worship) will prosper in this period, for only they will be permitted to buy and sell. In contemporary interpretations of this notion, cash will have been withdrawn from circulation, to be replaced by a sort of debit card, issued only to bearers of the mark, which will be readable by some form of scanner like those used in supermarkets.

This period and the three and a half years following it together will make up the tribulation, a time of unique suffering for Christians, at first, but finally for everyone, as Antichrist tries to enforce universal worship of himself as God. Satan and a false prophet will assist him in this effort, making up an unholy triumvirate, a satanic counterpart to the Holy Trinity.

Antichrist will set up an unspecified "abomination of desolation" in the holy of holies, inside the rebuilt Third Temple of the Jews, in Jerusalem. This is usually taken to refer to a colossal statue of himself that everyone must worship. This desecration will provoke an attack on Israel by armies of the North, which Antichrist will defeat with a coalition of other nations. This will give him unchallengeable power and total despotic rule over the earth for the short period until the true Christ appears and defeats him for good at Armageddon.

Antichrist is recognizable by his wickedness, that is, his rejection of God and Christ. He is a great liar and gains allegiance by bribery. Most tellingly for our purposes, he is a "satanic reformer," one who intends to change "times and laws" (Dan. 7:25). He may even try to change the calendar. He will also be the greatest anti-Semite known to history. Though the Jews initially will accept him as their Messiah, they will repudiate this covenant after the "abomination of desolation," and Antichrist will then seek to destroy them all.

This story relies on the arcane visions reported in Daniel 7 and in the Book of Revelation, where the ten horns of the beast from the sea symbolize Antichrist and his ten-nation alliance, in typical readings of the text.

Antichrist is not Satan, but stands in relation to him as Christ stands to God; Judeo-Christian eschatology constantly invokes complementary counterparts. As the New Testament recapitulates the Old, and is conceived by some Christian thinkers to complete it, every aspect of God has its satanic but unequal counterpart.

Antichrist will be the leader of the forces of evil on the earth, Satan's tool as Christ leads the faithful for God. Antichrist appears in Islam as al-Dajjal, the deceiver or denier, and fills much the same function there as in Christianity (see chapter 1). There is a similar figure in Judaism called Armilius.

In Zoroaster's apocalypse duality is absolute. For each protagonist there is an antagonist, and these paired beings fight one another exclusively. But the figure of an absolutely evil human opponent to the human/divine savior only begins to appear in the Jewish apocalypses of the late Second Temple era.[11] Like apocalyptic in general, the emergence of an Antichrist seems to be a direct consequence of Antiochus IV Epiphanes's persecution and attempted forcible conversion of the Jews. It is relatively commonplace to find a supernatural proponent of total evil in religious systems; in dualistic systems it is a requirement. At least for Christians a human acolyte of Satan has a peculiar fascination. Antichrist's legend emerges full-blown only in Christianity and has been elaborated constantly for most of two millennia. It is as though Christ's full majesty could be realized only in the defeat of an all-but-omnipotent force of evil.

Evil, like everything apocalyptic, oscillates between polar positions. Bernard McGinn identifies two of these in Christian thought. The first concerns evil's location: Is it some external force attacking the community of believers or some component of the believers themselves, perhaps one's own soul? The second polarity, perhaps a complement of the first, involves dread and deception. Antichrist's most vivid portrayals make him an immense worldly power, an emperor of the last days who will do his awful worst to destroy the church and all its believers. Although the faithful are assured of ultimate salvation, Antichrist still has the power to cause terrible death and destruction before Christ finally kills him.

Antichrist's pride in demanding worship is conspicuous and would inspire loathing in good Christians, but in terms of his character it is little more than a plot device and was not at all unusual among emperors at the time of the early Christians. This arrogance requires Christian refusal, which in turn requires Antichrist's best efforts to exterminate the

Christian community. It is impossible for Antichrist to tolerate repudiation, just as it is impossible for a Christian to submit. Confrontation becomes inevitable.

What is nearly as important as Antichrist's fearsomeness is his subtlety. He is the great deceiver, the perverter and betrayer of true Christianity, and he sometimes can fool even the elect. This aspect of Antichrist is usually cast as a religious leader or his office—typically the pope or the papacy. The deceiver also operates internally and can be seen in those Christians who profess Christ and still do wickedness.

The first Christian treatment of Antichrist is in Paul's second letter to the Thessalonians.[12] Here Paul makes it clear that Antichrist's presence must be made known before the Second Coming can occur. In an interesting aside, he observes that Antichrist opposes every so-called god, not just Jehovah. Christians should expect many false alarms from pretenders claiming to be, or to know of, Christ's return. Only when Antichrist institutes worship of himself in the Temple can they be certain. For now Antichrist is restrained, but the mystery of evil is still at work.

The mystical identifier 666 is, in McGinn's view, best read as a numerical encoding of the Hebrew for *Neron Caesar* (Emperor Nero). Nero's number has been applied ever since in attempts to assign the role of Antichrist to this or that powerful historical figure. In fact there is now a shareware computer program called "666 Searcher" that will analyze any name for its accordance with this number.

In McGinn's view, the most interesting conceptions of Antichrist are now to be found in fiction, and this part of the book will deal with apocalyptic and millenarian ideas that derive from that genre.

During Antichrist's long history, the conception has arisen that he might be collective rather than a single powerful man. But even if Antichrist is individual, he cannot work alone. In the final battle with Christ he has the armies of Gog and Magog on his side, as well as kings of the south and east, yet nevertheless he is beaten. A question that devils a great many of today's apocalypticists is, Who are these allies in today's world? Who is busily preparing his way? More often than not, the answer they arrive at is the West's favorite enemy: the Jews. We can thus begin to consider the place of fiction in apocalyptic rhetoric with the *Protocols of the Learned Elders of Zion.*

Notes

1. Michael Ortiz Hill, *Dreaming the End of the World: Apocalypse as a Rite of Passage* (Dallas: Spring Publications, 1994), 10.

2. Quoted in Catherine Keller, "The Breast, the Apocalypse, and the Colonial Journey," in *The Year 2000: Essays on the End,* ed. Charles B. Strozier and Michael Flynn (New York: New York University Press, 1997), 51.

3. Hill, *Dreaming the End of the World,* 10.

4. Ibid., 11.

5. H. G. Wells, *The World Set Free* (London: Unwin, 1926).

6. Hill, *Dreaming the End of the World,* 13.

7. Ibid., 19.

8. Stephen O'Leary, *Arguing the Apocalypse: A Theory of Millennial Rhetoric* (New York: Oxford University Press, 1994), 51ff.

9. This is a condensation of a generalized fundamentalist Christian version of the story. Sects differ on the details, but the fundamentalists are the most active believers in this aspect of the millennium myth.

10. There is endless debate over this doctrine. Will the rapture happen at all, or will Christians test their faith in the tribulation? If it does happen, when will it happen? Pre-trib, post-trib, mid-trib, in the jargon of contemporary belief? The rapture received special prominence in the work of the nineteenth-century divine John Nelson Darby and his doctrine of dispensationalism.

11. This sketch relies on Bernard McGinn's *Antichrist: Two Thousand Years of the Human Fascination with Evil* (San Francisco: Harper, 1994).

12. 2 Thessalonians 2:1–12. See also McGinn, *Antichrist,* 41–45.

CHAPTER 5

A ROYALIST APOCALYPSE

The Protocols of the Learned Elders of Zion

The Protocols of the Learned Elders of Zion was written partly in response to Karl Marx and his "spectre of Communism" with which the *Communist Manifesto* begins. It is a famous forgery purporting to reveal a plot of world Jewry to enslave the planet under its own rule through a series of Machiavellian manipulations of greed and liberal impulses. In fact it was composed (in large part plagiarized) by Czarist secret police as a rationale to divert criticism from the Romanovs for the decadent condition of their empire and to blame the Jews instead.

Russia at the end of the nineteenth century was the last surviving despotism in Europe, the last holdout of pure autocracy in the Western world. The Czars' reign was close to collapse in its economic stagnation, its backwardness, and above all the paralysis of its government.[1] Nicholas II, Russia's last Czar, believed passionately in his own divine right. He wrote, "I am absolute and I answer only to God."[2] He had taken his throne utterly unprepared to rule and expended little effort on changing that condition.

One of the Czar's ministers pressed the country's efforts at modernization; the rest strongly opposed them. Russia's industrialization under Nicholas was catastrophic for the peasants and might have served as the textbook case for Marx's critique of capital. One of the Czar's less progressive ministers, Konstantin Pobedonestsev, proposed a solution to the country's "Jewish problem" prescient of Hitler: he proposed to convert one third, deport another third, and allow the remainder to die out.

As these events drew together, an apocalyptic mood occupied much of the country and intensified as disaster followed upon neglected disaster. A stampede of the huge crowd gathered to witness Nicholas's coronation killed nearly 1,500 people. In Otto Friedrich's words, "Confronted by the dragon of chaos, the all-powerful Emperor proved powerless."[3] There were droughts and crop failures, plagues, and economic depression followed by famine. Desperate peasants looted and burned estates.

The government's primary response was to organize the Okhrana, an enormous network of political police and spies, to report on any organized opposition. This was a fascinating structure, a clear predecessor to the NKVD and other arms of the Soviet state. Once caught in the Okhrana's web, the only way to clear oneself of suspicion was to become another spy, adding to the 2.5 million rubles this apparatus cost every year. Spies were watching spies, and so much information was gathered that it became nearly impossible to make sense of it all.

In fact, there seems to have been little real organized opposition, but, like the Inquisition before them, the police were busily creating enemies. The chief of the Okhrana explained his tactics to some leftists: "We shall provoke you to acts of terror and then crush you." Hysteria rather quickly found an outlet, as a wave of political assassinations began.

The Czar's fervent Christianity led him to equally fervent anti-Semitism. He is quoted as saying, "We must never forget that it was the Jews who crucified our Lord and spilled his precious blood."[4] He "rejoice[d] when they [were] beaten" and blamed the pogroms on his people's outrage at "Jewish" socialists. Jews had been in Russia since before the birth of Christ, and they had been perceived as a "problem" nearly all that time, though there was no systematic persecution until Ivan the Terrible (1530–1584) instituted a ban against them. This was replaced by Catherine the Great's policy of containment (begun 1783), when Russia acquired nearly a million Jewish citizens after the partition of Poland. Jews were forbidden to leave the area where they already lived (the Pale) and were taxed at double the rate of Christian subjects.

Earlier pogroms had largely been confined to looting, but under Nicholas's reign they became increasingly bloodthirsty. A government-sponsored anti-Semitic newspaper in the city of Kishinev published a renewed version of the blood libel (slanderous rumors to the effect that Jews slaughter Christian children to drain their blood for ritual use). This story was repeated, accompanied by clearly organized provocation, clearly the work of the secret police. In 1903 fifty Jews were killed and hundreds wounded in two days of rioting that the local chief of police called "a use-ful bloodletting."[5] Russia's interior minister associated the pogrom with revolutionary activity and told Jews that he would stop the attacks when they renounced socialism.

This was the context in which the *Protocols of the Learned Elders of Zion* appeared. The notion of a secret cabalistic and rabbinical pan-despotism has medieval roots, but the idea of secret societies disrupting the feudal *ancien régimes* of Europe seems to originate with Abbé Baruel's attribution of the French Revolution to Freemasons in 1797. He makes no mention of Jews, but the notion of secret societies at work to enslave the world was introduced. Even today, many people do not distinguish between Jews and Freemasons. Baruel's idea was nonsense on its face, since the French nobility of the time was itself largely Masonic, but dystopian faith is not subject to contradiction by fact. The basic idea persists and flourishes even today.

The direct source of the *Protocols* is Maurice Joly's 1864 pamphlet *Dialogues in Hell between Machiavelli and Montesquieu.* This satire also fails to mention Jews, but it sets forth most of the plot they were later supposed to hatch in its attack on the ambitions of the French Emperor Napoleon III.

Joly went to jail for his writings, but his pamphlet inspired a German anti-Semite named Hermann Goedsche, who worked as a postal clerk and spy for the Prussian secret police. He forged evidence against a Prussian democrat in 1849 and was forced out of his job.

Goedsche took up writing fiction under the pen name Sir John Ret-cliffe. In a novel called *Biarritz* (published 1868) he adapted Joly's pamphlet in a chapter called "The Jewish Cemetery in Prague and the Council of Representatives of the Twelve Tribes of Israel." It describes a sort of Jewish witches' sabbath, where one representative from each of the twelve tribes of Israel comes to a once-a-century-meeting with their master, Satan, to discuss the progress of their plans for domination.

Goedsche's novel was translated into Russian in 1872, and a condensed version of the cemerty chapter, called "Rabbi's Speech," was published there in 1879. The connection between these books and the Russian secret police is not firmly established, though they are similar to the *Protocols* that the police later produced.

Goedshe's works were useful in support of Nicholas II and in damag-ing the reputation of liberal reformers. The *Protocols* first appeared in

Paris during the Dreyfus case (1893–1895), courtesy of the Okhrana, combining elements of the novel and Joly's satire. A Russian edition appeared in 1897, but the work attracted little attention until the Russo-Japanese War and subsequent revolution of 1905. The revolution led to the institution of a constitution and parliament, which aroused strong reaction in the Union of the Russian Nation. This movement, also called the Black Hundreds, blamed the revolution on the Jews and worked to arouse popular resentment against them. The *Protocols* suited this purpose well, and when Sergius Nilus, a "mystic priest," published his first Russian edition in 1905 the Black Hundreds quickly adopted it for their propaganda campaign.[6] This effort was closely orchestrated with pogroms incited by the Okhrana.

The *Protocols* has proved a useful political tool to reactionary movements ever since. The anti-Bolshevik White Army used it to incite pogroms in 1917, even as escapees from the Bolsheviks carried the book to Western Europe and the United States. It was translated widely, despite its exposure as plagiarism in 1920, just after Victor E. Marsden translated it into English. A recent publisher credits the work with no fewer than eighty-one printings. The fact that most of the debunkers were Jews made it a simple matter for anti-Semites to dismiss their efforts. Henry Ford sponsored an American edition until 1927, and the Nazis drew upon it to justify their holocaust.

The document is clearly a royalist apocalypse, or better, an anti-apocalypse. Richard Landes calls opponents of the millennium "owls," as opposed to prophetic roosters who are always crowing about a new dawn. The owls are wise birds, urging caution and restraint.[7] This doesn't quite fit the authors of the *Protocols*. As originally presented, however, it is owl propaganda. The authors call for the suppression of an evil cabal, a word whose derivation from Kabbalah is not insignificant. In presenting this Gnostic lore, the *Protocols* seek to protect, above all, the despotic order of Russia from "Jewish" socialism.[8] In the best thriller tradition, it presents a hair's-breadth escape. It is only by the merest accident that we, the good, have knowledge of this immense evil, hence the means to oppose and finally conquer it.

According to the *Protocols,* aristocracy is the only hope, the source of the stability and peace of nations, which is what this sinister organization with its alleged global control of finance has been wrecking for centuries. It alone can dominate the world and enslave it in a monstrous police state.

The Jews, it was supposed, planned to reintroduce aristocracy, but a new one, which they alone would administer and could gain admission to. Wouldn't everyone be an aristocrat, given the chance?

Jews provide the perfect scapegoat for this kind of magical thinking. They are a tiny minority nearly everywhere, often despised, frequently attacked and forced into exile, but still they have survived thousands of years of almost constant persecution. Notwithstanding all racist logic and justice, not only do they survive the most rigorous oppression and persecution, they have often thrived despite it. Jewish control of powerful institutions is disproportionate to their numbers. What can account for this, the thinking goes, but magic?

In the minds of the anonymous authors of the *Protocols,* democracy was the tool of choice for bringing about world domination. In an odd echo of Marx, the authors of the *Protocols* bitterly attack capital and its wage-slavery. Remember that these reactionaries supported a precapitalist feudal order that survived, barely, in Russia alone.

It would be possible to multiply examples, but it is perhaps more interesting to consider Nilus's commentary on this extraordinary work, which he claimed to have discovered.

The appeal of the *Protocols* does not end with the revelation of their forgery; that is generally known among scholars. But information coming from such sources is inherently suspect in the world of conspiracy. After all, scholars, or most of them, are part of the establishment, like the media. They know quite well where the butter lies on their bread, and so, conspiracists tell us, they tell the most egregious lies in the face of what the conspiracist knows is solid fact. No faith is ultimately subject to rational argument.

The appeal of texts like the *Protocols* is emotional. They continue to inflame passions on the radical right in America and elsewhere. Most of Nilus's themes of rage and repression reappear in conspiracist texts today.

• • •

The Protocols of the Learned Elders of Zion

From Protocol No. 1

In all corners of the earth the words "Liberty, Equality, Fraternity" brought to our ranks, thanks to our blind agents, whole legions who bore our banners with enthusiasm. And all the time these words were canker-worms at work boring into the well-being of the *goyim*, putting an end everywhere to peace, quiet, solidarity and destroying all the foundations of the *goya* States. As you will see later, this helped us to our triumph; it gave us the possibility, among other things, of getting into our hands the master card—the destruction of the privileges, or in other words of the very existence of the aristocracy of the *goyim*, that class which was the only defense peoples and countries had against us.

On the ruins of the natural and genealogical aristocracy of the *goyim* we have set up the aristocracy of our educated class headed by the aristocracy of money. The qualifications for this aristocracy we have established in wealth, which is dependent upon us, and in knowledge, for which our learned elders provide the motive force.

The abstraction of freedom has enabled us to persuade the mob in all countries that their government is nothing but the steward of the people who are the owners of the country, and that the steward may be replaced like a worn-out glove. It is this possibility of replacing the representatives of the people which has placed them at our disposal, and, as it were, given us the power of appointment.

From Protocol No. 3

Republican rights for a poor man are no more than a bitter piece of irony, for the necessity he is under of toiling almost all day gives him no present use of them, but on the other hand robs him of all guarantee of regular and certain earnings by making him dependent on strikes by his comrades or lockouts by his masters. The people under our guidance have annihilated the aristocracy, who were their one and only defense and foster mother for the sake of their own advantage which is inseparably bound up with the well-being of the people.

Nowadays, with the destruction of the aristocracy, the people have fallen into the grips of merciless money-grinding scoundrels who have laid a pitiless and cruel yoke upon the necks of the workers. We appear on the scene as alleged saviors of the worker from this oppression when we propose to him to enter the ranks of our fighting forces—Socialists, Anarchists, Communists—to whom we always give support in accordance with an alleged brotherly rule (of the solidarity of all humanity) of our social masonry.

The aristocracy, which enjoyed by law the labor of the workers, was interested in seeing that the workers were well fed, healthy and strong. We are interested in just the opposite—in the diminution, the killing out of the *goyim*. Our power is in the chronic shortness of food and physical weakness of the worker because by all that this implies he is made the slave of our will, and he will not find in his own authorities either strength or energy to set against our will. Hunger creates the right of capital to rule the worker more surely than it was given to the aristocracy by the legal authority of kings. By want and the envy and hatred which it engenders we shall move the mobs and with their hands we shall wipe out all those who hinder us on our way.

When the hour strikes for our Sovereign Lord of all the World to be crowned it is these same hands which will sweep away everything that might be a hindrance thereto. The *goyim* have lost the habit of thinking unless prompted by the suggestions of our specialists. Therefore they do not see the urgent necessity of what we, when our kingdom comes, shall adopt at once, namely this, that it is essential to teach in national schools one simple, true piece of knowledge, the basis of all knowledge—the knowledge of the structure of human life, of social existence, which requires division of labor, and, consequently, the division of men into classes and conditions.

Concluding Passage from the Epilogue of Nilus
(Edition of 1905)

According to the testament of Montefiore, Zion is not sparing, either of money or of any other means, to achieve its ends. In our day, all the governments of the entire world are consciously or unconsciously submissive to the commands of this great Supergovernment of Zion, because all the bonds and securities are in its hands: for all countries are indebted to the Jews for sums which they will never be able to pay. All affairs—industry, commerce, and diplomacy—are in the hands of Zion. It is by means of its capital loans that it has enslaved all nations. By keeping education on purely materialistic lines, the Jews have loaded the Gentiles with heavy chains with which they have harnessed them to their "super-government." The end of national liberty is near, therefore personal freedom is approaching its close; for true liberty cannot exist where Zion uses the lever of its gold to rule the masses and dominate the most respectable and enlightened class of society. "He that hath ears to hear, let him hear."

It is nearly four years since the *Protocols of the Elders of Zion* came into my possession. Only God knows what efforts I have made to bring them to general notice—in vain—and even to warn those in power, by disclosing the causes of the storm about to break on apathetic Russia who seems, in her misfortune, to have lost all notion of what is going on around her. And it is only now when I fear it may be too late, that I have succeeded in publishing my work, hoping to put on their guard those who still have ears to hear and eyes to see.

One can no longer doubt it, the triumphant reign of the King of Israel rises over our degenerate world as that of Satan, with his power and his terrors; the King born of the blood of Zion—the Antichrist—is about to mount the throne of universal empire. Events are precipitated in the world at a terrifying speed: quarrels, wars, rumors, famines, epidemics, earthquakes—everything which even yesterday was impossible, today is an accomplished fact. One would think that the days pass so rapidly to advance the cause of the chosen people.

Space does not allow us to enter into the details of world history with regard to the disclosed "mysteries of iniquity," to prove from history the influence which the "Wise Men of Zion" have exercised through universal misfortunes by foretelling the certain and already near future of humanity, or by raising the curtain for the last act of the world's tragedy.

Only the light of Christ and of his Holy Church Universal can fathom the abyss of Satan and disclose the extent of its wickedness. I feel in my heart that the hour has already struck when there should urgently be convoked an Eighth Ecumenical Council which would unite the pastor [*sic*] and representatives of all Christendom. Secular quarrels and schisms would all be forgotten in the imminent need of preparing against the coming of the Antichrist.

Notes

1. Otto Friedrich, *The End of the World: A History* (New York: Fromm International, 1986), 217ff.

2. Quoted in ibid., 218.

3. Ibid., 222.

4. Ibid., 229.

5. Ibid., 232.

6. Nilus had been a candidate for spiritual adviser to the royal family. He seems to have been mad and wrote a book called *The Great in the Small*, which foretold Antichrist's coming and a satanic reign over the earth. Members of the royal family who opposed the incumbent supported his appointment, and they succeeded in having Nilus move into the royal compound, though the post eventually went to Rasputin instead.

7. See, for example, Richard Landes, "The Apocalyptic Year 1000: Millennium Fever and the Origins of the Modern West," in *The Year 2000: Essays on the End,* ed. by Charles B. Strozier and Michael Flynn (New York: New York University Press, 1997).

8. The fact that a good many socialists, their leaders in particular, did indeed have Jewish backgrounds (Marx's grandfather was an important rabbi, though his father converted in order to keep his job in anti-Semitic Germany) does not make of their system a particularly Jewish doctrine. As we have seen, the roots of Enlightenment thought, and hence of socialism's egalitarian principles, lie in the work of Christian thinkers.

CHAPTER 6

MYTHS OF POWER

Conspiracies, Revenge, and The Turner Diaries

Conspiracy theory is frequently at the heart of millenarian thinking; we have seen examples already in *Mein Kampf* (chapter 3) and the *Protocols of the Elders of Zion* (chapter 5). An important point about conspiracy theory is that it very often has some basis in fact.[1] One such fact is that no organization can conduct all its business in public. If it had to consult its constituency about every decision, none of them could be carried out. Another fact is that organizations often work toward purposes they don't divulge. The CIA and the National Security Agency, to name just two, work this way.

The nature of conspiracist thought is no better conveyed than in this quotation from one of Jeffrey Kaplan's informants: "I'm a student of Bible prophecy. . . . I'm also a Vietnam veteran who has fought Communism. Partly because of that I was determined from the start to fit Communism into Bible Prophesy [*sic*], if at all possible. I looked for evidence that the Antichrist, the Beast, the Man of Sin, Gog (all names of the same man) was a Soviet leader. I found it."[2] Like many theologians before him, this student found evidence to support what he was "determined" to show.

Conspiracy theory is an inversion and doubling of Gnostic ideas about salvation through arcane knowledge. Gnostics believe that they possess exclusive access to this divine, or at any rate hidden, knowledge about the secret workings of the world; conspiracists believe that other people have such knowledge and use it to control the world and nearly everyone in it. This knowledge is not exclusive, however, because another tiny minority also knows the secret: the conspiracists themselves. In the conspiracists' view of the workings of the world, the controllers are intent only on domination and oppression; salvation lies in their own hands.

As Kaplan points out, believers in theories of this kind perceive themselves to be on a "promethean" quest: to reveal to the rest of mankind the truth behind the world's wickedness, though it may cost them friends, jobs, and marriages.[3] Still they find comfort with one another, in the occult milieu where these ideas circulate and come to roost.

Conspiracy theorists conduct thorough, painstaking research (much conspiratorialist history of the Bavarian Illuminati, for instance, is accurate: It really was a secret benevolent society founded in 1776 on the model of the Freemasons, then an important source of progressive ideas) leading to completely unjustified conclusions. There is always a leap of dystopian faith into the realm of the utterly implausible, if not the downright impossible. It is as certain as anything can be that the Illuminati as an organization did not survive its suppression. It is even more certain that the society cannot claim credit for the French Revolution, despite the fact that it promoted many of the same ideas. But these ideas had been in general circulation throughout Europe for about a generation before the society came into existence.

Conspiracy theory generally attributes much greater power to elites than they actually possess. In this kind of thought, nothing happens that is not ordained; there are no unintended consequences, and literally everything the Establishment says is a lie. Conspiracy theory allows no room for mistakes. Literally everything the elite does is somehow part of its satanic aims, no matter how self-destructive some of its behavior might seem to the rest of us.

We might contrast this view with the regular blundering and foolishness of state-sponsored programs. Public housing projects destroyed within a generation of their construction provide one example. So does Vietnam, or nearly any war for that matter. Many more instances, as well as fascinating observations on the reasons for these failures, can be found in *Seeing Like a State* by James C. Scott.[4] These failures generally rest on a mirror image of conspiracy thought: Planners convince themselves that the goal they have in mind can be reached through the application of rational abstract principles that fail to take real, local conditions into account. Their oversight dooms the plan. By assuming their own infallibility, the planners behave exactly like the omnipotent behemoths the conspiracists think they are.

Conspiracy theory, even when it is not overtly apocalyptic, shares attributes of apocalyptic thinking. Nothing less than total victory will satisfy the conspiracy thinker, for his enemy is all-powerful and totally ruthless. The enemy controls literally everything—history is the record of his works—except for the thinker himself and whatever tiny band of friends he may have. The enemy's almost total power and complete amorality make him utterly free, while the brave resister labors heroically under the constraints he imposes.

Researchers into conspiracies reject all authority: political, religious, mainstream media, and perhaps especially scientific. Anything that comes from a source of acknowledged power is ipso facto suspect. Such sources are only interested in maintaining the status quo and their own profitable place in it. There is some factual basis for this belief. Establishment resistance to innovation has been readily apparent at least since Thomas Kuhn's *The Structure of Scientific Revolution,* which describes the process whereby new theories gain acceptance in the scientific canon. Some of the people hatching and investigating these conspiratorial ideas carry their disillusionment so far that they maintain that power is incapable of truth, even when it would be beneficial to its interests.

This principle is perhaps nowhere better demonstrated than in one Christian apologist's test of the truth of his favorite doctrine, the "pre-trib rapture."[5] When the devil (i.e., the world and its minions) attacks or ignores an idea, you can be fairly certain that it comes from God. "If the devil-controlled world displays an[d] ignores or disfavor [*sic*] towards a teaching, it's almost a sured [*sic*] that the teaching, in question, can be noted as scripturally sound." Scripture remains his "foundational proof," but the worldly press's neglect is a close second.

When the networks (except the godless ABC) began to run shows on prophecy, they completely neglected the rapture, even when they discussed "every [other] conceivable prophetic topic." This puzzled the believer. Christian bookstores are crammed with works on the subject, but the mainstream media flatly ignore it. This can only indicate Satan's intense desire to keep it secret.

The believer's reflections on the media reveal a common and intense ambivalence. Millenarians generally loathe the media, which they see as a stooge of Antichrist, a stepson of the Father of Lies. At the same time, they yearn to have their messages broadcast and discussed seriously in the media. They know that in this way they could finally get the hearing they think their message deserves and the world needs.

To conspiracists, the elites who rule the world—especially those they consider to be the Antichrist—are people who combine two anomalies in their careers: power and mystery. Power is itself a mystery to some extent. It ought to function according to the rules of moral order that believers think control their own lives, but it seldom does. As for the mystery, it lies in the question of how people who have power get it in the first place, and why do they so often abuse it when they have it. From the point of view of the devotee who considers himself virtuous and submissive to the will of whatever ultimate principle he dedicates himself to, it must appear strange that people who so often are utterly unlike him enjoy so much of the world's material blessings. It is morally senseless that pushy, crass, destructive, and often downright wicked people should command so much of the world and its wealth, but that is exactly what happens. The world does not make moral sense for the believer shut out of life's rewards. The millenarian's aim is to restore moral sense to a world that conspicuously lacks it.

The Turner Diaries

A chillingly frequent focus of this vengeful rage is racism. William L. Pierce's 1978 racist novel *The Turner Diaries* is a fantasy about turning America and the world into a fascist and racist state. It is presented as a historical record of events during a revolution at the end of the twentieth century that brought about a new era of racial purity in which America is exclusively occupied by an Aryan society. All others have been purged in a series of titanic bloodbaths.

Purporting to be the reminiscences of a low-level "Organization" functionary named Earl Turner, the book pretends to chronicle events of that time, presenting along the way instructions on building and maintaining underground terrorist cells and equipping them for their grisly tasks. It records the activities of Turner and his colleagues in their own clandestine group, as their terror tactics progress from blowing up the FBI building in Washington through a mortar attack on the Capitol Building to a nuclear attack on Tel Aviv. In this book one can learn how to encode communication or build a bomb from ammonium nitrate and bunker oil (as Timothy McVeigh and Terry Nichols did in Oklahoma City), in terms just vague enough to save the book from becoming simply a manual of terror.

Its characters are pure cardboard, amounting to nothing more than names and actions, heroic or squalid according to Pierce's racist morality. Pierce uses the word "racist" in quotation marks whenever it is applied to his secret underground movement, as though it were a false accusation. This is odd, because the book and its protagonists are devoted exclusively to ridding the world of "niggers" and "kikes" in the most bloodthirsty and expeditious manner possible.

Death is the only life in this book. Martyrdom for the cause is a foregone conclusion and a sort of glorious millennium in itself. It vindicates the martyrs and their cause. Turner finds his martyrdom flying a cropduster biplane in a nuclear attack on the Pentagon. Pierce writes with gruesome relish of murder, rape, lynching, and war. Everything else is colorless boilerplate: pseudo-heroic posing, musty racist rhetoric, and musings about the "infantile" nature of liberalism and the corruption and inefficiency of central government. Conditions are almost postapoclyptic already: electric power is unreliable, and roads go unrepaired for years, all the while the ZOG (Zionist Occupation Government) plans ever more repressive measures against its own citizenry.

Turner and his group are presented as a finer breed even than most other Aryans, who remain apathetic to their struggle. The others can't "smell the stink" of the decaying "System." Most whites are "brainwashed" idlers, devoted to TV and a fatty diet and caring nothing for the loss of their freedoms, which they do not even notice. The racist apocalypse is perfectly clear, but its millennium—its vision of paradise—is not easy to identify. *The Turner Diaries* presents a dim version of it, but the real appeal for some of these believers seems to be that it will never arrive. They will perish in the deathless glory of a lost cause. The Reichsfolk web site, for example, contains this vision of renewal:

"For a true warrior, a true Aryan, all living is *either* a tiresome waiting for those moments of glory when sacrifice is possible, *or* a living of those divine moments of war, adventure, discovery and overcoming."[6] Their millennium is combat.

Pierce's book remains what the FBI called it, "a bible of the racist right." It begins as most "patriots" expect the New World Order to make its debut: with raids seizing guns from law-abiding white citizens, leaving them helpless against the depredations of black rapist gangs.

When a copy of this book was found in Timothy McVeigh's possession, Pierce tried valiantly to distance himself from the Oklahoma City massacre, despite the fact that it was clearly modeled on the attack on the FBI building described in the *Diaries*. It is widely available on web sites and seems to attract a large readership.

• • •

THE TURNER DIARIES

Chapter 1

September 16, 1991. Today it finally began! After all these years of talking—and nothing but talking—we have finally taken our first action. We are at war with the System, and it is no longer a war of words.

I cannot sleep, so I will try writing down some of the thoughts which are flying through my head.

It is not safe to talk here. The walls are quite thin, and the neighbors might wonder at a late-night conference. Besides, George and Katherine are already asleep. Only Henry and I are still awake, and he's just staring at the ceiling.

I am really uptight. I am so jittery I can barely sit still. And I'm exhausted. I've been up since 5:30 this morning, when George phoned to warn that the arrests had begun, and it's after midnight now. I've been keyed up and on the move all day.

But at the same time I'm exhilarated. We have finally acted! How long we will be able to continue defying the System, no one knows. Maybe it will all end tomorrow, but we must not think about that. Now that we have begun, we must continue with the plan we have been developing so carefully ever since the Gun Raids two years ago.

What a blow that was to us! And how it shamed us! All that brave talk by patriots, "The government will never take my guns away," and then nothing but meek submission when it happened.

On the other hand, maybe we should be heartened by the fact that there were still so many of us who had guns then, nearly 18 months after the Cohen Act had outlawed all private ownership of firearms in the United States. It was only because so many of us defied the law and hid our weapons instead of turning them in that the government wasn't able to act more harshly against us after the Gun Raids.

I'll never forget that terrible day: November 9, 1989. They knocked on my door at five in the morning. I was completely unsuspecting as I got up to see who it was.

I opened the door, and four Negroes came pushing into the apartment before I could stop them. One was carrying a baseball bat, and two had long kitchen knives thrust into their belts. The one with the bat shoved me back into a corner and stood guard over me with his bat raised in a threatening position while the other three began ransacking my apartment.

My first thought was that they were robbers. Robberies of this sort had become all too common since the Cohen Act, with groups of Blacks forcing their way into White homes to rob and rape, knowing that even if their victims had guns they probably would not dare use them.

Then the one who was guarding me flashed some kind of card and informed me that he and his accomplices were "special deputies" for the Northern Virginia Human Relations Council. They were searching for firearms, he said.

I couldn't believe it. It just couldn't be happening. Then I saw that they were wearing strips of green cloth tied around their left arms. As they dumped the contents of drawers on the floor and pulled luggage from the closet, they were ignoring things that robbers wouldn't have passed up: my brand-new electric razor, a valuable gold pocket watch, a milk bottle full of dimes. They were looking for firearms!

Right after the Cohen Act was passed, all of us in the Organization had cached our guns and ammunition where they weren't likely to be found. Those in my unit had carefully greased our weapons, sealed them in an oil drum, and spent all of one tedious weekend burying the drum in an eight-foot-deep pit 200 miles away in the woods of western Pennsylvania.

But I had kept one gun out of the cache. I had hidden my .357 magnum revolver and 50 rounds of ammunition inside the door frame between the kitchen and the living room. By pulling out two loosened nails and removing one board from the door frame I could get to my revolver in about two minutes flat if I ever needed it. I had timed myself.

But a police search would never uncover it. And these inexperienced Blacks couldn't find it in a million years.

After the three who were conducting the search had looked in all the obvious places, they began slitting open my mattress and the sofa cushions. I protested vigorously at this and briefly considered trying to put up a fight.

About that time there was a commotion out in the hallway. Another group of searchers had found a rifle hidden under a bed in the apartment of the young couple down the hall. They had both been handcuffed and were being forcibly escorted toward the stairs. Both were clad only in their underwear, and the young woman was complaining loudly about the fact that her baby was being left alone in the apartment.

Another man walked into my apartment. He was a Caucasian, though with an unusually dark complexion. He also wore a green armband, and he carried an attaché case and a clipboard. The Blacks greeted him deferentially and reported the negative result of their search: "No guns here, Mr. Tepper." Tepper ran his finger down the list of names and apartment numbers on his clipboard until he came to mine. He frowned. "This is a bad one," he said. "He has a racist record. Been cited by the Council twice. And he owned eight firearms which were never turned in."

Tepper opened his attaché case and took out a small, black object about the size of a pack of cigarettes which was attached by a long cord to an electronic instrument in the case. He began moving the black object in long sweeps back and forth over the walls, while the attaché case emitted a dull, rumbling noise. The rumble rose in pitch as the gadget approached the light switch, but Tepper convinced himself that the change was caused by the metal junction box and conduit buried in the wall. He continued his methodical sweep.

As he swept over the left side of the kitchen door frame the rumble jumped to a piercing shriek. Tepper grunted excitedly, and one of the Negroes went out and came back a few seconds later with a sledge hammer and a pry bar. It took the Negro substantially less than two minutes after that to find my gun.I was handcuffed without further ado and led outside. Altogether, four of us were arrested in my apartment building. In addition to the couple down the hall, there was an elderly man from the fourth floor. They hadn't found a firearm in his apartment, but they had found four shotgun shells on his closet shelf. Ammunition was also illegal.

Mr. Tepper and some of his "deputies" had more searches to carry out, but three large Blacks with baseball bats and knives were left to guard us in front of the apartment building. The four of us were forced to sit on the cold sidewalk, in various states of undress, for more than an hour until a police van finally came for us.

As other residents of the apartment building left for work, they eyed us curiously. We were all shivering, and the young woman from down the hall was weeping uncontrollably. One man stopped to ask what it was all about. One of our guards brusquely explained that we were all under arrest for possessing illegal weapons. The man stared at us and shook his head disapprovingly.

Then the Black pointed to me and said: "And that one's a racist." Still shaking his head, the man moved on. Herb Jones, who used to belong to the Organization and was one of the most outspoken of the "they'll-never-get-my-gun" people before the Cohen Act, walked by quickly with his eyes averted. His apartment had been searched too, but Herb was clean. He had been practically the first man in town to turn his guns over to the police after the passage of the Cohen Act made him liable to ten years imprisonment in a Federal penitentiary if he kept them. That was the penalty the four of us on the sidewalk were facing. It didn't work out that way, though. The reason it didn't is that the raids which were carried out all over the country that day netted a lot more fish than the System had counted on: more than 800,000 persons were arrested.

At first the news media tried hard to work up enough public sentiment against us so that the arrests would stick. The fact that there weren't enough jail cells in the country to hold us all could be remedied by herding us into barbed-wire enclosures outdoors until new prison facilities could be readied, the newspapers suggested. In freezing weather!

I still remember the Washington Post headline the next day: "Fascist-Racist Conspiracy Smashed, Illegal Weapons Seized." But not even the brainwashed American public could fully accept the idea that nearly a million of their fellow citizens had been engaged in a secret, armed conspiracy.

As more and more details of the raids leaked out, public restlessness grew. One of the details which bothered people was that the raiders had, for the most part, exempted Black neighborhoods from the searches. The explanation given at first for this was that since "racists" were the ones primarily suspected of harboring firearms, there was relatively little need to search Black homes.

The peculiar logic of this explanation broke down when it turned out that a number of persons who could hardly be considered either "racists" or "fascists" had been caught up in the raids. Among them were two prominent liberal newspaper columnists who had earlier been in the forefront of the antigun crusade, four Negro Congressmen (they lived in White neighborhoods), and an embarrassingly large number of government officials.

The list of persons to be raided, it turned out, had been compiled primarily from firearms sales records which all gun dealers had been required to keep. If a person had turned a gun in to the police after the Cohen Act was passed, his name was marked off the list. If he hadn't it stayed on, and he was raided on November 9-unless he lived in a Black neighborhood. In addition, certain categories of people were raided whether they had ever purchased a firearm from a dealer or not. All the members of the Organization were raided.

The government's list of suspects was so large that a number of "responsible" civilian groups were deputized to assist in the raids. I guess the planners in the System thought that most of the people on their list had either sold their guns privately before the Cohen Act, or had disposed of them in some other way. Probably they were expecting only about a quarter as many people to be arrested as actually were.

Anyway, the whole thing soon became so embarrassing and so unwieldy that most of the arrestees were turned loose again within a week.

The group I was with—some 600 of us—was held for three days in a high school gymnasium in Alexandria before being released. During those three days we were fed only four times, and we got virtually no sleep.

But the police did get mug shots, fingerprints, and personal data from everyone. When we were released we were told that we were still technically under arrest and could expect to be picked up again for prosecution at any time.

The media kept yelling for prosecutions for awhile, but the issue was gradually allowed to die. Actually, the System had bungled the affair rather badly.

Notes

1. Richard Hofstadter's *The Paranoid Style in American Politics and Other Essays* (Cambridge: Harvard University Press, 1965) is a classic brief survey of the history and characteristics of this genre in American history.

2. Jeffrey Kaplan, *Radical Religion in America: Millenarian Movements from the Far Right to the Children of Noah* (Syracuse, N.Y.: Syracuse University Press, 1997), 172.

3. Ibid., xvii.

4. James C. Scott, *Seeing Like a State: How Certain Schemes to Improve the Human Condition Have Failed* (New Haven: Yale University Press, 1998).

5. That is, the teaching that Jesus will rescue his Saints and meet them in the air before the worst of the tribulation's terrors strike. "How the World's Rejection of the Pre-Trib Rapture Proves Its Validity," http://www.novia.net/~todd/rap22.html (December 11, 1996).

6. The Reichs Folk website, http://reichsfolk.com/renewal.htm (April 15, 1998). There is also a Gay Nazi web site in poor repair at http://www.io.com/~rufftr88/nazi.html.

CHAPTER 7

THE NEW WORLD ORDER

George Bush's 1991 State of the Union Address aroused right-wing excitement over supposed plans for world hegemony. He called that occasion, in the middle of the Gulf War, a "defining hour." "Halfway around the world, we are engaged in a great struggle in the skies and on the seas and sands. We know why we're there. We are Americans—part of something larger than ourselves. . . . What is at stake is more than one small country, it is a big idea—a new world order, where diverse nations are drawn together in common cause to achieve the universal aspirations of mankind: peace and security, freedom, and the rule of law." And that rather neatly sums up the benefits that supporters of world union propose.

Bush was instantly demonized by conspiracists as a tool of Illuminist plots, in part because of his membership in the secretive Skull and Bones Society while at Yale. The term New World Order was not Bush's invention. It had come into inconspicuous right-wing use in a publication of a neo-Nazi group called the Covenant, the Sword, and the Arm of the Lord in 1981, though it surely was in general use before that.[1]

In conspiracy theory the New World Order (NWO) sums up the global Antichrist conspiracy. It is a catchall term covering all the objects of suspicion discussed so far. It is a secret society with arcane knowledge and immense power; instead of helping humankind toward enlightenment, these men—they are all male, apparently—want to dominate and crush us and will use any means to that end.

In its most common contemporary guise, the NWO is thought to be an avatar of the Bavarian Illuminati, an actual secret society closely modeled on Freemasonry, which at the time was itself a new and secret organization of rationalists founded for humanitarian purposes. These purposes immediately became suspect in the eyes of their opponents, principally churchmen, because the Illuminati and others like them not only met in secret to conduct arcane rituals, they promoted free thought and democracy, both anathema to the established churchly and aristocratic order of the time. Adam Weishaupt (1748—1811) founded the society on May 1, 1776.[2] He had been educated by Jesuits and had just been appointed professor of canon law at the University of Ingolstadt. The appointment caused offense and opposition in the Church, for previously the post had always been held by a cleric. The society's avowed aims were to improve its members' virtue and integrity, "and to lay the foundation for the reformation of the world by the association of good men to oppose the progress of moral evil."[3] It can be seen as a form of Gnosticism, even if there is no direct connection with the older mystery cults.

Weishaupt wrote a description of the ideal candidate for membership, which, in its compassion for the poor and disconsolate, foreshadows Marx and Lenin's critique of capital:

> Whoever does not close his ear to the lamentations of the miserable, nor his heart to gentle pity; whoever is the friend and brother of the unfortunate; whoever has a heart capable of love and friendship; whoever is steadfast in adversity, unwearied in the carrying out of whatever has been once engaged in, undaunted in the overcoming of difficulties; whoever does not mock and despise the weak; whose soul is susceptible of conceiving great designs, desirous of rising superior to all base motives, and of distinguishing itself by deeds of benevolence; whoever shuns idleness; whoever considers no knowledge as unessential which he may have the opportunity of acquiring, regarding the knowledge of mankind as his chief study; whoever, when truth and virtue are in question, despising the approbation of the multitude, is sufficiently courageous to follow the dictates of his own heart,—such a one is a proper candidate.[4]

Following the suppression of the Illuminati in 1784–1785 by the Elector of Bavaria, apparently on the grounds that the movement was anti-Christian, it quickly faded from view, though at one point it had as many as two thousand members throughout Western Europe. There were attempts to revive it under different names, but these too were speedily quashed.

Illuminati Now

In the view of the conspiracy theorists who fear the Antichrist potential of elite societies like Weishaupt's—its early membership lists included members of the nobility and the Church—piety like Weishaupt's is always and only a smoke screen.

The Illuminati live on, they say, in the persons of members of such covert, elite, and, above all, internationalist organizations as the Trilateral Commission (TC), the Council on Foreign Relations (CFR), and the highly secretive Bilderberg Group. The Trilateral Commission, in its own words, "was formed in 1973 by private citizens of Japan, Europe (European Union countries) and North America (United States and Canada) to foster closer cooperation among these principal democratic industrialized areas with shared leadership responsibilities in the wider international system."[5] The Council on Foreign Relations is a similar association, calling itself "a unique membership organization and think tank that educates members and staff to serve the nation with ideas for a better and safer world."

The CFR and the TC both maintain a public presence, with offices, mailing addresses, and web sites. The Bilderberg Group is something else. They have no web site that appears on search engines, and they appear to have no headquarters or public accessibility. By the reports of their opponents, they meet at least once a year, in heavily guarded seclusion. One meeting, according to their self-appointed watchdogs, took place in a hotel so exclusive that it is not listed with travel agencies. Their name comes from the Dutch hotel where they held their first meeting in 1954.

One such watchdog is *The Spotlight*, the organ of a right-wing group called the Liberty Lobby. As the only news outlet that regularly covers these meetings, *The Spotlight* prides itself on its splendid journalistic isolation. It claims to have covered the group, and penetrated its meetings, for more than twenty years.[6]

By *The Spotlight's* account, no records are kept of Bilderberger meetings, no votes are taken, and no outsiders are allowed to attend. Meetings are rarely or never covered in the mainstream press, though there was an exception in 1997, when the *Toronto Star* carried several stories about their meeting near that city. The reason for this silence, according to the group's opponents, is that the owners and publishers of the most powerful Western media all belong to the organization and respect its code of *omertà*—absolute silence. The term derives from Mafia usage.

The supposed code was broken in 1997, when the organization provided a press release listing attendees. The membership list does indeed include some of the Western world's most powerful people: Monarchs and CEOs, prime ministers and press lords, professors, presidents, and pundits are named among those who regularly attend. In 1997 the meeting included a gentleman so arcane that his nationality was given as "International" and his occupation "High Representative"—of and to what was unspecified.[7]

The agenda of the meeting was not stated. Watchdog groups report that the Bilderbergers are eager to unify the European Community in preparation for further consolidation and, in the view of the movement's critics, surrender of national sovereignty, in an "American Union" and an "Asian-Pacific Union." It is said that the Bilderbergers worry about increasing nationalism around the world, which, if successful, would hinder any such plans for global unification and eventual world government.

Internationalism, especially when carried out in such secretive ways, invokes predictions of Antichrist's arrival because of his prophesied world leadership role. His plot requires an international power base, and it would greatly assist his goals if that structure were already in place when he arrived. For that reason, believers watch the workings of the United Nations with particular suspicion and revile every peace initiative. This may seem paradoxical, given that most anti-NWO activists profess devout and sometimes literalist Christian belief. We might expect pious followers of the Prince of Peace to applaud attempts to fulfill his agenda, but they are too subtle for that. In conspiracy theory, every attempt to exert control over nationalist squabbles amounts to suppression of sovereignty.

Ultimately what is at stake in conspiracy thinking is identity. Identity is the source and basis of the purity that devotion demands of the disciple. Pollution, and perhaps social pollution in particular, threatens the purity of identity and finally identity itself. All movements that foster diversity at whatever level threaten this core of the believer's being. We are back at the combat myth: Chaos is that which disrupts identity's order; it must be repelled.

The text that follows is the modest apocalypse on which so much fear and fantasy build: the "Mission Statement" of the Council on Foreign Relations. Perhaps the main reason the CFR arouses so much suspicion is because it is of and by the elite. Founded by wealthy professionals, it still consists of and addresses itself to that class. The fact that members nominate new members assures that the CFR remains closed to those excluded from the highest reaches of power. The CFR proclaims lofty ideals and stern disinterest, but that carries little weight with the conspiracy theorists, who can see quite well that the elite prosper apparently without limit, while their own fortunes are at best variable. In their worldview the reason for that disparity has to lie in secret dealings. To some extent this is accurate, but the leap from an internationalist agenda to world hegemony remains fantastic.

• • •

MISSION STATEMENT OF THE COUNCIL ON FOREIGN RELATIONS

The Council on Foreign Relations was founded in 1921 by businessmen, bankers, and lawyers determined to keep the United States engaged in the world. Today, the Council is composed of men and women from all walks of international life and from all parts of America dedicated to the belief that the nation's peace and prosperity are firmly linked to that of the rest of the world. From this flows the Council's mission: to foster America's understanding of other nations, near and far, their peoples, cultures, histories, hopes, quarrels, and ambitions; and thus to serve America's global interests through study and debate, private and public.

The Council is a national membership organization, 3,300 members strong, divided almost equally among New York, Washington, D.C., and the rest of the nation. Its ranks include nearly all past and present senior U.S. government officials who deal with international matters, renowned scholars, and leaders of business, media, human rights, humanitarian, and other nongovernmental groups. Its members choose new members, who aim to educate themselves and then others.

These members strictly maintain the Council's nonpartisan and non-ideological heritage. The Council, headquartered in New York City with offices in Washington, D.C., is host to the widest possible range of views and advocate of none. The Council takes no institutional stand on foreign relations issues. The views expressed in task force reports, by members of study groups, or in articles in *Foreign Affairs* are solely the responsibility of the respective authors or the members of committees or task forces. This tradition of neutrality enables the Council to gather contending voices for serious and civil debate and discussion. That special convening power is almost unique in American society.

In keeping with its mission, membership, and heritage, the Council now pursues three goals:

1. To gain new insights into the rules and rhythms of international affairs and to provide analysis and ideas for U.S. foreign policy. The Council does this by talking with world leaders and thinkers, and by bringing together its unmatched membership with its own expert staff of Fellows. These Fellows—with backgrounds in government and scholarship, and with expertise in almost every world issue and region—constitute one of the country's largest and most active think tanks.

2. To share these insights, analyses, and ideas beyond Council members, with others who have a stake in international matters. The Council does this in many ways. It publishes *Foreign Affairs* magazine, the most respected publication in the field of international relations. It produces books, monographs, and policy reports, and holds numerous conferences. It runs a vibrant and exclusive Corporate Program for some 200 of the world's leading firms. It also produces a series of televised debates and hearings on major policy issues.

3. To find and nurture the next generation of foreign policy leaders and thinkers. The Council does this primarily through a special membership program for younger Americans and a variety of fellowships. The aim is to spark interest in world affairs and U.S. foreign policy. The diverse group of 350 younger Council term members with remarkable backgrounds is increasingly active in Council events.

In recent months, Council members have heard former U.N. Ambassadors Madeleine Albright and Jeane Kirkpatrick debate the future of the United Nations; Henry Kissinger muse to younger members about the lessons of history; the four Joint Chiefs of Staff discuss strategy; House Speaker Newt Gingrich sketch his vision of our future world; CNN

founder Ted Turner talk of television's next phase abroad; Israeli leader
Benjamin Netanyahu and Palestinian leader Yasser Arafat give their visions of peace; Prime Minister Ryutaro Hashimoto explain Japan's foreign and economic policies; Chairman of the Federal Reserve Alan
Greenspan; former British Prime Minister Margaret Thatcher; European
economist and banker Jacques Attali; President Ernesto Zedillo of Mexico; South African leader Thabo Mbeki; Prime Minister Mahathir bin
Mohamad of Malaysia . . .

The Council on Foreign Relations is a unique membership organization and think tank that educates members and staff to serve the nation
with ideas for a better and safer world.

Notes

1. Michael Barkun, *Religion and the Racist Right: The Origin of the Christian Identity
Movement* (Chapel Hill: University of North Carolina Press, 1996), 257.

2. The source for this information is "A Bavarian Illuminati Primer," http://www.bc-
freemasonry.com/Writings/Illuminati.html (June 27, 1998); and Richard Hofstadter, *The
Paranoid Style in American Politics and Other Essays* (Cambridge: Harvard University Press,
1965).

3. Albert G. Mackey, *Encyclopedia of Freemasonry* (Richmond, Va.: Macoy Publishing,
1966), 474, cited in "Bavarian Illuminati Primer."

4. Adam Weishaupt, *An Improved System of the Illuminati* (Gotha, 1787), quoted in "A
Bavarian Illuminati Primer."

5. "About the Trilateral Commission," http://www.trilateral.org/MoreInfo/ABOUT.htm
(June 27, 1998).

6. "Bilderbergers Found Again: Meeting Scheduled in Eastern Canada," *The Spotlight*
22, no. 20 (May 20, 1996).

7. This information is from the Bilderbergers' premeeting press release, found at
http://www.ccnet.com/~suntzu75/pirn9735.htm (June 28, 1998).

PART III

Well-Known Contemporary Movements

ALL THE GROUPS discussed here achieved a measure of fame or notoriety as the twentieth century neared its close. They all committed, or threatened, large-scale violence against themselves or others, or else had it thrust upon them, bringing media attention and notoriety.

It is one of history's sadder facts that explosions of violence involving millenarian believers recur from time to time. We have already discussed the Bar Kochba revolt against Rome. Two centuries later the Zealots massacred themselves when faced with Roman defeat. The rebellions of the Czech Taborites and German Anabaptists come to mind as examples of comparatively large-scale millenarian movements that met violent ends. Any number of groups under colonialist rule have imagined a restoration of the paradise they used to know once they defeat their oppressors, frequently under a millenarian leader.

The outcome of these struggles is always the same. The power of the world is overwhelming and always wins. The end of the twentieth century saw more of these bloody confrontations than most times do. Perhaps this was due to the influence of a mysterious millenarian mindset as the end of the millennium neared. It was a popular assumption in the media that nearly everyone was, or would be, afflicted with a peculiar "millennium madness" brought on by the calendar's turn and the synonymy of the time and the theological concept. Whatever the cause, the end of the twentieth century endured more than its share of millenarian violence. We move now to consider these groups and the fates they met.

CHAPTER 8

THE BRANCH DAVIDIANS

Probably the best-known prophet of the late twentieth century is David Koresh, the leader of the Koreshite Branch Davidians, most of whom died in the apocalyptic destruction of the community they called Mt. Carmel, outside Waco, Texas, on April 19, 1993. The date is important; it's the date of the Battle of Concord that opened the American Revolution, a point that escaped few members of "patriot" movements, who regard themselves as all but enslaved by an unconstitutional federal despotism. It's also the date the Warsaw ghetto uprising began in 1943, and the patriots commonly call the government Nazis. Timothy McVeigh planned his Oklahoma City bombing to correspond with it. The horrific events at Waco have a resonance for some Americans, and militia members in particular, that will not soon abate.

The Branch Davidians were an offshoot of the Davidian Seventh-Day Adventists, and a number of communities still operate under the Davidian name.[1] All the Davidian sects sprung from the Seventh-Day Adventist (SDA) Church, which traces its origins to William Miller's millennialist movement, a group some fifty thousand strong that expected the Second Coming in 1843, and again in 1844. The Millerites' "Great Disappointment," when the Second Coming failed twice to occur on their schedule, led Ellen G. White to build the Adventist movement on Miller's ideas. The failure of Miller's prediction did nothing to discredit his ideas as far as White and her followers were concerned.

White's revised theology of the Second Advent relied heavily on interpretation of the Book of Revelation, an enterprise that never abated among her successors.[2] This dogma included the idea that Miller had erred, not in naming the date, but in understanding its meaning. What really had happened, White proclaimed, was that Christ had entered an inner room in the heavenly temple to prepare for the Advent, not yet to bring it about. Thus the Adventists could extend their expectation indefinitely. This innovation also endowed the Adventists with unique knowledge of the *parousia* (Second Coming) and an obligation to set themselves apart from Babylon, that is, the world. White also honored Miller's prophetic role by proclaiming that there was a prophet for each age who alone could interpret the Bible properly for the faithful. The Bible's truth is evolutionary in that it is progressively revealed to each generation. White's death in 1915 left the Adventists without a prophet to lead them for the first time in almost a century.

Victor Houteff, a Bulgarian immigrant and convert to Adventism, tried to step into the breach in 1929 with his own interpretation of Revelation, which he called "Shepherd's Rod" and proclaimed without permission to the students in his California Sabbath School class. The popularity of his heterodox teaching led the church to ban him, and Houteff eventually left. In Adventist theology there is room for only one prophet in each generation.

Houteff hit upon Waco, Texas, as the gathering place of the faithful and led a band of followers there in 1935, though he expected them to travel to Jerusalem for the Second Coming in a year. The group remained in Waco, where it went by the name "Shepherd's Rod," after Houteff's publication. In 1942, the group needed to incorporate in order for its pacifist membership to avoid the draft. It was not eligible for the SDA's automatic conscientious-objector status, so it took the name Davidian Seventh-Day Adventist. Houteff predicted that someday the group would take a six-letter name, which indeed they did in becoming the Branch Davidian. The DSDA thrived for a while, building a mailing list of some 100,000.

Houteff's wife Florence assumed his mantle upon his unanticipated death in 1955. She predicted his resurrection some 1,260 days later, preceded by a number of signs in the world at large, and called for all Davidians to assemble at Mt. Carmel to await his return.[3] When Houteff failed to arrive and Florence defected for California with $20,000 in Davidian funds, the group was left in disarray.

After some months' negotiation with the parent SDA, it was finally decided that Houteff had been wrong and that the Davidians should disband, with a warning not to try to revive his teaching. This they did, except that a Davidian named Benjamin Roden arrived on the date Florence had set, April 22, 1959, aiming to continue the Davidian movement under his own rule as the new prophet. He declared himself the "Branch" spoken of by the prophet Zechariah and gave the group its new name, fulfilling Houteff's six-letter-name prediction. A lawsuit ensued over the Davidians' holdings: Florence proposed to return them to the donors, while Roden claimed they belonged to the group under his leadership. Roden and his followers won the suit but were evicted from Mt. Carmel anyway. Seventeen of them stayed on, claiming squatter's rights, which they eventually won.

Benjamin, who called himself the "Fifth Angel," died in 1978, and his son George claimed the prophet's title. (Roden, like many another millenarian prophet, seems to have failed to name a successor, as is logical for someone who expects there to be none.) Nevertheless, Benjamin's widow, Lois, wound up in command. She had begun advancing her claim a year previous, with the visionary announcement that the Holy Ghost was God's feminine principle. Benjamin criticized this claim, but she made it a central part of her own theology anyway. This device also served to explain why Benjamin "the Branch" didn't live to see the Second Coming: he embodied only the male principle, and the Branch wasn't complete without its feminine aspect.

This part of Lois's teachings, which she publicized during her tenure in a magazine called *SHEkinah*,[4] gained her wide recognition, and as Bishop Roden (also known as the "Sixth Angel of Revelation") she took part in a number of shows with Christian televangelists. With a seven-year prophecy dating from 1977 she also prepared the way for the "Seventh Angel," David Koresh, then known as Vernon Howell.

But George Roden, who had been part of the group since he was ten and had fully expected to assume its leadership one day, was not pleased when his mother took over. He seemed to lack the charisma necessary to persuade the group to accept him—they called him "Poor George"—but he had seen his father obtain God's judgment in court and felt confident that he would fare no worse. He sued his mother in 1979 and lost. Not only was he barred from leadership of the Branch, but his mother won an injunction against him.

George won control of the compound by vote of the membership in 1985, using mailing lists in his control. Lois sued him the same year for violating the injunction. By that time no lawyer would take the litigious George's case, so he defended himself. Part of his case consisted of virtually the same criticisms that anticult activists and others would later level at Koresh:

> This Vernon W. Howell is a cult leader who uses hypnotism, mind-altering drugs and sex to seduce people. He restricts their intake of food and all of them have lost weight, especially my mother. . . . He says that he owns all the members' property, including their wives and daughters and that he can have them anytime he wishes and no one can say a word about it. . . . His tactics are to keep them up all hours of the night and deprive them of their sleep.[5]

Despite these and other charges, including that Howell had raped Lois—who, George claimed, desperately needed her son to protect her from Howell—George lost the case and the allegiance of the Davidians, who united behind Howell. George still had an important claim, however, since he held title to the land where Mt. Carmel lay. So between his repeated and invisible campaigns for president of the United States in 1987 George challenged Howell to a "resurrection contest:" whoever could raise from the dead the body of Anna Hughes, a DSDA member who had been dead for twenty years, would win the leadership. He apparently dug up her remains for this purpose.

Howell and the Branch were outraged at this desecration and went to the sheriff to demand an investigation of George Roden. The lawman refused to believe their story and asked for proof. Howell and some followers tried to sneak into Mt. Carmel to take pictures of the cadaver, but George met them with an Uzi and a forty-five minute gunfight followed.

The sheriff broke up the skirmish, apparently without injury to anyone, though Howell was jailed. George filed a motion calling down God's plague of AIDS and herpes on any judge who would dare liberate Howell. He got six months in jail for contempt of court for his trouble. Howell's followers were acquitted at trial, and his own case received a split verdict, which the prosecutor declined to retry.

George Roden met an unhappy end. In 1989 a Davidian called Adair met Howell and learned from the meeting that he, Adair, was "God's chosen prophet." He rushed off to Mt. Carmel to proclaim the good news there, and George, apparently maddened by this proliferation of prophets, killed him. By report he has spent the rest of his life in a state hospital for the insane.

Howell now had complete control of the group. In 1990 he took the name David Koresh: David for the hero-king of the Jews and Koresh for the Persian King Cyrus (Koresh in Hebrew) who ended their Babylonian captivity. During his own Babylonian captivity in the compound near Waco, Koresh told some of his followers that his new name would fulfill Isaiah 44:28 and 45:1.[6] He also told them Koresh means "death."[7]

Howell's early life was chaotic. According to Charles Strozier he was born into a violent and criminal family and showed early signs of emotional distress.[8] He did very badly in school, where his repeated failures earned him the nickname "Mr. Retardo." However, he had a gift for expression, which he exercised in religion. His mother was raised in the SDA church but rarely attended. His grandmother occasionally took him to services, and this experience opened him to biblical poetry. Televangelists provided a model for his style, which included massive memorization of Scripture. The second major influence on his life was guns, which Strozier calls "a predictable source of power" in the turmoil of his life.[9]

He found refuge in an SDA church, but it disfellowshipped him for asking inappropriate questions. He heard about Lois Roden and Mt. Carmel in 1981 and made the trip there right away. The bishop's prophecy had called for major events to influence the Davidians in 1981, and for major change to occur in 1984. She was a wise predictor, for Howell arrived in 1981 and split the group in 1984. This contributed a good deal to the group's eventual recognition of his legitimacy as the "Seventh Angel," or "sinful messiah," as he came to call himself.

His arrogance alienated many believers at first, and they assigned him the worst jobs and meanest quarters. However, he seemed to be seriously interested in salvation. He soon earned Lois Roden's support and she urged the others to suspend judgment and listen to what he had to say. This entrée was important in his eventual assumption of the group's leadership.

By 1983 he was warning the Branch against impurity. He assured them that unless they changed their ways they, like Houteff, would never see the

Second Coming. He said it was urgent for the Branch to attain true purity and assigned them a rigorous new diet.

Privately, he told Lois Roden that the two of them were mentioned in Isaiah 8:3: "And I went unto the prophetess; and she conceived, and bare a son." There were rumors that they were secretly married in 1983, but Howell married fourteen-year-old Rachel Jones in 1984, at the end of Lois's seven-year prophecy. Lois was so enraged that she lost her support among the Branch members, who adopted Howell as their new leader.

Howell's charisma was potent. Outsiders testify that he could make anyone feel like the center of the universe. The evident change in his personality from a neurotic loner to a charismatic leader was, in Davidian eyes, testimony to God's interest in him. He had knowledge of the Bible that seemed miraculous. He had the courage to do and say outrageous things, which also made him seem to be a true prophet. This status entitled him to flout all the Branch's (i.e., his own) rules. When he suffered no punishment, that too added to his power. When he broke a fast in front of the others, he would tell them that when they knew as much as he did, then they could do it too.

Behavior like this is typical of prophets and enhances their power, which is beyond the reach of the rules that govern the lives even of other believers. The followers of Sabbatai Zvi and perhaps especially of Jacob Frank exercised this principle, as we saw in chapter 1. So did Hitler. The change in Howell's personality amounted to a conversion and was further testimony to his special status.

Howell claimed his followers' sins literally made him sick, that God punished him because of their failings. But he "married" as many as fourteen young girls in his group by the simple expedient of climbing into their beds, according to a disaffected former member.[10] This was the correct thing for him to do, he said, because God had given him the mission of fathering a new race. By 1989, when he claimed rights over the married women in the group, his sexual monopoly was complete, though he assured his male followers that their mates would arrive in heaven, after the manner of Eve. Everyone in the group was celibate except Koresh and those women he chose as his mates, and their indulgence was only to serve his purpose.

This doctrine, called "New Light" within the group, had come to Koresh (as he now called himself) in a vision during a trip to Israel. It was revolutionary for the Davidians and added immensely to Koresh's charisma, both positive and negative. Koresh rationalized the innovation on biblical grounds, as we might expect, but also pointed out that God's laws are not man's. The arrangement was what God wanted; it had to be followed. The idea was not without precedent, as Strozier points out. Religious experimentation with food and sex (usually in the direction of abstention rather than indulgence) is seen to have a transfigurative power. Raising his personal power to this new level immensely enhanced Koresh's charisma, at the same time that it set in motion the final confrontation with the law.

The new doctrine drove away one of Koresh's most powerful disciples, Mark Breault, who returned to his native Australia and began evangelizing to other Branch groups to disavow Koresh. Other members left, and some swore out warrants against him for child abuse and kidnaping, but these were not prosecuted. Reports of his behavior began to appear in the press, and the State of Texas began investigating the charges.

Agents of the U.S. Treasury's Bureau of Alcohol, Tobacco and Firearms (BATF) had been watching Koresh and his community of end-time believers for about a year, suspecting them of keeping and dealing in illegal weapons. The BATF made its move on Mt. Carmel on February 28, 1993, with apparent lack of appropriate caution. Koresh reportedly offered to negotiate with them but was rebuffed. Among the Davidians was a Harvard-trained lawyer with a local practice.[11] Instead of resorting to a "dynamic entry," the BATF could easily and quite peacefully have handed a search warrant to Koresh or the lawyer.

Instead, the agency mounted an elaborate and supposedly secret raid, but their intricate preparations involved telling nearly everyone in the area to be ready. Koresh clearly knew of their highly inept surveillance, and seems to have known of the raid. It seems quite clear that the raid was as much a public relations effort as law enforcement: The BATF budget was due for congressional review in a few weeks, and the agency assigned special Public Information Officers to "Operation Trojan Horse," known to its participants as "Showtime." These officers' duties included providing television outlets with footage of the operation made by the agency itself.[12]

When the BATF agents arrived, a firefight ensued in which four agents and six Davidians were killed and Koresh himself was badly wounded. Who fired first remains an open question. In Texas it would not have been unlawful for the Davidians to forcibly resist an unannounced entry or to return fire. Following this debacle, FBI agents assumed control of the situation. During the fifty-one-day siege it became painfully obvious that the FBI had no idea what they were dealing with.[13] Scholars of religion were unanimous in the perception that the FBI's tactics were doomed to tragic failure. Despite advice that Koresh's biblical beliefs needed to be taken seriously, the FBI assumed that Koresh was a con man and that his followers were hostages and treated them accordingly, using clumsy attempts at psychological warfare to drive the Davidians out of their compound. Nancy Ammerman attributes law enforcement's skepticism about Koresh's religious beliefs in part to cynicism from long experience with "conversions of convenience" and a reckoning that belief makes no difference: A devout criminal is no different than a skeptic, and should be treated the same.[14] The misleading and pejorative rhetoric of the anticult movement also strongly affected law enforcement's views; there was little information available to counter the sensationalism of this rhetoric in the media. Yet another factor might be a general indifference to religion on the part of government officials, who may perceive it as none of their business under the American system. The FBI was not the only agency that was remiss in this respect. The BATF has no social science division comparable to the FBI's, and it sought no advice from any outside source except informers. Many of these were anticult activists whose information should have been taken with a grain of salt but wasn't.

It is interesting that no one in the FBI or among its advisers would take credit for the psy-war tactics employed, which included playing Nancy Sinatra's "These Boots Were Made for Walking" at maximum volume in the middle of the night, along with the recorded screams of butchered rabbits, among other things. The FBI seemed to believe these tactics would make the Branch want to surrender.

The effect was to demonstrate the accuracy of Koresh's prophecies: The world, it seemed, really was ruled by Antichrist. The final battle with Babylon was at hand and, given the global media coverage the event received, it must have seemed that Koresh was what he proclaimed himself to be: the most important person in the world. All the FBI's efforts only strengthened the Davidians' faith.

Koresh told incredulous FBI agents that he had been commanded by the Lord to write his interpretation of the seven seals of the Book of Revelation, which only he could open. He was, in his belief, the Lion of Judah in Revelation 5:1-5:

> And I saw in the right hand of him that sat on the throne a book written within and on the backside, sealed with seven seals. And I saw a strong angel proclaiming with a loud voice, Who is worthy to open the book, and to loose the seals thereof? And no man in heaven, nor in earth, neither under the earth, was able to open the book, neither to look thereon. And I wept much, because no man was found worthy to open and to read the book, neither to look thereon. And one of the elders saith unto me, Weep not: behold, the Lion of the tribe of Judah, the Root of David, hath prevailed to open the book, and to loose the seven seals thereof.

In the following verse, this lion is revealed as a mystic lamb "as it had been slain," with seven eyes and seven horns representing God's seven spirits over the world. It is this lamb/lion that can break the seals and read the scroll in this pivotal moment of the world's salvation.

Koresh clearly staked the meaning of his mission on this text. He believed that he was in the Branch's succession of prophets. There is some ambiguity as to whether he also believed he was the Second Coming of Jesus of Nazareth, on the one hand, or a Christ, a messianic figure for his people and their time, on the other. But that he saw himself as the Lamb is unquestionable. Support for the lesser claim seems to be undermined by this admission, for the Lamb is clearly intended in Revelation to represent Jesus as the Messiah. In Strozier's view, Koresh was quite free in associating biblical figures with himself, though he stopped "just short of actual madness."[15]

The text that follows is Koresh's interpretation of the first seal in the Book of Revelation. He wrote it, as he said, at God's command. As the Branch's anointed prophet, only he could open the seals. He intended to cover all seven seals, but the FBI forestalled him by moving against Mt.

Carmel with gas and tanks. It turned out to be Koresh's last cryptic message to the world.

According to James D. Tabor and Eugene V. Gallagher's interpretation of Koresh's apocalypticism, his key to the first seal in the Book of Revelation was Psalm 45.[16] It describes the anointing and triumph of a king, whom Koresh took to be the messiah. Gallagher and Tabor note this section, but oddly ignore the rest. This psalm is also an erotic poem, describing the gift of a king's daughter given to the new messiah. Verse 14 reads: "She shall be brought unto the king in raiment of needle work: the virgins her companions that follow her shall be brought unto thee." Could this have been a "proof text" for Koresh's new sexual dispensation?

There is a very interesting double meaning to be found in this text, not unlike the coded references that John embedded in the original Book of Revelation. Koresh used the Bible not only as the unquestionable authenticating source of his visions, but as an encrypted affirmation of his own self-description and mission. After negotiating with the FBI, he learned that the Bible was to them exactly what one of them called it in a press conference: "babble."[17] He knew he would be safe in using his pious platitudes of Christian redemption to mask what he was actually saying about himself as the messiah. The "hidden" message is insurgent and subversive, a brilliant and quite simple defiance of Babylon.

These texts also clearly contain a symbolical biblical charter for the Branch, legitimizing its actions and at least some of Koresh's identification with the messiah. The piety about "standing in the counsel of the Lord" may have been intended for the followers, but it seems safe to assume that Koresh cannot have missed the other significance of this passage.

These verses form a sort of mini-apocalypse. In fundamentalist thought Old Testament literature is full of such "types": foreshadowings of Christ's new covenant that underline their apparent fulfillment in the New Testament. If you believe, as the fundamentalists do, that every verse is the fresh word of God without reference to what has gone before, then such correspondences can only mean that God was hiding in the earlier testaments meanings that would emerge only in the fullness of time.

The Church is the New Israel in fundamentalist belief. God's promises to Israel must be reinterpreted in the light of Christ's ministry—hence the notion that the Christians are in a diaspora, waiting only for a final purification before their salvation. It is possible that this might also be for Koresh a covert reference to the defection of Breault and the others.

In Hebrew Baal means "master" or "lord." Ishi, on the other hand, means "husband." God is changing his relationship with the Israelites/Church, and Koresh may well have seen this as a reference to his own situation. By the time he wrote this treatise, he had fathered twelve children with his various "wives."

Koresh promised the agents that he and his followers would surrender once his interpretation of the seals was complete. He got no further than the first chapter before the FBI mounted their final apocalyptic raid in which almost everyone inside Mt. Carmel died. A surviving member took the manuscript from Mt. Carmel on a computer disk.

It is ironic that Koresh's last written words are so full of imagery of marriage. After the FBI attacked with CS gas, a compound outlawed for use in war by the Geneva Convention, the compound went up in flames. How the fire started remains a matter of dispute, but in any case it was so intense that the Texas coroner reported that some of the bodies had melted together—a parody of a marriage embrace in a dance of death.[18]

• • •

CHAPTER 1: THE FIRST SEAL

Jeremiah 23:5,6,7,8,18,19,20:

> "Behold, the days come, saith the Lord, that I will raise unto David a righteous Branch, and a King shall reign and prosper, and shall execute judgment and justice in the earth. In his days Judah shall be saved, and Israel shall dwell safely; and this is his name, whereby he shall be called, the Lord is our righteousness. Therefore, behold, the days come, saith the Lord, that they shall no more say, The Lord liveth, who brought up the children of Israel out of the land of Egypt, but the Lord liveth, who brought up and who led the seed of the house of Israel out of the north country, and from all the countries to which I had driven them, and they shall dwell in their own land. . . .

Copyright 1994 by Phillip Arnold and James Tabor. Reunion Institute, PO Box 981111, Houston TX 77098).

For who hath stood in the counsel of the Lord, and hath perceived and heard his word? Who hath marked his word, and heard it? Behold, a whirlwind of the Lord is gone forth in fury, even a grievous whirlwind; it shall fall grievously upon the head of the wicked. Then the anger of the Lord shall not return, until he have executed, and till he have performed the thoughts of his heart; in the latter days ye shall consider it perfectly."

This beautiful prophecy, the Desire of Ages, entails of Christ the Lord our Righteousness and also warns us of the latter days should we be found not standing in the counsel of the Lord. If we, the church of God, stand in the counsel of Christ, especially in the light of the seven seals, shall we not be a part of that beautiful bride spoken of in Jeremiah 33?

Jeremiah 33:14–16:

"Behold, the days come, saith the Lord, that I will perform that good thing which I have promised unto the house of Israel and to the house of Judah. In those days, and at that time, will I cause the Branch of righteousness to grow up unto David; and he shall execute judgment and righteousness in the land. In those days shall Judah be saved, and Jerusalem shall dwell safely; and this is the name of which she shall be called, the Lord, our righteousness."

She, the city, she, the saints, those who are clothed with the righteousness of Christ and His Word, for it is also promised in verse 17, "David shall never want a man to sit upon the throne of the house of Israel." For Christ remains a King "forever." (Psalm 45:6)

Ezekiel 37:24–25; Daniel 12:1:

"And David, my servant, shall be king over them, and they all shall have one shepherd; they shall also walk in mine judgments, and observe my statutes, and do them. And they shall dwell in the land that I have given unto Jacob, my servant, in which your fathers have dwelt; and they shall dwell in it, even they, and their children, and their children's children forever; and my servant, David shall be their prince forever."

"And at that time shall Michael stand up, the great prince who standeth for the children of thy people, and there shall be a time of trouble, such as never was since there was a nation even to that same time; and at that time thy people shall be delivered, every one that shall be found written in the book."

If we are to be found written in the book, surely we should be found in the first seal for there Christ is revealed, shall not we also be revealed as one who "hearkens and considers" for is not He "our Lord" and shall not we "worship" him "in spirit and in truth" (John 4:24).

In Hosea 2:14 we read, "Therefore, behold I will allure her and bring her into the wilderness, and speak tenderly unto her." The Christian Church being scattered from Jerusalem went throughout all nations. Being amongst the Gentiles, the gospel was to impart unto the Gentiles the riches of God's mercy.

Verse 15: "And I will give her her vineyards from thence, and the Valley of Achor for a door of hope; and she shall sing there, as in the days of her youth, and as in the day when she came up out of the land of Egypt."

Here it is promised that once the unfaithful ones as Achan are taken from amongst God's people we will definitely have a deliverance and all the prophets agree.

Verse 16: "And it shall be at that day, saith the Lord, that thou shalt call me Ishi, and shalt call me no more Baali."

If we are to call God by such an endearing term, we are to know Him a little better and what better way to know him than in the revelation of Jesus Christ.

Verse 17: "For I will take away the names of Baalim out of her mouth, and they shall no more be remembered by their name."

All false teachers and false prophets are to be forgotten for there is one God, and one Lamb and one seven seal truth.

Verse 18: "And in that day will I make a covenant for them with the beasts of the field, and with the fowls of the heavens, and with the creeping things of the ground; and I will break the bow and the sword and the battle out of the earth, and will make them to lie down safely."

Just as Isaiah 11 has promised, so Hosea also promises, peace for those who are called to the Marriage Supper of the Lamb.

Verses 19 and 20: "And I will betroth thee unto me forever; yea, I will betroth thee unto me in righteousness, and in judgment, and in lovingkindness, and in mercies. I will even betroth thee unto me in faithfulness; and thou shalt know the Lord."

So again, here we see the importance of this opportunity of learning these seven seals and the complete entailment of what that includes.

Verse 21: "And it shall come to pass in that day, I will hear, saith the Lord, I will hear the heavens, and they shall hear the earth."

Are we not a part of this event by faith? Is not heaven in total unity to the receiving of these seals from God? Is not God's word supreme in heaven? And it being the Word which reveals Christ now is the time like never before to pray that we may be worthy to understand these things more clearly.

Joel 2:15,16: "Blow the trumpet in Zion, sanctify a fast, call a solemn assembly. Gather the people, sanctify the congregation, assemble the elders, gather the children, and those that nurse at the breasts; let the bridegroom go forth from his chamber, and the bride out of her closet."

Yes, the bride is definitely to be revealed for we know that Christ is in the Heavenly Sanctuary anticipating His Marriage of which God has spoken. Should we not eagerly ourselves be ready to accept this truth and come out of our closet and be revealed to the world as those who love Christ in truth and in righteousness.

Amos 9:11,14,15: "In that day will I raise up the tabernacle of David that is fallen, and close up the breaches of it; and I will raise up his ruins, and I will build it as in the days of old . . . And I will bring again the captivity of my people of Israel, and they shall build the waste cities, and inhabit them; and they shall plant vineyeards [sic], and drink their wine; they shall also make gardens, and eat the fruit of them. And I will plant them upon their land, and they shall no more be pulled up out of their land which I have given them, saith the Lord, thy God."

Notes

1. William L. Pitts, Jr., "Davidians and Branch Davidians 1929–1987," in *Armageddon in Waco: Critical Perspectives on the Branch Davidian Conflict,* ed. Stuart A. Wright (Chicago: University of Chicago Press, 1995), 20–42.

2. Charles B. Strozier, "Apocalyptic Violence and the Politics of Waco," in *The Year 2000: Essays on the End,* ed. Charles B. Strozier and Michael Flynn (New York: New York University Press, 1997), 100.

3. The number 1,260 recurs constantly in Christian millenarian prophecies. It is a reflection of the span of time given God's two witnesses to testify against Antichrist in Revelation 11:3. There are two of them, by the way, because that is the canonical number required to establish sin in Deuteronomy 17:6.

4. The Hebrew word refers to God's presence in the world. It is interesting to observe that Jewish commentators refer to this principle as feminine. See, e.g., Gershom Scholem, *The Messianic Idea in Judaism and Other Essays in Jewish Sprituality* (New York: Schocken Books, 1971), 74.

5. Paul Broyles, "A Brief History of the Branch Davidian Seventh Day Adventist," http://www.geocities.com/CapitolHill/Senate/1400/koresh1.html (March 26, 1998). Pitts's account does not mention this particular suit or George Roden's testimony.

6. "[The Lord] saith of Cyrus, he is my shepherd, and shall perform all my pleasure: even saying to Jerusalem, thou shalt be built; and to the temple, thy foundation shall be laid. Thus saith the Lord to his anointed, to Cyrus, whose right hand I have holden, to subdue nations before him; and I will loose the loins of kings, to open before him the two leaved gates; and the gates shall not be shut."

7. U.S. District Court, Waco, TX. *United States vs. Brad Eugene Branch, et al,* 1994, docket no. W-93-CR-046 4139.

8. Strozier, "Apocalyptic Violence," 101.

9. Ibid., 102.

10. Koresh undertook this sexual buccaneering with the consent of all parties, apparently—though as Strozier observes legal and ethical questions remain where the underage girls are concerned. Ibid., 103.

11. Ibid., 97.

12. Dick J. Reavis, *The Ashes of Waco: An Investigation* (Syracuse, N.Y.: Syracuse University Press, 1995), 31–38.

13. The source for this material is Nancy Ammerman, "Waco, Federal Law Enforce-

ment, and Scholars of Religion," in *Armageddon in Waco: Critical Perspectives on the Branch Davidian Conflict,* ed. Stuart A. Wright (Chicago: University of Chicago Press, 1996), 282–96.

14. Ibid., 285.

15. Strozier, "Apocalyptic Violence," 103. Strozier is in one respect almost alone among those who pronounce such judgments on prophets and their followers: as a practicing psychoanalyst he is qualified to do so.

16. James D. Tabor and Eugene V. Gallagher, *Why Waco? Cults and the Battle for Religious Freedom in America* (Berkeley: University of California Press, 1995), 206.

17. Ibid., 52.

18. Strozier, "Apocalyptic Violence," 97.

CHAPTER 9

THE ORDER OF THE SOLAR TEMPLE

Early in October 1994 the world was shocked to hear of the deaths of fifty-three members of an organization called the Order of the Solar Temple (OST). The bodies were found in three groups. The first group was discovered in a villa in the prosperous Quebec town of Morin Heights. The next day, the others were discovered in a house in Cheiry, Switzerland, whose nearby barn was ablaze, and in some villas in nearby Granges-sur-Salvain that had also been set on fire. In the latter instance the bodies were arranged in a star pattern on the floor and appeared to have died in a religious sacrifice.

The religious connection between these deaths was quickly apparent. The Canadian and Swiss police made some of the same assumptions that U.S. federal officers had made with regard to the Branch Davidians.[1] They assumed that the leaders of the group must have been con artists who murdered everyone and then escaped with the loot. A lengthy investigation established that the Quebec victims had indeed been murdered, while the deaths in Switzerland seem to have been suicides. The leaders died there.

The press and many academics assumed that the group's founder, Dr. Luc Jouret, was responsible for the group and its actions. However, it later appeared that he was actually working for, or with, the shadowy Joseph Di-Mambro, who was the real leader.

Jouret met DiMambro in Geneva in 1976. DiMambro led an occult organization called the Golden Way Foundation and later became the real leader of the OST, which Jouret founded in 1977. DiMambro also headed a secret group called La Pyramide and had belonged to other neo-Templar organizations known to have associations with right-wing paramilitary and private intelligence groups: SAC in France and P2 in Italy. It appears that

DiMambro exercised some clandestine influence over affairs of state through these connections, or tried to.

As founder, Jouret continued to influence the OST. He also established a name for himself as a lecturer on New Age topics, concentrating on healing and "self-realization," which seems to have meant the acquisition of supernatural power. He lost a good deal of his cachet in Europe when disaffected apostates revealed his apocalyptic leanings. However, he continued to get a warm reception in Quebec. In fact, it later became a minor scandal that he had lectured to executives of the province's power company, Hydro-Quebec, and recruited some of them to OST.

The full name of the group was the International Order of Chivalry Solar Tradition (OICST). Jouret, who seems to have functioned primarily as the group's charismatic front man and recruiter, was a Belgian citizen and native of the Belgian Congo. His parents left Africa under threat of reprisal during decolonization. He entered the Free University in Brussels and graduated in 1974 with a medical degree, after attracting police notice for Communist activities. In 1976 he joined the Belgian paratroop force and took part in a raid to rescue Belgian hostages in Zaire. According to a classmate, he joined the army with the purpose of infiltrating it with Communist doctrine.

Jouret constructed a complex arrangement of front organizations around the secret, inner OICST, known as the Solar Temple. This inner OICST was both a splinter group from and a continuation of a group called the Order of the Reformed Temple (ORT), headed by Julien Origas, to which Jouret had briefly belonged. Origas was active in esoteric neo-Templar circles as early as 1952, when he took part in a meeting that aimed to unite European Templar organizations. Origas seems to have converted to these beliefs following a reported jail sentence for activities with the Gestapo during World War II, but his career is otherwise obscure. Jouret tried to assume leadership of the ORT after Origas's death in 1981, but Origas's daughter Christine beat him out and he left to found the OST.

According to Gerry O'Sullivan, the ORT was a neo-Nazi magical society founded by Origas.[2] Jouret's OST was a synthesis of Gnostic Christianity and the occult and drew in particular from Rosicrucianism, Kabbalah, some eastern religions, and Hermetic Freemasonry.[3]

The OST's dogma derived from the doctrines of Bernard-Raymond Fabre-Palaprat, an occultist at the time of the French Revolution. Palaprat claimed to be the last Grand Master of the Knights Templar, a secretive and wealthy Catholic order that had been suppressed in the fourteenth century, and which historians generally agree did not survive, even in secret. Modern Templars usually claim descent from this order, and assert that their doctrine is the same as Rosicrucianism, which is part of the same esoteric tradition and arose at about the same time as Freemasonry. Palaprat's organization thrived and underwent a series of schisms, so that there are now more than thirty separate organizations claiming succession from Palaprat. These groups generally have their best success in Latin countries.

Jouret's teachings borrowed from three main streams: the ecocide predictions of many New Age believers; the notion of a cosmic alchemical *renovatio* (renewal) claimed to have been revealed by the Ascended Masters to their neo-Templar successors; and extremist political notions of a final ideological apocalypse from various left- and right-wing groups Jouret maintained contact with. The alchemical connection is interesting because alchemy is ultimately devoted to transformation, the essence of the millennial project, and yet it is seldom referenced in other millenarian texts.

Jouret claimed to have received a series of revelations, as Origas had done before him, from 1986 to 1993. These emphasized four sacred objects: the Holy Grail, King Arthur's mystical sword Excalibur, the menorah, and the Ark of the Covenant. The Holy Grail is the legendary goblet used at the Last Supper and later to catch the blood of Christ on the cross. It was the supreme object of the medieval knightly quest, accessible only to the purest of spirit, a symbol of the spiritual quest itself. Excalibur was the augury of Arthur's heroic status, the sword that he alone could pull from the stone in which it was embedded. Swords generally symbolize power and justice. The menorah is the seven-branched candlestick of Jewish custom. Candlesticks generally represent spiritual truth; seven represents totality and also refers to the seven planets and seven heavens of cosmic lore. In the Hanukkah story, the menorah is miraculous because it burns a day's supply of oil in a week, while the priests look for more oil for the renovated Temple. This seems to be a symbolic reference to the presence of God in the burning bush on Sinai, which also is not consumed. The Ark of the

Covenant is the symbolic seat of God's presence and concern for humanity, and it symbolizes the entire indestructible structure of sacred knowledge as well the messenger of salvation.

Jouret's final revelation informed him that, between 1993 and 1994, the last "guardians" of the planet would leave for higher realms. These guardians were six "'entities' hidden in the Great Pyramid." Their departure from the planet would signal the beginning of the end. Then three more Masters would depart, after getting a special revelation at Ayer's Rock, Australia. This might have been a metaphor for some experience of the three leaders of OICST, mentioned in the letter reprinted below.

The group's total membership at the time of the deaths in Quebec and Switzerland is estimated to have been close to three hundred. Many of the dead were members of the *haute bourgeoisie* and even the elite of the Francophone west, which puzzled many investigators.[4] Why would people with everything to lose take this route out of life and away from all their privileges? Members of apocalyptic movements are generally supposed to be relatively deprived, but the Solar Templars could by no means be considered poor.

In fact, this is not such a mystery. DiMambro and Jouret promised their followers life among an exclusive spiritual elite who alone had been given Gnostic understanding of the way to divinity and eternal life. An anonymous survivor told a Swiss television audience, "We went about our daily lives, but we didn't belong to this world. Jouret made us feel we were a chosen and privileged congregation."[5] Elaborate and impressive rituals enhanced that impression. The Order provided a "mystical mood" for all its members, even those lacking spiritual gifts. The group seems to have mastered the manipulation of emotion.[6]

According to Jouret's "most secret teachings," the rift with Origas and his ORT had finally come at the command of the Ascended Masters of the Grand Lodge of Agartha.[7] Imagery of lodges and grand masters derives from the Freemasons and various groups with similar mysterious aims and practices. These groups promise their members secret knowledge of the world's workings, made plain only to an esoteric elite of the specially illuminated and initiated. These occult and humanist movements had their origins around the time of the French Enlightenment, and some of their ideas strongly influenced the French and American revolutions.

Groups like these figure prominently in American right-wing fantasies of the nefarious New World Order. It is ironic that Origas and DiMambro seem to have had inclinations in this direction, especially since they were staunch right-wing neofascists. At the same time, ideas of an esoteric secret order are invoked by progressivist groups calling for a rational order of the world. These doctrines resonate with Theosophical ideas of "Ascended Masters" who inhabit an ethereal realm from which they watch affairs on earth, and who return here at propitious times to impart bits of their divine wisdom.[8]

Jouret began to encounter opposition to his ideas and his organizations in Europe as early as 1984. He seems to have been deeply upset by any criticism. After an anticult organization called his group "very dangerous,"[9] Jouret pronounced Europe finished and observed that Quebec, with its "strong magnetic field," would protect his flock against the apocalypse.[10] Jouret began "curing" cancers unseen by anyone else, and he called for one hundred of the faithful to follow him to the New World, where they would start a new race after the destruction of the old.

But even there they came to feel persecuted. Most members of the Order were Catholic by upbringing, but the disaffected Protestant spouse of one member, who already found OST's mystical trappings repugnant, rebelled when her husband told her that Jouret had decided he was to live with a new woman. Eventually the wife, Rose-Marie Klaus, complained to a friend in the police. She sued the OST, and word of the lawsuit reached Canadian anticult organizations. Complaints from Martinique, where the Order operated from time to time, also began to reach the Canadian anticult movements. When the suit was settled, Klaus mounted a public campaign against the Order.

In the meantime, Jouret had been replaced as Grand Master of the Order because his apocalypticism was becoming too urgent for comfort. He founded a new organization called l'Academie de Recherche et Conassiance des Hautes Sciences (Academy for Research and Knowledge of the Higher Sciences) and took some of the Order's members with him. One of them helped Jouret set himself up as a spiritual guru to business executives, lecturing on topics such as "the real meaning of work." In 1992 a member of this group tried to buy a pistol with a silencer from someone who turned out to be a police informant. The police decided there must be a connection between this attempted purchase and assassination threats they had been receiving from someone claiming to represent a terrorist organization called Q37, which later proved not to exist. The person calling in the threats was never found.

Not the least of the OST's complaints with the world was that the provincial police, the Sureté de Québec, (SQ) arrested and investigated members for these illegal weapons charges around the time that a group of Mohawk protesters armed with assault weapons that they flaunted on national television were disrupting traffic near Montreal with perfect impunity. This offended the OST's notions of racial superiority. Also at about this time, Klaus turned up in tabloid headlines with complaints that the OST had robbed her. Anticult activists compared the group to the Branch Davidians, whose siege was just beginning.

As a result of the investigation, Jouret's chief lieutenant lost his job at Hydro Québec, along with some fifteen other executives who had joined the OST after hearing Jouret lecture. The group was also accused of sabotaging some power transmission towers, a charge that proved baseless.

The effect of this opposition on Jouret was powerful. Like most millenarians, he demanded that the world take him as seriously as he took himself. These attacks on his legitimacy were deeply threatening to his plans. He despised the publicity, which he felt could threaten his whole network.

The illegal weapons trial ended in a plea bargain and a sentence of probation and a fine for Jouret and the others implicated in the purchase. But their legal troubles were not over, for the SQ mounted an investigation into Jouret's finances. The inquest quickly became global, and by early 1994 Australian federal police, the Royal Canadian Mounted Police, and the French Sureté had all joined in. The Temple's leadership probably was not aware of all these investigations, but they were suspicious. One of the letters they left calls it all a plot. It is a strange set of circumstances that leads from an attempt to buy a silenced pistol to an international investigation for arms trafficking and money laundering.

The document that follows is one of four the group posted to the Swiss scholar Jean-François Mayer just before their deaths, under the pseudonym "D. Part." It was widely circulated among scholars at the time of the murder-suicides and excerpted in the press.

I chose this one because its tone seems to me to exemplify best the spiteful world-rejection common to many millenarian movements. The world refuses their message of salvation, often even laughing at it. Since the message is conceived to be divine, the only explanation possible is that the world is too ignorant and sinful to recognize its own salvation, and in fact interferes with salvation through its obtuseness. Self-destruction comes to seem like a form of martyrdom for the group, and a message of ultimate rejection of the world that remains so intransigent. This text is my own translation from the French.

• • •

WE ADDRESS THIS FINAL MESSAGE TO ALL THOSE WHO CAN STILL UNDERSTAND THE VOICE OF WISDOM.

The chaos of this world inescapably leads humanity toward the failure of its destiny.

Throughout time cycles have followed one another according to precise rhythms and laws. Various societies have disappeared in destructive but regenerative disasters. None has fallen to our civilization's level of decadence. It cannot escape sudden self-destruction, subject as it is to devastating individual and collective egocentricity and in its total ignorance of the Laws of Spirit and Life.

Since the beginning of time philosophers, prophets and avatars have come in succession to help mankind take its place as creator. Its refusal every time to See and Hear has caused the plans of Cosmic Evolution to go astray.

We servants of the Rose + Cross possess an ancient and authentic Wisdom and affirm that we have worked since the beginning of time for the Evolution of Awareness. Philosophies, sciences, and sacred shrines and temples remain as living witnesses.

These Beings devised their plan of action in the crypts and sanctuaries of the order, following strict guidelines. The result is secret from the profane world, but well known to the Initiate.

We servants of the Rose + Cross declare that from all eternity the Universal Solar Temple has shown itself among men according to cycles of activity and dormancy. After the solemn opening of the Gates on March 21, 1981, in Geneva at the Sanctuary of its Secret Lodge, a former domain of the Order of Malta, its last overt activity will last eleven years. During this cycle the Holy Grail, Excalibur, the Seven-Branch Candlestick, and the Ark of the Covenant are revealed to living witnesses, the last faithful servants of the Eternal Rose + Cross. After this the lies and libels, all the betrayals, the scandal carefully orchestrated by the powers that be, have sounded the death knell for the last attempt to regenerate the Plans of Awareness. Those who have breached our code of honor are traitors. They will suffer the punishment they deserve for ages of ages.[*]

Everything happens according to the dictates of Justice. We affirm that we execute justice according to the commands of a Higher Order.

In view of the present unchangeable situation, we, servants of the Rose + Cross, forcibly reaffirm that we are not of this world and are perfectly aware of the coordinates of our origin and our future.

With no wish to start an empty polemic, we proclaim that:

The Great White Lodge of Sirius has decreed the Recall of the last to carry the authentic Ancestral Wisdom; a Just Sentence will be executed according to the guidelines of a Universal Superior Order with the full rigor of the Law.[**]

---

[*]The ominous reference to treachery probably accounts for the fate of Antonio and Nicky Dutoit and their infant son Charles Emmanuel. They were murdered with particular cruelty in Morin Heights for the crime of giving their son the same name as DiMambro's daughter Emmanuelle. She was the group's "divine child," apparently a potential savior until this disgrace to her "sanctity." She died in a "kind" murder in Switzerland.

Hall and Schuyler (op. cit.: 306) dispute this view, saying that Antonio Dutoit, disenchanted with the Order, had begun giving away secrets of his electronic stagecraft that produced "miracles" at their ceremonies. The tale of the infant Antichrist came initially from the Sureté de Québec, which made some rather self-serving public remarks during the investigation. However, Introvigne claims that DiMambro's daughter, the "starry child" mentioned in another note, was said to have a divine future. She was not allowed any contact with other children who had to stay a meter away from her while at play.—*Ed.*

[**]The Great White Lodge of Sirius is, in Theosophical doctrine, the pantheon: the Ascended Masters who watch over us and appear from time to time to help us along our spiritual path, but never intervene, because that would contravene our sacred free will.—*Ed.*

The Seven Entities of the Great Pyramid of Gizeh left the Secret Chamber during the night of March 31, 1993, and took with them the main Energy-Awareness of the seven fundamental planets of our solar system.*

The last Ancient Brothers of the Rose + Cross have planned their transition according to criteria they alone know. After transmitting to their servants the means to finish the Work, they left this world on January 6, 1994, at four minutes past midnight, in Sydney. Their destination is a new cycle of Creation.

We servants of the Rose + Cross, faced with an urgent situation, affirm:

That we refuse to take part in any system put in place by this decadent humanity;

That we have made plans in full awareness and with no fanaticism whatever. Our transition will only appear to be a suicide in human terms;

That, according to a commandment from the Great White Lodge of Sirius, we have closed and chosen to blow up all the Sanctuaries of the Secret Lodges to prevent their desecration by ignorant people or impostors.

That we will recall the last Servants who can understand this last message, according to the Plan we will work on in the future and the just law of magnetism.

Every slander, lie or libel about what we do can only be taken as refusal once more to understand and to penetrate the Mystery of Life and Death.

Space is bent, time is ending. We leave this world with unfathomable love, unspeakable joy, and no regret whatever.

Man, don't weep for our fate, but cry instead for your own. Ours is better than yours.

Those of you who are receptive of this last message, know that our Love and our Peace will go with you in the terrible trials of the Apoca-

---

*In astrology, planets regulate earthly life; their absence would suggest a period of chaos. The pyramids have been the focus of intense metaphysical speculation ever since their rediscovery by Napoleon's armies at the beginning of the eighteenth century.—Ed.

lypse that await you. Know that from where we will be, we will always keep our arms open to receive those who are worthy to join us.

Notes

1. John R. Hall and Philip Schuyler, "The Mystical Apocalypse of the Solar Temple," in *Millennium, Messiahs, and Mayhem: Contemporary Apocalyptic Movements,* ed. Thomas Robbins and Susan L. Palmer (New York: Routledge, 1997), 285–311.

2. Personal communication.

3. Rosicrucianism is a mystical and occult organization with roots in fifteenth-century Germany, where it was invented by some Lutheran mystics under the guidance of Johann Valentin Andrae as "a game," according to Peter Washington, *Madame Blavatsky's Baboon* (New York: Schocken, 1995), 38–39. It involved elaborate redactions of medieval chivalric myth. Hermetic Freemasonry brings the occult alchemical tradition of material and spiritual transformation into the Masonic secret society.

4. Hall and Schuyler, "Mystical Apocalypse," 288.

5. Richard Lacayo, "Cults: In the Reign of Fire," *Time,* October 17, 1994, archived at http://www.rickross.com/reference/S_Groups5.html.

6. Hall and Schuyler, "Mystical Apocalypse," 295.

7. In Buddhist belief, Agartha is a pure land, the heavenly capital of light and meditation. See below, chapter 10.

8. The history of Theosophy is well set forth in Washington's *Madame Blavatsky's Baboon.* Its founder, Madame H. P. Blavatsky, seems to have been heavily influenced by the esoteric novels of Edward Bulwer Lytton as well as her time's fashion for spiritualism. Theosophy is a major influence on today's New Age movement.

9. Hall and Schuyler, "Mystical Apocalypse," 293.

10. Ibid., 294.

AUM SHINRI KYO AND THE POLITICS OF TERROR

On March 20, 1995, eleven people were killed and more than five thousand injured in simultaneous poison gas attacks aboard Tokyo subway trains, all converging on a station near the city's government center. Shoko Asahara, the leader of a new religious movement called Aum Shinri Kyo, was arrested for planning and directing the attacks. At this writing, his trial is still working its glacial way toward its foregone conclusion: Asahara, like everybody else, knows he will hang. But the trial continues its work, one hearing a month.

Aum's religious and social system combines traditional Buddhism with elements of Christianity, popular culture, the newest scientific breakthroughs, and immense amounts of cash. Though this mixture may seem odd, it is not unique. Syncretistic borrowings of this kind are quite common in Japanese religious systems generally. Strict pacifism is a core component of Buddhism, but Buddhist armies are not unknown to history. It was common for Japanese Buddhists to arm themselves throughout the medieval period. The practice began as a self-defense measure, but eventually Buddhist temples had standing private armies that they used on occasion to pressure emperors into doing the temple's bidding. In the sixteenth century these warlord priests were gradually disarmed by the state.[1]

Both Buddhism and Shinto condemn violence, and most Japanese new religions have followed this lead. The glaring exception is Aum Shinri Kyo. As one observer commented, it "caused the collapse of what Japanese had for 400 years believed to be common sense."[2]

Aum urged its members to prepare for a dismal postapocalyptic future. The group built bomb shelters for its members and stockpiled air filters, clothing to ward off electromagnetic radiation, and supplies of food and medicine. The acquisition of supernatural powers of various kinds was also part of this preparation. Aum was going to be the ark of the millennium. At least one of its members found a measure of shivery, perhaps orgasmic, delight in the prospect of the sudden death of most of the world's population. Robert Jay Lifton quotes an ex-Aumist he interviewed on his feelings on learning that Armageddon had started with the release of the poison gas sarin in the subway: "I didn't ask who did it. . . . I didn't care who did it. . . . This was Armageddon. . . . We're going to be the savior of the world!" He said it was like "the feeling of being a star."[3] Even though the world is going to die, Aum will save it.

Lifton introduces the important concept of *poa* to discussion of Aum and its doings. This is yet another of those twisting leaps of faith that resolve contradiction by turning it on its head. The notion arises in Tantric Buddhism, where it is used to shorten a dying person's journey to nirvana by killing him. This "healing by killing" converts the victim into an immortal, but only when performed by "spiritually advanced beings" such as Asahara and his minions believe themselves to be.[4]

The imported idea of Armageddon seems to have destroyed for Aum the Japanese religious ideal of nonviolence. Aum was prepared to cause the apocalypse it feared by recruiting members of the military and police and allegedly engaging in terrorist activities.

In Buddhism's eternal circle of time (see chapter 1), Armageddon's terminus appears to be a contradiction, but Aum's followers seem to have no trouble with this problem. Asahara's Armageddon involves Christianity's defeat of Buddhism, except for Aum's elect. The idea of Buddhism's defeat is known in Japan from the work of Kanji Ishiwara, who is quoted in Aum's publications. Ishiwara was a Kwangtung officer and prophetic Nichiren Buddhist guru who created the puppet Manchukuo state in China in the 1930s, which he saw as a base for a final global struggle between Japan and the U.S. in the year 2000. He planned some failed germ warfare attacks against Beijing and other cities.[5] He predicted in the 1940s that America would defeat Japan in their final war. In Aum's beliefs, this final war will be the result of a plot involving Jewish financiers, Freemasons, and war profiteers.

The idea of Armageddon is well known in Japanese popular culture, fed by cartoon television shows such as *Uchusenkan Yamato* (Spaceship Yamato), first broadcast in 1974, and *Akira,* a comic book serial that began to run in 1983. (Interestingly, the air filters made by Aum apparently are identical in design to "cosmo cleaners" used to remove radioactivity in the fictional *Uchusenkan Yamato*.)[6] Dedicated fans of these science-fiction epics are called *otaku* in Japanese. The term is commonly used to describe people who live somewhat apart from others, in a dream world of their own. So it seems that Aum is, in part, an amalgamation of World War II–era alarmism and pop culture details.

This "*otaku* generation" is also called the "deviation value generation." This name refers, not to social alienation, but to the extent to which one's exam scores deviate from the standard mean, whether for better or worse. The best jobs go to students with the highest "deviation values," as we might expect. So it seems surprising that a great many of Aum's highest-placed recruits came from the ranks of these overachievers. Most of Asahara's "cabinet"—he established a shadow government in preparation for ruling Japan—held advanced degrees from Japan's most prestigious universities, and his minister of science, Hideo Murai, who was later assassinated, was reported to be "the most intelligent Japanese who ever lived."

These young people seemed already to have been promised everything Japanese life had to offer; they were assured first-class seats in Japan's economic bullet train as it raced to exceed America. But in the 1980s the race did not seem as easy as it once had, and Japan fell behind. The deviation value generation was faced with a road that was not so smooth. New values had begun to creep into the culture, and the national vocabulary was now salted with words such as "leisure" and "environment." New goals began to attract some of Japan's elite.

Members of the deviation value generation were utterly unprepared for these developments. Their options were to forsake their goals when they failed even to approach them; to retreat into "a delayed adolescence," searching for new personal aims; or to find the meaning they sought in new religions such as Aum.

A teacher remembered Chizuo Matsumoto (Asahara's given name) as "just a dreamer, a complete fantasist. He did have a strange, almost spiritual tranquillity in the way he talked to people."[7] Poor eyesight led to his enrollment at a school for the blind, where he made pocket money by leading blind students and telling fantastic tales. He and a brother developed an interest in traditional Chinese medicine as practiced by "Magicmakers." By the time he was fifteen Chizuo had a reputation as a guru and healer based on his illegal practice of this art. He told of out-of-body travels to China, where, he said, the best "Magicmakers" taught him levitation, the art of making robots, and how to reach "true enlightenment." He also told fortunes.

In his early twenties he vanished for a few years, claiming on his return to have been on a pilgrimage to Tibet and remote China, where he achieved nirvana. He reappeared ready to proclaim himself the chosen savior, a descendant, not just of Buddha, but of Jesus Christ, Muhammad, and other spiritual heavy hitters. It was later revealed that in fact he had been a short-order cook in Tokyo during that time.

It appears that Asahara belonged to a Buddhist movement called Agon-shu before he started his better-known Aum Shinri Kyo. Agon, in turn, seems to have emerged from a little-known movement called Kannon Jikei-kai, originally formed to worship a goddess of mercy, and later given to bellicose commemorations of the dead of World War II. Agon, like Aum, drew most of its members from among left-leaning, educated young people.

In 1985 Asahara "levitated" for the first time, in front of several Agon members. The experience led Asahara and some of his friends in the movement to split off and form their own yoga-teaching society. The "miracle" established Asahara's superiority over his master in Agon; there was nothing more for him to learn there.

Asahara is not a physically attractive man, as some of his devotees acknowledge. Yet his charismatic hold over his followers is complete. Much of their worship is devoted to Asahara's person as their guru, the source of their enlightenment and salvation. Lifton notes that one of the most prized benefits Aum had to offer was the opportunity to pay handsomely for the privilege of owning a "brain wave transmitter" that would tune the wearer in to Asahara's divine essence. He might also have noted reports that Asahara sold his bathwater as a sacrament, an idea not without precedent, as we have seen in the case of St. Anselm (chapter 1). Ian Reader reports that Asahara's blood was said to contain a special form of DNA that would lend enhanced spiritual powers to anyone who drank it. This he also sold for large sums.[8] He is reported to have done the same with his semen. One way

to holiness is mortification of the flesh, which can be accomplished by in-
gesting disgusting substances.

Lifton also observes that Asahara's grandiosity was immense. It led him
to subsume the world into himself, merging his identity with the cosmos.[9]
This idea is perhaps rarely far from such prophets, given the essential
course of millenarian prophecy. The prophet's vision converts and heals
him; at the same time, it inspires him to repeat the process through a select
circle of followers, and may lead him to try to convert the entire world.

At the beginning, Aum Shinri Kyo was no different from swarms of
other tiny new religions in Japan. The country has enough religions to provide one for every five hundred inhabitants, all of them untaxed. Many observers think that this cult-glut results from materialist Japan's spiritual vac-
uum. According to some analysts, ever since Emperor Hirohito renounced
his divine status after World War II, in a gesture of spiritual *seppuku* (ritual
suicide), there has been a hollow at the center of the country's spiritual life,
which these hosts of small group vie to fill.

The core beliefs of Aum Shinri Kyo derive from Buddhism but also
cover all bases. Aum's cosmology begins in a fourfold universe structured
in hierarchical levels. The lowest is the realm of desire, which is where unfortunate ordinary mortals reside. The highest is Maha Nirvana (great
peace) a state that Asahara alone among all Japanese has attained. In the
"beginningless past" all souls could roam at will through these levels of
being. They could also take up and leave bodies at will, as needed in their
celestial frolic. There were no consequences to any action the soul might
take; there was no karma.

But now we are caught up in karma, eternal prisoners of cause and effect until we find Absolute Truth through the teachings of Master Asahara.
We are "gagged up" by information from television and other sources, until
it is no wonder we are "like comedians." Fulfillment of desire drains us of
"joy energy," leaving us ever more subject to the energy of suffering.[10]

The aim of Asahara's teachings is to assist the souls of his followers to return to the state of divine bliss through the process of *samadhi*: freeing the
True Self from desire. In the last stage of the procedure, one seems to be
near death: "One's subtle body called 'the body of emanation' is released
from the top of one's head at this time, and one experiences various kinds
of worlds."[11]

Beliefs from other sources quickly joined Aum's pantheon. One of these was modern science—and science fiction. Asahara taught that the change in our condition, our fall, came about when the forms of energy called *Gunas,* consisting of heat, sound, and wisdom/light, attracted the joyous True Self to plunge into them, leading to the Big Bang of modern physics. For Asahara this did not contradict Shakyamuni's (that is, Buddha's) teaching that the fall was due to ignorance of mystical wisdom. The notion that there might be something better in the world of desire than the absolute freedom, happiness, and joy they had known seduced the fallen beings a second time. We ordinary humans, their offspring, share the realm of desire (in Asahara's terms, "The Heaven of Degenerate Consciousness"[12]) with the beings that pilot UFOs.

Asahara's teachings about the body and its relation to the levels of being seem to follow pretty closely the classical Hindu and Buddhist teachings of *chakras.* The realms of existence are subdivided into complex levels of levels, in a Dantesque assignment of rewards and punishments according to karma. However, Asahara seems to depart from these sources a bit in talking of "Karmic Rebound," or the recovery from cause and effect, which he asserts comes much faster to his followers than to others, even other practitioners of yogic discipline. Since karma is morally neutral, the speedy rebound Aum's followers experience means that they suffer now for errors of this lifetime. If they seem to be suffering under Asahara's regime, it is only a sign of their salvation working for them. Once again, faith conquers common sense.

In a clear departure from Hindu and Buddhist teachings, Asahara offers an image of Judgment Day, when he will return to act as a sort of defense attorney for his followers. Christ will appear then as well, as the Christians' guru. Without a guru to speak to Yama (the god of death) on our behalf, others can only anticipate the most miserable reincarnation. It seems that this Judgment Day is ongoing, rather than a conclusive cosmic event.[13]

Asahara's historical teachings are something of a novelty. He foresees an imminent split within victorious capitalism, whereby one of two "seeds" will accept materialism while retaining a higher purpose: *samadhi.* The other will remain purely materialist. This separation is what Christians refer to as the Last Judgment. The Book of Revelation, for Asahara, describes this postcapitalist world order. Christians, he says, believe that

Chinese Communism will collapse at the end of the twentieth century and that "unimaginable disasters" will ensue. This does not bother Buddhists, who disdain the things of this life, but for Christians it is like cramming for a final exam.[14] In Aum's view they must frantically prepare to survive. Buddhists should not ignore these predictions, though, because if properly used they can contribute to happiness. Asahara finds consistency among all truth-systems, including Marxism, and seeks to integrate them as supreme truth.

Aum's eschatology is clearly and expressly based on Christianity. The world is under the devil's control. That would be all right with Asahara if Satan could bring us to true happiness, but of course he can not.[15] Satan's minions control the flow of both money and information. As our nature falls to the level of animals under this malign influence, the world correspondingly falls into disorder. Aum is a force for order and the restoration of the world's "homeostasis." Aum is a "menace" to these materialistic values because it actively combats them. Asahara tells his followers that even if he were offered a position of world leadership, he "would not comply."[16] Asahara names his enemies as "X" but leaves little doubt that Jews— equated with Freemasons—are meant. For instance, he says that X claims the Ten Commandments as its exclusive property. However, these X are actually pretty spiritually advanced, in Asahara's view.

Asahara views the present state of comparative world peace as akin to that of 1939. World War III is just over the horizon. Accordingly, Asahara told an audience in late 1992 of Aum's construction plans and its acquisition of broadcast facilities to spread the gospel across Japan and Russia. Another element in the movement's preparation was the construction of a computer-based divination process called "Grand Universe Truth Astrology," which would reveal individual karmic stages "as well as activation of the intensity of sunlight, gravity of the sun and moon out of the powers of the sun and the moon."[17]

The final battle will be the result of the merging of an evil stream with a good one, focused on the United States. The "evil stream" will try to unify the world and eventually will come into conflict with the truth (that is, Aum). In this conflict, Aum's awareness of spiritual truth will protect it. Its broadcasting activity and especially its music programs are especially potent in the effort to spread this message.[18]

The evil stream is personified as the Freemasons, who are not distinct from Jews or any other internationalist group in Asahara's eschatology. Aum's web site, based in Russia, offers a complete version of *The Protocols of the Elders of Zion* on a page marked "Freemasons." Asahara sees Freemasons behind what he took to be manipulation of the Japanese stock exchange in 1993. When they cause the next crash, "phenomena like spitting at heaven will occur."[19] Asahara also had a research program devoted to the works of Nostradamus, who he said foretold Armageddon for 1997. He knew, even though he hadn't yet checked the translator's version of the poem by meditating on it to determine its truth, because it is poem (century) 97 and mentions Armageddon.

The battle of Armageddon will reduce humanity by as much as three-fourths of its present size. Armageddon will not be the last battle, though. It will leave the Western powers largely unscathed. According to Asahara's reading of Nostradamus, Christ will take part in Armageddon and then attack the smug Western powers. He also says that Nostradamus foretold an American-led Western nuclear attack on Japan. The end will come in 2000 or 2006. But even if it does not arrive on schedule, believers should "count [their] karma" and prepare for death.

World War III, says Asahara, will be fought with plasma weapons (i.e., hypothetical arms that radiate particle beams capable of heating a target to 8000 degrees) of the same kind that "vaporized" the cadavers of 92,000 Iraqi soldiers in the Gulf War.[20] Asahara is intensely interested in such weapons of mass destruction; he describes with evident relish the superiority of plasma ("no soldier is required") over "conventional" weaponry such as chemical and biological arms. Since Japan lags in the production of this super-weapon, there is but one recourse: high-level Aumists must learn to generate plasma (super-heated gas) with their own bodies, by manipulating their magnetic fields. "Frantic practice" is required.

Aum carefully documents experiments that claim to prove the ability of adepts to spend twelve hours in a sealed tank without breathing, for example. This is taken to be evidence of the attainment of *samadhi*. Holiness in Aum's system seems to be in inverse proportion to physical health, not an unreasonable conclusion given their premises.

Asahara's reading of Christian texts and his proclamation that he is, in effect, the Second Coming, seem bizarre actions for a Buddhist guru.[21] An article in a Japanese web-based investigative journal called *Archipelago* suggests that he may have had a political motive: the seduction of Russia, or at least of some members of its political apparatus. He made a serious attempt in a book called *Declaring Myself the Christ* to reconcile the doctrine of the Second Coming with certain Buddhist dogmas. According to *Archipelago* it was intended as a missionary tool in Russia, and apparently it succeeded: Asahara amassed thirty thousand recruits there in three years, three times his estimated total of Japanese followers. According to Ian Reader, the number may also have had some mystical significance. He reports that thirty thousand was the number of devoted believers Asahara said it would take "to eradicate the negative energies of the material world" and bring Aum to paradise.[22] It might also have been simply the number of followers he had on hand.

According to *Archipelago,* Asahara also established intimate clandestine relations with important members of the Russian government, as well as with some elements of Japan's political leadership. It is not clear from these accounts exactly who may have manipulated whom, but all sides may have benefited. It is known that Aum had some success in buying Russian weapons.

Archipelago explains the Russians' eagerness to work with Asahara in the light of what Aum had to offer: hard currency, high technology, and cooperation in Russia's proposed new Asian security arrangement. Russia would open up its client states in Asia to Japanese entrepreneurs, and Japan would cold-shoulder the United States and its security umbrella. Russia also might have hoped to restrain China's ambitions by short-circuiting U.S. influence in the area.

After the subway attack two anonymous terroristic threats were sent to government offices and newspapers in Tokyo, in apparent response to plans to use Japan's anti–subversive activities law to shut down Aum Shinri Kyo. The obviously false signature on the threats was that of Honda Sigekuni of "Project MV." Sigekuni is the narrator of Yukio Mishima's *Sea of Fertility* tetralogy, whose theme is reincarnation. MV is described as "the underground militant wing of Aum."

The message of the first warning was lifted from the Book of Matthew, larded with a Japanese passage that translates: "We, on November 30, in war will enter and attack forcefully, do it, Tokyo station, warning, beware of the anti-subversive law, if you do it, do it if you dare."[23] In the message Judas is replaced by the name of Fumihiro Joyu, Aum's former press representative.

The second note was signed in the same way, but was written in an alphanumeric code translatable by word processor.[24] It noted that an attack against a nuclear plant had failed, but that another would be mounted against a facility somewhere in southeast Asia. Shortly after, there were two mishaps at Japanese plants and a fire at another.

The second message quotes from Fredric Jameson's essay "Metacommentary":

And since I have mentioned Susan Sontag above . . . to . . . a language that hides what it displays beneath its own reality as language, a glance that designates, through the very process of avoiding, the object forbidden.[25]

Whatever Jameson might have had in mind when he wrote the passage, in this context it becomes postmodern terrorism of the image, psy-war as cultural criticism. To attack the nation's plutonium stocks is to cast a pall of doubt over the question of the terrorist's identity in a reversal of roles. An assault on "the Japanese corporate-neocolonialist enterprise" raises the issue of who it is that threatens international order, and attacking the subversion law throws the accusation of subverting the constitution in a new direction. This is identity terror, where the accusation cuts both ways, and leveling it eviscerates the accuser.

Jameson's essay critiques Susan Sontag's famous essay on science fiction movies, "The Imagination of Disaster."[26] In the note, "Sigekuni" replaces Sontag's name with Shoko Egawa's. The implication is that Egawa, an investigative reporter known for attacking Aum, thinks of herself as a person like Sontag, "a high priestess exorcising a hostile, evil force lurking out there—science fiction monsters, Aum, whatever renders humanity powerless to act."[27]

In Jameson's terms, science fiction really reveals a deep-seated envy of the Godlike scientist who has real power and authority, though he does no "real" work. Money is not the object of his life, and his work has that rarest of attributes, a fascination in itself. This "folk-dream" of the scientist's life

also suggests an ironic quasi-Luddite return to an older epoch of community and collegiality of work, of guilds and apprenticeship.

This almost perfectly describes the scientific organization Hideo Murai
established for Aum at Kamikuiishiki village. There Aum's elite recruits,
alienated overachievers all, worked on the most advanced projects in this
atmosphere of close and cooperative collaboration. From another point of
view, they were sinister if jolly versions of Snow White's seven dwarves,
happily at work on "genetically manipulating biological anti-toxins, developing plasma technology, experimenting with brain waves, and living the
myth of Isaac Asimov's *Foundation* series."[28] They were building Aum's
postapocalypse paradise, a new and higher civilization.

Groups such as Aum that attract society's elites perplex their observers
in the media and especially in academia. How is it possible for the privileged, well-educated few to abandon everything that life offers them—
fame, wealth, respect—and go off in pursuit of the millennial chimera? For
academics, the question comes perilously close to home, for the believers
are like them: the best-educated, the brightest their nation has to offer. The
case of Hideo Murai offers an example.

Murai, the assassinated minister of science and technology in Aum
Shinri Kyo, had an IQ "higher than Einstein's."[29] His studies of astro-
physics and specialty in X-rays gave him the capacity to head up the sect's
research into "new types of weapons more powerful than nuclear bombs."
He claimed that the earthquake that destroyed Kobe in January 1995 was
actually caused by laser-powered seismic weapons.

Murai was specifically interested in (hypothetical but conceivable)
plasma weapons. As we have seen, such talk held a fascination for Asahara.
Murai discussed some of his ideas with Asahara on one of their radio
broadcasts.[30] For instance, he talked of electron-beam weapons that could
produce plasma at $4,000°C$, hot enough to destroy missiles in flight and
cook the inhabitants of hardened bunkers. Murai's major interest was in
protecting Aum from these weapons. He designed special goggles for Asahara's driver and was developing protective gear to shield other members of
the group, but he thought that the only real protection would be a magnetic field.

Aum was looking into the work carried out by Nikola Tesla earlier in the
century. Tesla (1856–1943) is a cult figure among believers in suppressed dis-

coveries, free energy, and miracle science. He is said to have created artificial earthquakes and definitely claimed he could "split the earth like an
apple." He is credited with a number of other inventions as well, and apparently challenged Edison to the extent that the latter destroyed Tesla's
reputation.

Tesla's theories depended on his accurate perception that the Earth creates massive electromagnetic forces that with relative ease could provide essentially free and limitless energy. Aum found that the U.S. government
classifies much of Tesla's work and that he is widely respected in Eastern
Europe, though little known in Japan.

The Aum document below is a part of a transcript of a radio broadcast
from a show called *Evangelion tes Basileis* (The King's Good News). Why it
was given a Greek name for a Japanese audience is not clear. This particular show, which must have occupied a good two hours of airtime, was
broadcast December 4, 1994.

I chose to include it because it neatly summarizes Aum's beliefs about
Armageddon and the new world to come. Each speaker addresses an area
of expertise, so the discussion covers most of the bases in Asahara's apocalypse. Its structure is also revealing, in that it pretends to offer Asahara's
acolytes an opportunity to speak freely. What they actually do is parrot the
party line and defer to Asahara. His authority is supreme.

It begins with a long discussion of the inevitability of World War III, the
hideous weapons to be used in it, and what the chances of survival are for
Asahara's followers. It takes the form of a discussion in which Asahara
quizzes his apostles about their expertise in such matters, which appears to
be formidable, but nothing when compared to Asahara's. The opinions he
asks them about are always correct. On this particular show the followers
include Murai, under his "sacred name" Manjusrimitra Seitashi (MM in
the text); Bodhisattva Vajrapani Shicho (VP), an elementary particle physicist from the University of Tokyo; Saint Tilopa Seigoshi, an architect and
landscape engineer; Bodhisattva Krishnananda Shicho, a heart surgeon;
Bodhisattva Vimala Shi, a translator at work on a Japanese version of Nostradamus's *Centuries*; and the secular Mr. Yukio Ishitani (I), an expert in
the I Ching, a Chinese divination system.[31]

The City of Shambhala mentioned in the text comes from Tibetan
mythology. In some accounts it is a locus of the power of evil, in

bitter rivalry with Agartha, the capital of Light and meditation. Shambhala seems to be a pure land invisible and certainly inaccessible to those of limited purity. Different authors ascribe disparate characteristics to it and locate it in various spots, but underground is a favorite. Shambhala and Agartha seem to be in an ambiguous relationship akin to the interdependence of heaven and hell; neither is complete without the existence of the other. But whereas heaven and hell are distinct and permanent entities—it would be unthinkable for heaven to become a place of endless torment—Agartha and Shambhala seem to change their locations and their natures depending on who is talking about them. In any case, the Pure Land is a generally recognized counterpart of paradise among Eastern religions in general and Buddhists in particular.

• • •

THE WORLD AFTER THE FINAL WAR
(THE MILLENNIUM)

MASTER: After the Third World War, I imagine that this world will be filled with love. Every person will overcome his or her own suffering and work for the good of others. But each person has a vision of the millennium. Let me ask what your visions are. Mr. Ishitani?

ISHITANI: As Master always says we are in the age of Kali Yuga. There are a lot of peculiar situations because of the transgressing of the precepts. Recently, for example, someone committed suicide as a result of being bullied. Armageddon will occur because of the vice people have accumulated. The world is like a hell. There is no religion in which the followers strictly observe its precepts, apart from Aum Shinrikyo. Master said in a lecture that during Armageddon many will regret what they have done, and they will begin to observe the precepts. They will be the survivors. The world will be like a heaven and people will be able to live without consuming their merit. We will enter a wonderful new age. This is what I believe.

Reprinted from Shoko Asahara, *Disaster Approaches the Land of the Rising Sun* (Shizuoka, Japan: Aum Publishing Co., 1995), 133–36.

VIMALA: According to the predictions of Nostradamus, the world population will dramatically decrease, and land formations will drastically change. The land and sea will not have their present shape. The Bible says that those who have seals impressed on their foreheads will survive. Nostradamus said the great Chyren (Christ) will become the ruler of earth.* He will be loved and feared, and inspire awe. His esteem and repute is above the gods. The victor will be satisfied with the one title. I imagine that in a world like this, a king will reign as a victor, and those who have the seal will survive.

KRISHNANANDA: Today's topics were mainly about the physical aspects and materials used for weapons and defenses. But the fundamental reason Armageddon must occur is that the inhabitants of the present human realm do not recognize that they are fated to die. We can also say that in contemporary society death is concealed from the public eye. However, life and death are closely connected and our life span is short. This is a characteristic of the human world. Therefore, any society that is unaware of death must be corrected. That is why wars happen.

I think that in the coming age the survivors of the final war will form a society in which they mindfully face death and stress the importance of the law of karma. People will extinguish their karma, accumulate merit through cooperative lifestyles, and acquire divine powers. Moreover there will be a concrete system of using the power of consciousness, especially the unconscious. That system will liberate all people from materialistic ideas. Aum Shinri Kyo is currently adopting that system.

TILOPA: Most governments have taken countermeasures against the final war, which I think will mainly be a nuclear war. In Russia subways can be used as shelters. Subways in Japan are approximately 20

---

*It is difficult to know which Century or Quatrain of Nostradamus is meant. It might be Century 4 Quatrain 34, which reads:

Le grand mené captif d'estrange terre,
D'or enchainé au Roy Chyren offert:
Qui dans Ausone, Milan perdra la guerre,
Et tout son ost mis à feu & à fer.

This refers to a captive from outlandish parts brought as an offering to King Chyren. He (presumably the captive, not Chyren) had lost a war over "Ausonia and Milan" and seen all his army put to the sword.—*Ed.*

meters deep. Russia's are about 40 meters deep. They constructed the subway system from its inception as a shelter. There is one area in Japan that is similar to the subway in Russia—Kasumigaseki station in Nagata-cho.* That is where the Diet Building and other government offices are located. This underground station looks like a shelter for a nuclear bomb. Those who run into such structures will surely survive. But people should not depend on the government because there are few such facilities in Japan. People should protect themselves from war on their own.

Those who acquire the necessary material protection by themselves or from the government will survive the first stage. Then radioactivity and other bad circumstances—poison gas, epidemics, food shortages—will occur. People will have to try to survive these situations, too. Those who survive in the end and create the new world must have a much higher wisdom and virtue. I think people with great karma will transcend the worst suffering ever faced by humankind. They will survive and create a new and transcendent human world.

VAJRAPANI: I think what will come will be the opposite of the present world. The world will be completely materially devastated by war. Yet I think that an affluent world of the mind will arise in which the laws of the truth will spread. It will not be an environment in which people lose their virtue and fall to lower worlds. It will be a place where people can jump up to higher worlds. If spirituality is reestablished and virtuous souls come forth, the world will also be materially abundant.

MM: Causes create effects. Since this world is nearly full of vice, the gods will pass judgment on it. Hence the battle will end in the triumph of Ahura Mazda over Griffon [sic]. Only those people selected by the gods will survive, and the entire world will become a Shambhala. The present world is connected to the realm of hungry ghosts and hell because vice is being accumulated. I think the future world will be connected to the heavens of the gods through the practice of the truth.

---

*This is the station where the trains Aum attacked all converged. No doubt there was a message in this choice—perhaps something about the futility of trying to hide.—Ed.

Notes

1. Yoshihiko Nomura, "Where AUM Shinrikyo Is Coming From," *Kansai Forum,* no. 20 (June–July 1995), archived at http://www.notredame.ac.jp/POETS/IBH/KansaiForum/ 20/Aum.html.

2. Ibid.

3. Robert Jay Lifton, "Reflections on Aum Shinrikyo," in *The Year 2000: Essays on the End,* ed. Charles B. Strozier and Michael Flynn (New York: New York University Press, 1997), 118.

4. Ibid., 114.

5. Nomura, "Where AUM Shinrikyo Is Coming From." Nichiren Buddhism is named for its founder, a thirteenth-century priest who taught that salvation was assured all those who professed simple belief in the Lotus Sutra. Much of this background information comes from a series in the web-based Japanese magazine *Archipelago,* which seems now to be defunct. Ishihara is said to have survived the war and worked undercover for the U.S. government developing biological warfare weapons. It is difficult to know how much of these tales to credit; many are reprinted with complete credence in conspiracy-theory journals such as the web-based *Deep Times.* However, *Archipelago*'s editor was Yoichi Clark Shimatsu, a former senior editor at the *Japan Times,* the country's premier English-language newspaper.

6. Ibid.

7. James Dalrymple, "The Day Mighty Japan Lost Its Nerve," *Sunday Times Magazine* (London), August 13, 1995, archived at irdial@irdialsys.win-uk.net.

8. Ian Reader, "Gas Clouds over Tokyo: Aum Shinri Kyo's Path to Violence," *NIAS Nytt: Nordic Newsletter of Asian Studies,* no. 2 (July 1995), archived at http://nias.ku.dk/ Nytt/Regional/EastAsia/Articles/aum.html.

9. Lifton, "Reflections on Aum Shinrikyo," 116–17.

10. Aum Shinri Kyo, "What Is Our Essence?" http://www.aum-shinrikyo.com/english/ index.htm/11-2.htm (October 4, 1998).

11. Aum Shinri Kyo, "What Is Samadhi?" http://www.aum-shinrikyo.com/english/index .htm/11-20.htm (October 4, 1998).

12. Aum Shinri Kyo, "Where Do Extraterrestrial Come From?" http://www.aum-shinrikyo.com/english/index.htm/11-10.htm (October 4, 1998).

13. Aum Shinri Kyo, "Guru Is Your Defense Lawyer at the Judgment after Death," http://www.aum-shinrikyo.com/english/index.htm/13-7.htm (October 4, 1998).

14. Aum Shinri Kyo, "Buddhism Encompasses Christianity," http://www.aum-shinrikyo .com/english/index.htm/buddhism.htm (October 4, 1998).

15. Aum Shinri Kyo, "Materialism—The Sermon of the Devil," http://www.aum-shinrikyo.com/english/index.htm/matter2.htm (October 4, 1998).

16. Aum Shinri Kyo, "The Intrigue behind Information," http://www.aum-shinrikyo .com/english/index.htm/matter6.htm (October 4, 1998).

17. Aum Shinri Kyo, "How to Live during the Time of Radical Changes," http:// www.aum-shinrikyo.com/english/index.htm/changes.htm (October 4, 1998).

18. The web site also contains a number of Aum's, and possibly Asahara's, compositions, as well as a photo of Asahara conducting an orchestra—at least, it shows him holding a baton.

19. Aum Shinri Kyo, "Preparing for the Appearance of Christ at the End of the Century," http://www.aum-shinrikyo.com/english/index.htm/christ.htm (October 4, 1998).

20. Aum Shinri Kyo, "World War III Is Coming Soon: The Control of Plasma," http:// www.aum-shinrikyo.com/english/index.htm/plasma.htm (October 4, 1998).

21. Jack Amano, "Enter the Red Dragon: How Japanese Politicians Used Aum to Penetrate the Kremlin," *Archipelago,* http://www.pelago.com/0101/story2.html (July 1, 1996). Amano is clearly an anticult conspiracist, so his conclusions cannot be taken at face value. However, the basic facts he presents are, like much of conspiracy theory, sound.

22. Reader, "Aum Shinri Kyo's Path to Violence."

23. http://www.pelago.com/Aumpedia/gospelofMatthew.html (April 25, 1996).

24. http://www.pelago.com/Aumpedia/susanSontag.html.

25. Fredric Jameson, "Metacommentary," in *The Ideologies of Theory: Essays 1971–1986* (Minneapolis: University of Minnesota Press, 1988).

26. See Susan Sontag, *Against Interpretation* (New York: Farrar, Strauss and Giroux, 1966).

27. http://www.pelago.com/Aumpedia/susanSontag.html.

28. Ibid.

29. Yoichi Clark Shimatsu, "Starwars and the Final War: The Life, Death and Secret Weapons Research of Hideo Murai, Science and Technology Minister of Aum Shinrikyo," *Archipelago,* http://www.pelago.com/0102/story2.html (July 1, 1996); Yoichi Clark Shimatsu, "Judea Cipher: Why Aum's Science Chief Had to Be Silenced," in ibid.

30. See, for example, Shoko Asahara's introduction in *Disaster Approaches the Land of the Rising Sun* (Shizuoka, Japan: Aum Publishing Co., 1995).

31. Seitashi means "saint," and a Bodhisattva is one who might enter nirvana but abstains in order to help others attain the same level. Manjusri is the wisest of the Four Great Bodhisattvas. Vajrapani is a rain god and protective deity. Tilopa was a tenth-century yogin. Krishnananda is a prominent Indian holy man. Vimala probably refers to a goddess of speech.

CHAPTER 11

THE MONTANA FREEMEN

The Montana Freemen movement offered its followers the dream of every wage and debt slave: sovereignty.[1] In its fantasy of total independence and Constitutional fundamentalism, its members could become millionaires with no labor simply by issuing their own money. Unlike leftist populist movements of the past, the Freemen and their "Constitutionalist" partners seek this dream not by empowering and reforming government, but by rejecting it. They seek a return to a supposedly ideal time before the federal government subverted the original intent of the founders by usurping power, enslaving us in an unending spiral of debt, taxes, and mercantile justice.

The Christian Constitutionalist movement of which the Freemen are a part believes that the Bill of Rights and the Constitution through the Twelfth Amendment are divinely inspired, nearly holy writ on a par with the Bible.[2] This is the "organic constitution" in their beliefs.[3] The later amendments establishing a federal government are in opposition to the original, which contains God's law. Since Constitutionalists are not "Fourteenth Amendment citizens"—women or nonwhites—they consider themselves free of requirements not set forth in the part of the Constitution they accept. Only sovereign citizens (i.e., the Freemen themselves) can judge the merits of laws, leaving them impervious, as all dualists are, to critical argument. As sovercigns they are subject to the feudalist common law principles set forth in the Magna Carta. Any failure to obey their dictates is treason and punishable by death.

Constitutionalists closely study the law and can recite it—especially the Uniform Commercial Code—as other Christians can recite holy writ. They observe the forms of legalism, Latin tags and all, with intense scruple. Mr. Burke Elder; Hale III, the national director of the

Fully Informed Grand Jury Association, punctuates his name in that fashion in order

> [t]o distinguish between the surname and the Christian name, with the intent to distinguish the character of the Lawful Christian man from a fiction, e.g., Burk E. Hale III, or Burk Elder Hale III, or Hale, Burk E., or Burk E. Hale III, all of which have the potential of being used as a "trust" under de facto corporate federal jurisdiction. The SS #, Drivers license, etc., use the fictional name designated to the fictional character activated by the consent of the freeborn character. The character is considered a thing, and chattel of "government," and as such is prosecuted "in rem" when the fictional character violates the statutes of the corporate federal jurisdiction. So, the punctuation is used to show character/status.[4]

Constitutionalists study the minutiae of legalism like any guardhouse lawyer, but they ignore all the principles of law that do not serve their own purposes.

The ideological underpinnings of the Freemen lie in the Posse Comitatus, an antigovernment group founded in 1969 by Henry L. Beach and William P. Gale, a retired colonel.[5] Beach had been a pro-Nazi "Silver Shirt" in the thirties. The Posse Comitatus argues that no government beyond the local level has any legitimacy. There is no genuine government power beyond that vested in the sheriff, with his powers to call juries and swear in posses of deputies to enforce the law.

Many antigovernment right-wing activist groups have appeared on the American scene in recent years. Some of these groups had been around for years and found themselves thrust into prominence following the 1995 bombing of the federal building in Oklahoma City. These groups are rarely or never unanimous in much of anything beyond their fear and loathing of the U.S. government. There is no central authority behind them, nor any dogma to which they must adhere.

Many of these groups also have a religious basis. The beliefs that inspire some of the groups, or at least some of their members, derive from a movement that arose in the eighteenth century called British-Israelism. The central tenet of this movement is that the English are descended from the lost tribes of the Kingdom of Israel, while the "other" Jews are descended from the Kingdom of Judah.[6] The very first inklings of this belief appear in some Puritan letters and other writings dating from as far back as 1666, as well as in the Sabbatian movement on the continent. There were rumors of immense armies of Jews sweeping through the Middle East attacking Muslims. The Puritans, ardent apocalypticists, decided that they themselves were the lost tribes emerging into history to assume their place in Jerusalem and the Second Coming.

However, the doctrine of British-Israelism did not take real shape until the eighteenth century, when it emerged as a belief that there was a "hidden Israel" among the peoples of Western Europe and the British Isles in particular. This claim was not based on faith alone. Some investigators used a kind of folk etymology to note similarities of sounds between Hebrew and English. They argued that these similarities meant that English is actually an adaptation of Hebrew, thereby "proving" what they wanted to believe.

The English were Jews, but so were the "other" Jews. They too had a place in "All-Israel," albeit a subordinate one. In Britain the movement remained benign if somewhat patronizing toward its non-English counterparts. In America the movement took an entirely different turn in becoming the Christian Identity movement.

The American offshoot retained the idea of Jewish ancestry for the white (i.e., Nordic) races with a bitterly anti-Semitic twist. It retained a strong millenarian tone in its expectation of a final showdown between the Zionist Occupation Government (ZOG; a key catchword in the movement) and the few lonely bands of Identity guerrillas wise enough to oppose its tyranny.

Starting with the premise of British-Israelism, some American Identity Christians added the belief that Jews were the result of Satan in the guise of the serpent literally seducing Eve. This was the original sin and Jews are the race of Cain, forever cursed. This "two-seed" theory is reportedly a direct result of Nazi influence in the movement prior to World War II.[7] An ancillary belief casts blacks as the servants of Satan's rebellion. Christian Identity treats *The Protocols of the Elders of Zion* as the purest truth, if not actual holy writ.

Beach and his followers in the Posse Comitatus rejected the authority of the federal government, in particular the Internal Revenue Service (IRS) and the Federal Reserve. They rejected the Sixteenth Amendment, the basis of the IRS's power, and argued that the revenue codes could be shown to hold payment of income tax optional for individuals. The Federal Reserve has no authority whatever, being, in their words, "a private monopoly which neither the people nor the states authorized in the constitution." Its issuance of paper money is clearly unconstitutional, in their view.

The Posse was not racist in its entirety, but it did include some anti-Semites who said the Federal Reserve was under the control of a cartel of European Jewish bankers whose aim was to profit by the destruction of the United States through irredeemable debt and spurious paper money. Many Posse Comitatus members base their ideology on the tenets of Christian Identity. Though there is little doubt that the militias draw many of their ideas from people who espouse these views, there is room to question the common conclusion that they all share this doctrine.

Jeffrey Kaplan makes it clear that there is no unanimity among the numerous rejecters of federal authority.[8] Most militia members vehemently deny racism, whereas Christian Identity groups, as well as many other racists, generally flaunt it. Following some of Kaplan's observations, it might be wiser to see Identity Christians and the extreme right wing as sharing a common "occult milieu" in which ideas like those of Identity meet and mingle with other conspiratorial notions.[9] The single idea that binds them is intense fear of an all-powerful inhuman government bent on total domination of its citizens and the extermination of all opposition.

Another, related influence on the Freemen was the Township movement, which argued for the establishment of small sovereign communities independent of all exterior government. The Posse set one of these up in Wisconsin, with border warnings of death to intruding federal agents. It chose its own judges and ambassadors.

The Posse showed no mercy toward those holding different ideas. Beach recommended hanging any federal official thought to violate the Constitution or his oath of office. The hangman's noose became a symbol of the movement, and members wore lapel pins in that shape.

The Wisconsin Posse (still operating under the name Family Farm Preservation) was the most aggressive of the many cells. Like the Freemen, it assaulted officials and disrupted meetings. The farm crisis of the 1980s significantly broadened the Posse's appeal, not least because it offered scapegoats for the farmers' failures: inept courts, an illegal money system, and Jews. Many farms failed in those days, often for reasons well beyond farmers' control. The Federal Housing Administration and banks had encouraged them to take out large loans in the 1970s. Then in 1979 the Federal Reserve raised interest rates. Land values dropped sharply at the same time that interest rates on the farmers' mortgages rose steeply. Multinational corporations took advantage of the situation by moving in and scooping up the discounted land for their "factory farms." It is little wonder the farmers felt that forces beyond their control had dispossessed them. These forces seemed to be in alliance with foreign interests while operating under the cover of U.S. government authority. As in all conspiracy theory, there was a strong element of truth underlying the belief. Catherine Wessinger cites a moving testimonial from a dispossessed farm couple:

Dear Sir:

No one can ever begin to imagine the stress, strain, frustrations, and total helplessness that the American farmer has had and felt the last few years in trying to stay afloat and fight the farm credit system. You get so desperate you do not know what to do or even where your next meal for your kids will come from.

We personally have been fighting Federal Land Bank of Enid and Wichita for the last seven years. FLB lied, cheated, and frauded us. One farmer by themselves can not fight them through the courts. So where do you turn to for help?

We wanted to give up so many times and walk away. You take your frustrations out on each other and on your family. You are always under tension. . . . This desperation often causes murder and suicides. They can not face failure and losing the family farm.

Our Plea is this, make the Farm Credit System, especially the FLB accountable to someone! No entity should be allowed to do these things to anyone and not be punished. . . . Please make the Farm Credit System accountable to someone!

Darrell and Sally Frech, 1989[10]

The range and intensity of the Posse's illegal activities also increased significantly in the 1980s. They took up counterfeiting, paramilitary activity, tax resisting, bomb making, and continued threats against government officials. Gordon Kahl, a North Dakota tax resister, became the movement's chief martyr after his death in a shootout with police.

The Posse's favorite tactic was legal harassment. They seem to have invented the tactic of placing fraudulent liens against anyone they disliked, especially IRS agents. Even though the liens had no merit, they were a major nuisance, since they impaired the victims' credit until they could get them removed. They function like booby traps left behind by retreating armies. Once in place they can lie dormant for years until victims try to sell or borrow against their property, when the lien pops up and blocks the process. The victim then has to spend a good deal of time and money to get it revoked.

Their second favorite approach was to flood the courts with useless paper of all kinds. This was related to their "common law courts," which amounted to vigilante organizations that, again, issued threats against government officials.

The Posse largely died out by the end of the 1980s. The only way they found to make any money resisting taxes was to run seminars, a favorite activity of the Montana Freemen as well.

Freemen leaders, Leroy Schweitzer in particular, were influenced by people peddling the techniques of tax evasion. Schweitzer was a crop-duster by trade, but his resentment of government was such that he refused to get a pilot's license, which led to a federal warrant for his arrest. His failure to pay taxes resulted in the seizure and sale of his plane, his home, and other possessions in settlement of liens dating back to the 1970s. His desire to turn this tool against his tormentors may have arisen from the Posse Comitatus meetings he is known to have attended. He may also have had contact with The Order, a notorious band of neo-Nazi outlaws.

Even in his deep legal trouble, Schweitzer had powerful charisma. Everyone seemed to love him. But his troubles continued to mount as he rejected any form of government control whatever. A safety inspector cited him for a minor electrical code violation at his business, explaining that the code was there to protect his employees. By report Schweitzer then fired his only helper, saying "now there are no employees who work here, so see how your regulations protected the man."

His partner, Rodney Skurdal, was a complement to Schweitzer's own charismatic bullheadedness. Skurdal developed an ability to manipulate the system "into a fine art."[11] He managed to string out an appeal of a Workman's Compensation suit for a whole year, on the grounds that he should be paid in gold bullion because paper money is illegal. The state supreme court refused to hear the case, calling it "perhaps the most frivolous appeal ever filed here." Skurdal's religious and racial beliefs mixed with his legal persuasions in an inextricable confusion of terms. For him the Uniform Commercial Code became scripture, and he could quote it like a legal deacon.

Skurdal seems to have settled down for a while, living in Montana, where some neighbors described him as peaceful and calm. But he still believed that government was enslavement. Its tyrannical methods include social security numbers, marriage and driver's licenses, insurance, car registration, welfare payments, building permits and inspections, and taxes. He was also a member of Christian Identity and an overt racist.

Skurdal's legal tactics eventually led the Montana judiciary to declare any documents coming from him frivolous so long as they lacked a lawyer's signature. He thought up an end run around this prohibition and began to send his writs to agencies in other states. They would assume the writs had been misaddressed and return them to Montana, where officials would file them as though they were valid. He filed a "Citizens Declaration of War" against "foreign agents" operating in the "country of Montana."

When the IRS seized his farm for nonpayment of taxes, no one quite had the courage to come and evict him, so he continued to live there. In 1994 Schweitzer moved in with Skurdal, and two others joined them shortly after. The farm became a "command center" complete with the latest communication gear.

The Freemen's tactic of turning the enemy's weapons against him is one part of a general trend of rage at government interference in every aspect of life. As one instructor in these tactics put it, "I sit here and expect a raid just because of the work I'm in, but does that mean I'm going to start shooting at the policeman? No! My solution is to go into court and defeat the jackbooted thugs."[12]

No matter how inane or frivolous the countless suits the Freemen filed, every defendant had to respond once a court accepted the filing. But this was not the Freemen's only tactic. Their false liens amounted to an attempt to create money for themselves, because banks often would list the liens as assets until they were shown to be invalid. The banks might then transfer funds against the liens, allowing the Freemen to deposit false money orders in other banks, which would draw against the liens. This kiting scheme allowed them occasionally to get away with a good deal of money.

They also sold the money order scheme as a way for people to get out of debt. They advised their clients to make out the order for double the amount of the debt, then to demand refund of the overpayment. Often they would get the refund before the bank discovered the fraud. About a hundred banks reported these phony money orders from different locations around the country.

The police were in a quandary. There was no precedent for this situation. Their small town had been severely disrupted and demoralized by the Freemen's aggressiveness. They wanted to arrest the Freemen, but it was clear that there would be a fight. The sheriff's department numbered six, so the odds were not good.

The group in Roundup also had company. The Clark family in Jordan were Freemen, and there were allies in other towns. The Clarks did not oppose government until they got in trouble with it. In fact, they accepted almost $700,000 in government aid, but they got into debt they could not deal with, and in 1981 they stopped repaying their loans. By 1995 they owed nearly $2 million. For a while, neighbors helped them to evade foreclosure.

The Clarks' plight made them prime believers in the antigovernment dogma of patriot "prophets," as a family member called them. But Ralph Clark was already close to belief. Back in 1982 he had told a neighbor it would take the National Guard to get him off his ranch. Foreclosure came eventually, and the ranch was sold at auction. In response, the Clarks set up their own common law court.

Early in 1994 three dozen Freemen created their own county government at a meeting held in the Garfield County courthouse, which they commandeered for the purpose. They charged the lawful judge and others they took to be opponents with contempt and offered huge rewards for the judge and other officials, promising the sheriff that he could collect his own reward if he turned himself in, but that he'd be hanged before he could enjoy it. What they had in mind can be gleaned from this "edict" issued by Skurdal:

We do not submit to foreigners nor aliens to rule over us nor are We the People subject to the laws of man nor the constitutions, for these only apply to their own corporations and their officer, agents, servants and employees. . . . We the People must follow our one and only Almighty God; or, you can go on worshipping your new false Baal's and de facto master, i.e., congress and legislators, etc., under their "color of law," for you are now their "slave;" which is contrary to the Word of our Almighty God.[13]

With a one-cell jail, the sheriff could do little against this group, but he did arrest Freemen for their threats when he could find one alone. Ralph Clark was ordered to stand trial for solicitation of kidnaping as his ranch was auctioned to pay his debts. He refused. The Freemen then "subpoenaed" the state's senators, its entire Supreme Court, and the district judge. They also threatened jurors in an upcoming Freemen trial.

The government finally won a conviction for "criminal syndicalism" (promoting political terrorism) against a Freeman named William Stanton, who also acted out of economic desperation. This conviction only inspired the other Freemen to escalate their challenge.

The FBI warned the district attorney and the judge who tried Stanton that his friends planned to kidnap the judge, try him, and hang him. On March 3, 1995, the day after Stanton was sentenced, a deputy stopped two Freemen (Dale Jacobi and Frank Ellena) for driving an unregistered vehicle without a license. Both men were also carrying concealed weapons without permits. The pickup contained an arsenal of guns and ammunition and a map and equipment suggesting a plan to kidnap the district attorney. He arrested them.

At 6 P.M. that day, two carloads of Freemen came to Jordan to demand the return of the confiscated property. A deputy noticed an ill-concealed handgun and arrested the three who had come to the jail. The deputies then confronted two more men who had stayed with the cars, arresting them on the same charge. One of them turned out to be John Trochmann, founder of the Militia of Montana (MOM), who had become a fan of the Freemen.

The sheriff's office immediately began receiving phone calls in support of the Freemen, many of them threatening violence against the sheriff and other officials and their families. Many seemed to come from MOM supporters, since they demanded Trochmann's release.

Few of the charges stuck, though more criminal syndicalism complaints were lodged. Two Freemen who were held eventually jumped bail.

These events made law enforcement officials even more leery of provoking violence, but local resentment of the Freemen escalated because of the "special treatment" they got in response to flouting the law. The Oklahoma City bombing on April 19, 1995, decreased tolerance for their antigovernment stance.

The federal government was disinclined to intervene, though its help had been requested, for fear of a shootout. Understandable reluctance to get involved in another Waco seems to have motivated this hesitation, but the delay added significant numbers to the Freemen's supporters. Skurdal and Schweitzer clearly understood that they controlled the situation, and they even refused press interviews unless the media gave them $100 million liens to ensure fair treatment.

Just the same, they appear to have felt some insecurity, for in September 1995 the Roundup group moved onto the Clark ranch in Jordan. The waiting game began anew, with the most radical Freemen assembled in this one refuge. They were wise to worry, for five of them were charged with threatening officials and three with impersonating officials. Other charges included soliciting kidnaping, criminal syndicalism, armed robbery, and obstruction of justice, and Richard Clark would soon be charged with stealing $70,000 worth of grain from his son, which he would not allow to be removed from the property.

Local law enforcement was clearly outnumbered, and even if they had been able to arrest the group, there would have been no cells in which to hold them. State officials were no more eager to confront the Freemen. Montana's attorney general put them last on his list of priorities. "We'll do everything we can not to put officers or others in harm's way," he said. Despite the fact that the local attorneys general had told Congress this was an "open insurrection," the federal government was in no more of a hurry to intervene.

The Freemen were busy running their little kingdom and offering seminars, which, though nominally free, required a fee to guarantee attendance. Students would come for a week, in groups of twenty-five. Skurdal called the Freemen "the new Federal Reserve" in one meeting, and claimed this competition was perfectly legal. If you disliked their beliefs, however, you were the enemy, especially if you were part of the press. There were several confrontations with journalists, notably the confiscation of an ABC television crew's gear.

The Freemen also attacked other opponents. Skurdal sent a $100 billion lien to a local pastor who had taken exception to his Christian Identity dogma. At this time the Freemen also tried to buy almost a million and a half dollars worth of weapons with a bogus money order.

They lost touch with everyone not of their persuasion and even put a bounty on Trochmann, who had removed MOM's support of the Freemen, perhaps in reaction to their irresponsibility or to the competition they offered to his local monopoly on patriot fervor.

Nevertheless, the Freemen's numbers grew, augmented by a variety of fugitives and former felons. Some locals also joined, and there was vocal support from other places, calling for the establishment of similar "common law" courts. But most of their neighbors continued to resent the Freemen, whom they called "the Freeloaders."

Despite the Freemen's isolation, Schweitzer's bad checks continued to spread across the whole country. Usually they did not pass successfully, though private individuals were frequently taken in. One car credit firm in San Diego said it got about one bad check every ten days. One of Schweitzer's clients succeeded in buying seven cars, four houses, and a condo in Hawaii with Freemen checks.

"Clients" of this scheme seem for the most part to have been quite aware that it was illegal, though others may have used the bogus money orders in good faith. As much as $150 million in fake obligations may have been created this way, but whatever their value, the sham instruments have caused great disruption in the financial structure of the United States.

The scam had a marvelous rationale. While getting rich, or trying to, "patriots" could preen themselves with the justification that they were actually fighting a war against tyranny and the Federal Reserve. "This is perfectly legal," said one believer. "They're just getting scared because we are winning."[14]

Early in 1996 the FBI succeeded in luring Schweitzer and Daniel Peterson into a trap and arrested them. They also nabbed Lavon Hansen as an accessory to another fraud involving more counterfeiting.

The Freemen surrendered without a fight, though they were armed. The next day, however, they disrupted their arraignment to the extent that the judge had them removed from the courtroom to watch via closed-circuit television. The Freemen lived up to their reputation for courtroom grand-standing; in their belief, as "sovereigns" no courts but their own have any jurisdiction over them.[15] One writer observed that for the Freemen a court appearance was a *jihad*; since they based their politics on religion, they be-haved toward the court with the same disdain as Yitzhak Rabin's assassin did.

On March 25, 1996, the standoff began. This time, the FBI was meticulous in its attempts to avoid a repetition of Waco. By report they delayed the arrests as long as they did in order to gather as much advance information as possible.[16] They may have been moved to take action by increased local pressure. The Freemen were threatening to take over much of northeast Montana. They warned that anyone on "their" land would be arrested and punished. They had begun disturbing their neighbors' lives, not just threatening government employees, and that may have been the last straw.

Neighbors had discussed in meetings the possibility of cutting the Freemen's phone lines and closing the roads to their ranch. This almost cer-tainly would have ended in confrontation, and may have forced the FBI's hand. But the Freemen themselves had videotapes of a meeting where Schweitzer announced plans to kidnap officials and shoot anyone who ob-structed their "justice."

The FBI's move was welcome to the neighbors, some of whom ex-pressed a wish that the FBI use force, calling for a massacre. When the siege was set up, there were no jackboots or black uniforms in sight. Instead of snipers the FBI used surveillance cameras and eavesdropping gear, which worked well in Montana's open terrain.

Richard Clark, who was not on the property when the arrests occurred, turned himself in but otherwise refused to cooperate, as did Peterson. Schweitzer began a hunger strike and was removed to a prison hospital in Missouri.

Six Freemen left of their own accord after Schweitzer and Peterson were arrested. The twenty or so who remained were unresponsive to promises of safety if they surrendered. Since they were not interested in negotiation, a stalemate quickly developed.

The FBI's tactics were quite different than those used at Waco. Agents were careful to tell the Freemen of their plans before making a move, hoping to forestall a violent reaction. They set up no tight perimeter and avoided the psychological warfare techniques they had used on the Branch Davidians. The FBI allowed the Freemen to meet with the press and permitted family visits. They also brought in some forty-five outside negotiators, an unheard-of precedent for the FBI.

An early FBI tactic was to let neighbors and family members try to talk some of the Freemen into surrender. There were still strong ties to them in Jordan, where people had raised $125,000 for an operation for one of the Clarks. Strangers, however, were turned away, including small numbers of armed militia men, or else the supplies they tried to bring in were confiscated when they were allowed to enter. None of these maneuvers was persuasive, and the Freemen stayed put.

Some militias praised the die-hards, a few even forecasting civil war over the dispute, but others distanced themselves from the Freemen and their bad image. MOM called for a "stand down" of other militias, warning them to stay away from Jordan, and praised the FBI's restraint. It is as well none of the militias turned up to support the Freemen, despite some promises to do so, for there was an unofficial posse patrolling the roads, ready to meet an incursion with weapons.

Norman Olson, former head of the Michigan Militia who was fired for saying that the Japanese had bombed the Murrah building in Oklahoma City, had ideas like the Freemen's. He saw the standoff as an opportunity to incite insurrection, or at least get some publicity. He issued a press release saying he feared the FBI had planned all along to massacre the Freemen. His call to arms to the nation's militias fortunately went unheeded. He waxed apocalyptic in expectation of a new civil war to start in Jordan. Other groups of supporters called for a rally in Lewistown, Montana, but organizers managed to entice only eight people to show up.

The Freemen began to negotiate on April 4, first with some Montana legislators. A sympathetic state senator named Casey Emerson publicly advocated concessions to the Freemen: dropping some charges, giving them money and a national TV appearance. He recommended that they get a hearing before a common law jury, "so they can get their bitching done."

The negotiations failed. The Freemen refused to give ground on demands for their own government and jury. A prosecutor experienced in dealing with the Freemen said that firm pressure needed to be applied from a position of strength. But the FBI relaxed its restraints even more, promising the Freemen a chance to get their story heard. Reports leaked out that the Freemen were prepared for a long siege.

Shortly after, the Freemen posted a "declaration of independence" on the ranch gate. "It should be further made known to all Men," they said, using their customary pseudo-legal boilerplate, "that this republic, Justus Township, Montana state, united [*sic*] States of America, so affirmed in Law is *not* that de facto fiction, the corporation, incorporated in London, England in the year of Yeshua, the Christ, eighteen hundred seventy-one, AD, the United States, a corporation, so defined as their own Title 28 U.S.C. 3005 (A)(15)."[17] It is particularly telling that the Freemen's first communication with the rest of the world defines the group. Identity is a prime concern in all millenarian thought, since it is crucial to "come out of [Bablyon]" (Rev. 18:4) and separate the believers from the rest of the rotten world. Purity is of the essence. This declaration is a concise if abstruse drawing of the boundary between the Freemen and everybody else. The abstruseness is not especially important from the Freemen's point of view, since it matters little to people in this state of mind whether the rest of the world understands them or not. Such a statement of difference allows for no compromise. It is an implicit declaration of war.

But things remained quiet, as both sides patrolled the perimeter in relaxed fashion. Elsewhere militias blustered and Norman Olson continued to rant, proclaiming his expectation to lead "the second American revolution." He came to Montana on April 16th, dressed in camouflage fatigues and promising to bring the Freemen children a teddy bear. He also promised to discuss surrender terms with the FBI. He was stopped at a roadblock on two successive days, and even the Geneva Convention could not get him in. Olson claimed rights of war under this treaty.

In the meantime, Peterson continued to swamp the state with paper from his cell, threatening to "fine" and jail the prosecutor. Schweitzer gave up his hunger strike.

The Freemen did not talk to the outside world again until April 17. They expected big things to happen on April 19, the anniversary of the final siege at Waco, but nothing did. On April 25, Bo Gritz, Jack McLamb, and Randy Weaver, all important figures to the "patriot" right, offered to negotiate, but the FBI would not let them in either.

In what seems like desperation, the FBI let Gritz and McLamb in to negotiate on the 27th, though Weaver was barred. But even their right-wing credentials did no good. The Freemen still demanded their own grand jury. They finally hinted at a surrender if they could address the Montana legislature, which would not be in session until 1997. Various authorities offered to reduce some charges, to no avail.

The FBI had agreed to step aside and leave matters up to a civil authority chosen by the Freemen in return for peaceful surrender. But the Freemen would settle for nothing less than their version of a "common law" grand jury made up of "sovereigns" who had renounced U.S. citizenship. The FBI even considered allowing this, which would have amounted to the Freemen's choosing their own jury.

The two negotiators reported that the Freemen were demanding the return of Schwietzer to Montana from the prison in Missouri where he was being held. The Freemen also professed themselves ready to surrender if the government would prove that Freemen proclamations did not reflect the law. They also dropped their demand to have their case heard in a "common law" court by a grand jury.[18]

Gritz's efforts to bring the standoff to a peaceful conclusion did him little good with some of his followers, who took his actions as nothing short of treason to their cause. He and Colorado State Senator Charles Duke, another supporter of antifederalist activism, who also made futile attempts to bring the Freemen out, were called tools of the establishment for this perceived "selling out" to the enemy. According to their critics on the right, the pair's work was "only window dressing" to convince others that "patriots" were actively involved in negotiations. Accusers said their planned failure gave "a green light" for the armed raid that the FBI planned and wanted to carry out all along.[19]

There seems to have been two factions among the Freemen. One was willing to compromise, but the other, which was in control, refused to budge. They began to play games with the FBI, demanding Robert Bork as a negotiator. In the end, they refused all offers. They claimed that they had vowed to God not to surrender. They said God had protected them with an invisible barrier that no one could cross. Gritz had said before he started negotiating that the Freemen were going to have to deal with reality, but this was something they could not or would not do.

The FBI made another attempt to negotiate, even offering the "legislative forum" the Freemen had requested, but the agents promised they would do whatever they thought necessary to end the situation if the Freemen rejected this offer. The Freemen responded by saying that the FBI "does not exist as a government agency." This declaration was accompanied by a media handout explaining the FBI's, and the entire government's, illegality.

The standoff ended peacefully on June 13, 1996, when the Freemen surrendered. It is not known exactly what persuaded them to give up, though their temporary leader Edwin Clark had visited Schweitzer in jail to discuss it and was credited with that intercession at his trial.[20] The group also arranged for a sympathetic Montana legislator to take custody of some documents they believed would vindicate them. They went to jail to await trial on the numerous charges pending against them.

One bit of Constitutionalist analysis in the storm of hype and high excitement surrounding the Montana confrontation seemed to have the ring of real insight. Peter Kay of the North Carolina Grand Jury—another Constitutional organization—wondered in a piece in the Liberty Newswire whether there might not be a "class system" at work within the pretended equality of our legal apparatus. "Is there a double standard?" he wondered. "Might there be an elitist class favoritism of the rich politicians, judges, attorneys, and bankers perpetrated by the judiciary and government agencies upon the unsuspecting common man? Is the average working class American simply run through the revolving door of the court system's revenue collection grinder and spit out of the courthouse door poorer, downtrodden, confused, frustrated, intimidated, and angry, yet powerless to do anything to change it?"[21]

Some of Kay's rhetoric goes beyond what a level-headed examination of the case warrants, yet there can be little doubt that the best justice goes to the person with the best lawyer, which is to say, the most money. That Skurdal, Schweitzer, the Clarks, and McLaren felt they had been victimized by a system they could hardly understand, let alone influence, is clear. Regardless of whether or not they got justice, the fact is that they clearly felt that they had been ill-treated by an unsympathetic and unjust system of courts and laws.

What is especially interesting is the remedy they found: a magical use of the system's own tools in a remarkably successful attempt to coopt and sabotage its workings. The Latin tags that some Constitutionalist writers are so fond of are part of this process. Latin is the language of lawyers and other highly educated people. Its effect, intended or otherwise, is often to conceal meanings from the uninitiated. So to take it over as part of one's own arsenal is to absorb at least part of that aura of power. The same can be said of the convoluted legalistic jargon Constitutionalists use with such enthusiasm. It functions as an invocation of the law's power to suit quite magical purposes. And finally, they observed with great rigor the physical form of legal documents, though they wrote them by hand.

It seems especially telling that Peterson drew a little notary seal on one of his legal documents, as though its shape and the correct wording were all that really mattered. This is make-believe taken into the arena of real power in an attempt to gather to the performer the special power inherent in the real law.

This logic has parallels in workings of the Melanesian cargo cults.[22] Like the Freemen, Melanesian natives under colonialism perceived that they were excluded from a system that governed their lives but denied them access to its extravagant riches. The perception was perfectly correct, as is the Freemen's perception that they can not get justice as they conceive it under American law. The Melanesians resorted to magic to redirect the riches their way. One approach they tried was to imitate the mysterious things they saw whites do. They practiced military drills carrying branches instead of rifles. They also built miniature airports to attract cargo planes.

The Freemen used some similar techniques. They made use of a partial understanding of the law, carefully picking those bits that served their purpose and ignoring the rest, to construct an elaborate fantasy of power wherein they could magically access the immense riches that elites control. They seemed to believe that manipulation of the symbols of power would be enough to get them their hearts' desire (obscene amounts of money, for one thing) by a sort of sympathetic magic.

If the patriots could not get justice, they would try to create it on their own terms. In the process, they hoped to gain what might have been the most important part of the whole scheme: respectful recognition as full participants in the life of their times. Like the New Guinea tribes, they caused immense harm to themselves, but they got what they were after—that is, a hearing from the ultimate source of power in their lives: the media and the courts, the Establishment.

Some of the Freemen—perhaps only Rodney Skurdal—professed Christian Identity beliefs, but that may be a smokescreen in the way of understanding their movement. Christian Identity promises the same thing in terms of the sacred that the pseudo-legalism of the Constitutionalists offers in the secular realm: access to power and self-justification. Both ideas offer a reversal of the social order and a return to a condition of original purity and justice, the essence of the millennium.

An important part of Constitutionalist schemes is that the officials of the present order will get their due justice, usually in extravagant form. The Freemen swore to hang the sheriff; Richard McLaren's faction of the Republic of Texas movement, a nonmillenarian scheme to remove Texas from the United States, wanted to sue the U.S. administration at The Hague. The talk of genocide at Justus symbolizes the extent of the grievance the Freemen felt at their losses to ignorance, debt, and unsympathetic justice.

The Freemen document reprinted in part below, entitled "Our de jure county government pursuant to the Word of Almighty God," is a textbook used in their teaching.[23] It sets forth and rationalizes their form of local theocracy, in which the church is the courthouse enforcing God's law. It relies heavily on literal interpretation of selected Bible passages to legitimize its authority. The reason for its heavy reliance on trinitarian form is not apparent, aside from its obvious Christian significance. The Trinity is not a biblical doctrine and was not adopted as Christian dogma until the fourth century. Like other millenarian creeds, the Freemen's text makes an end run around Babylon and appeals to higher authority. Every point of doctrine, even the Lord's Prayer, is cited chapter and verse, regardless of whether it comes from the Bible or from law.

The Freemen, like other millenarians, set enormous store by symbols. Many Constitutionalists proclaim that courts other than their own lack jurisdiction because the flags they display have yellow fringes. The reasoning behind this is convoluted, but one theorist set forth the position. The

Emergency Banking Act of March 9, 1933, and Roosevelt's Proclamation of Emergency and War Powers three days previous were turning points in the abandonment of constitutional rule. "This act effectively suspended the Constitution and granted dictatorial powers to the President, a situation which continues to this day."[24] In effect, they say, it suspended the Constitution under the guise of stretching its provisions. Since the "law of the land" was no longer ruling us, it follows that the United States is now clandestinely governed by the law of the sea: admiralty law. All federal courts are admiralty courts, exercising martial law over America. This rule is symbolized by the U.S. flag bearing a yellow fringe, which the patriots take to be a military device. As is the case with most conspiracy theories this nubbin of fact is correct. It is stated in an executive order of 1959 that the fringe is to be used on military flags.

From there it is a simple, if perilous, leap of faith to the conclusion that any place the yellow-fringed flag is shown is under military control and the Constitution is suspended there. Under this "king's law" we are no longer sovereign, but subject, and our ownership of land is replaced by tenancy. Like Hitler's mystical *Heimat,* land has special meaning to Constitutionalists. It is every man's power base, from which he may resist all government intrusion, armed or otherwise.

In view of the Freemen's punctilious use of Latin their extreme sloppiness in English is difficult to understand. It seemed to me that to correct their mistakes would be to rob their document of its character, and to indicate each mistake with [*sic*] would make it unreadably choppy and insufferably pedantic. Here it is, warts and all.

• • •

OUR DE JURE COUNTY GOVERNMENT PURSUANT TO THE WORD OF ALMIGHTY GOD

"Blessed are those persecuted for righteousness' sake, for theirs is the kingdom of heaven."
"Blessed are you when men revile you and persecute you and utter all kinds of evil against you falsely on my account. Rejoice and be glad, for your reward is great in heaven, for so men persecute the prophets who were before you." Matthew 5:10–12.

"Thy kingdom come, Thy will be done, <u>on earth</u> <u>as it is</u> <u>in</u> <u>Heaven</u>." the Lord's Prayer, Matt. 6: verse 10.

And Jesus, full of the Holy Spirit, returned from the Jordan, and was led by the Spirit for forty days in the wildnerness, tempted by the devil. . . . And the devil took Him up, and showed Him all the kingdoms of the world in a moment of time, and said to Him, "To you I will give all this authority and their glory; for it to whom I will. If you then, will worship me, it shall be yours." And Jesus answered him, "It is written, 'You shall worship the Lord your God, and him only shall you serve,'" Luke 4:1–8.

See I Samuel 8:1–22 at 8:10–19; as to what will happen if we accept a king of this earth, i.e., man. . . .

Our Constitution of Montana, 1889, clearly mandated the following; 'Preamble' and <u>our</u> 'Bill of Rights':

ARTICLE III, SECTION 1; "<u>All political power is vested in and de-</u><u>rived from the People</u>; <u>all government of Right originates with the</u> <u>People</u>; is founded upon <u>their will only</u>, and is instituted solely for the good of the whole." <u>CORRECT IN LAW</u>. [NOTE: <u>Our</u> public hire-lings/servants/officials/officers/agents **possess no power over the Peo-ple, i.e., 'government' in fact; for the servants is never to be above their Master, i.e., "We the People";** see <u>Texas v. White, 7 Wall. 700–</u><u>743, 1869</u>]

ARTICLE III, SECTION 2; "<u>The People</u> of the State <u>have the sole and ex-</u><u>clusive right of governing themselves, as a free sovereign and independ-</u><u>ent State</u>, and to alter and abolish <u>their</u> constitution and form of gov-ernment, whenever they may deem it necessary to their safety and hap-piness, provided such change be not repugnant to the Constitution of the United States." <u>CORRECT IN LAW</u>. SEE REV. 1:6.

This is a restatement of our commandments from our **Almighty God,** to establish **His** de jure [Lawful] government pursuant to the **Holy Scrip-**tures, i.e., "self-governing," for did not our **Lord and King,** "**Emmanuel,**" i.e., '**Jesus**' [Isaiah 7:14; Matt. 1:23], clearly states and mandates several times that '<u>every man must take up the cross upon his shoulders</u>', i.e., "self governing" by carring the weight of [self] government {ones own "<u>Cross</u>"} upon one own shoulders pursuant to the Commandments of our Almighty God in His 'good book', i.e. the "Bible." See Matthew 10:38; 16:24; Mark 8:34; 10:21; Luke 9:23; and 14:27. How many times does Emmanuel have to tell us; Israel to follw His/Gods Laws? Do you have eyes to see and ears to hear?

"Our" Lawful Chain of Command

1. Almighty God, pursuant to His Holy Scriptures, creator of all good and evil; ['So be it']

2. Adam, i.e., White race of Man/Israel, God's chosen People;

3. We the People [Adam] of the Posterity, obedient to the Laws of Almighty God, a.k.a., our 'Common Law';

4. Constitution(s), [1] States' then, [2] National, with limited powers;

    a) Article IV, Section 4 of our national Constitution, mandates a 're-publican form of government', i.e., [1]'of the people'—[2]'by the people'—[3]'for the people'; [1]legislative, [2]executive & [3]judicial offices; pursuant to the Word of All Mighty God, i.e., "[1]God, [2]Son and [3]Holly Ghost," a "trinity" form of government pursuant to the Word of All Mighty God.

5. which created public offices filled by our 'public officers/officials/agents/servants'; either [1]appointed or by [2]election; [Note: Appointive Power supersedes elective powers.]

6. 14th Amendment, creating a 'second class of citizens', and at the bottom of the chain, i.e., corporations, persons, subjects, and citizens of the United States, subject to its jurisdiction, Article 1, Section VIII, clause 17, and via the Fourteenth Amendment.

"America," i.e., 'United States of America', is the new "Land" of 'milk and honey', the new 'Zion', as contained in the Bible, [q.v.] in which Israel-Adam cities will no longer have walls around them, and the Land which Almighty God promised Israel, which we will never move from again. q.v. {'q.v.' means to look elsewhere; such as the Bible}

God made two covenants with Abraham, or rather, one with Abram and the other with the same man after Almighty God changed his name to Abraham. . . .

We all know that there are three distinct and separate forms of government in this Great Nation called "America," i.e., the "United States of America"; each having a 'supreme court', by common knowledge and practice.

1] County	2] State	3] National

In our "republican form of government" ['republican' means "three"] as contained within our National Constitution, **Article IV, Section 4**, i.e., it is a "trinity form of government," if you will, pursuant to the Word of **Almighty God**;

[1]**God**	[2]**Son**	[3]**Holy Spirit"**
[1]**of the [white] People**	[2]**by the [white] People**	[3]**for the [white] People**
[1]**Judicial**	[2]**Executive**	[3]**Legislative**

[county governments= most being three voting districts/three grand divisions]

[1]**voting/district/**precinct 1	[2]**voting/district/**precinct 2	[3]**voting/district/**precinct 3
[1]**commissioner one**	[2]**commissioner two**	[3]**commissioner three**
[1]**supreme court justice 1**	[2]**supreme court justice 2**	[3]**supreme court justice 3**
[1]**district judge 1**	[2]**district judge 2**	[3]**district judge 3**

The main problem is that 'We the People' (most) have abandon our de jure/**God's** county government, a.k.a. "church," contrary to the word of Almighty God, **Amos 5:14–15**, and that of our Constitution of Montana, **Article V, Section 26** and that of **Article XX, Section 6**; to wit: "**Upon a change from Territorial to State government the seals in use by the supreme court and the Territorial district courts in and for the several counties respectively, shall pass to and become, until otherwise provided by law, the seals respectively of the supreme court and of the district courts of the State in such counties.**" . . .

The justices', meaning all white men, from each township/precinct/district, either **appoints** or elects one 'good Man' who know the law and means to keep it well, which is reaffirmed in chapter 45 of Magna Charta; "**§ 45. We will not make any justices, constables, sheriffs, or bailiffs, but of such as know the law of the realm and mean duly to observe it.**"; pursuant to the Word of Almighty God, Exodus 18:21.

Each **county** is in fact a '**church**', meaning a geographical/territorial area whereby said county is **self-governing, pursuant to the Word of our Almighty God.** U.C.C. 1-105, territorial application of the law, our Common Law.

On the Lord's day, '**Saturday**', all the people in the county gather together to first, **Worship our Almighty God, our Creator** then to establish **His laws** within said county by the gathering of the men to establish **His Laws** in each county. Sunday is not our Lords de jure Sabbath but the first day of the week of the creation, 'Sun'-day, the separation of day [Sun—worshipers/Baal] and night [**moon/mon**-day], Genesis 1:3–5; one must remember that this information is only for those who have eyes to see and ears to hear.

This is done by all the people within the county gathering together at the county seat, in the morning, example - about 9:00 A.M. o'clock. This gathering place, most commonly called a 'church' by most, could also be our local school gym or even the county court, i.e., in our 'court room'. Is not all court rooms set up the same as a church, but only use different names for the terms within the same room. To wit:

```
                              Cross/flags

                      bench/justices or de facto judge
   winess box/piano player    Preachers pulpit/pulpitum   .


   *******
   *j - c  *
   *u-h    *
   *r- o   *
   *y- i   *
   *   r   *
   *       *
   * box   *
   ********
           Plaintiff/Alter boy              Defendant/Alter boy

           The 'Bar'            i.e.,       The "Communion Rail"
   ########################     i.e.,   ########################
           congregation                     open/public court

   _____                      _____

   _____                      _____
                      church/court
```

This gathering of the People throughout the county gives everyone an opportunity to meet his neighbor and to understand his needs and personal views and vice versa.

After the first half of our church services, all will break for lunch, whereby all the wives have brought a pot luck diner for all to share. After lunch, the women and children will go to one side, to allow the children to play and the wives to talk about house hold needs, cooking, sewing, and etc. . . .

The word "<u>church</u>" has a **dual meaning**, most believe that it is some sort of "**assembly**," 'ekklesia' (Greek), that is devoted to Christian worship, preaching, praying and prophesying. This is only half of the true intent of the word. Using 'Vine's Expository Dictionary of New Testament Words', one will again find the national intent of that word "**assembly**" translated "**church**." According to Vine's, a "**church**" is "<u>a body of citizens gathered to descuss the affairs of state</u>." To claim that there is a seperation between the words 'church and state' is contrary to the definition of the word church/assembly. In essences, a church is used both for the worshipping our **Almighty God** and the establishment of **His** government here on earth, pursuant to **His Law.**

An example of this would be someone within the county on our county roads who needs or believes that the bridge on said road needs replaced. At our church/government meating, this man would bring this to the attention to the congregation that possibly the bridge may need replacing whereby the elders/commisssioners would appoint 12 good men to inspect the bridge and to bring back the report as soon as possible. Either the bridge would be replaced or maybe put off for another year or two with inspections of the bridge from time to time. This only applies to the people within the county as a whole, we do not provide for private interests/self-interests. . . .

On some the the major advantages in returning to **God's Law** and passing ordinances pursuant to the **Word of Almighty God;**

1) **Taxes;** [elimination of all taxes on your private property, i.e., your labor, land, automobiles and all other personal private property.]

a) What did 'Jesus', "Emmanuel," say about taxes on Israel?

"**What do you think, Simon? From whom do the kings of the earth take toll or tribute? From their sons or others*?**" And when he said, "**From others,**" Jesus said to him, "**Then the sons are free.**" Matt. 17:25-26. . . .

We the People of the Posterity in each county would not be paying any taxes on our "private" land, labor, perosnal private business nor other personal private property. Think of it, no more 'direct taxes' pursuant to the Word of Almighty God and pursuant to the National constitution.

What would be taxed is a corporation that may wish to come into our county for its protection. We could offer a lower tax burden on said corporation. An example would be that most corporations pay up to 80 to 90 per cent on their product via state and federal taxes. Here within our county said corporation would ouly pay maybe three to ten per cent on said product for our county does not need that large of revenue to run on being under God's Law. The corporation would see all of it production from within the county, therefore no state or federal taxes would be placed upon the products, meaning less costs to the People within the county and the other customers ourside of the county.

By such though, we will take care of our own first. Lets say one of our People has a cafe, yet McDonalds wants to come into our county and establish a business in our county seat. As long a 'John Doe' provides good service at reasonable and fair prices at his cafe, we would reject McDonalds offer in order to allow our People to provide for their needs first. 'John Doe' would not pay any taxes within the county not to the corporate state nad feds, **for is not a Man's private labor, "<u>worthy of his hire</u>," see Matt. 20:8; Luke 10:7. No Taxes!!** . . .

Another sample closer to home would be the "Brandin Iron Saloon." Kevin would bring up the fact that he wished to open a saloon on Highway 87, before the **congregation** at church, the **congregation** would then approve such, even though in Law they have no power to do such for it is an old common Law Right, without going to the de facto corporate state of Montana for permission. This is our county, not the state of Montana. The only tax that Kevin would be paying is the tax on the liquor that he has to have imported. No local, state nor federal taxes for again, **a Man's private labor, is "<u>worthy of his hire</u>." This is <u>his Private business</u>.** By such he would be able to sell his product for less and still maintain a good living. . . .

Constitutional de jure county government

The phrase '<u>law of the land</u>' as used in Article VI, Section 2, of our National Constitution, applies only to the Man formed by our Almighty God on the Seventh day, Genesis 2, who **formed "<u>Adam</u>"** from the **dust of the earth**, i.e., **"land"**; in order to till the earth.

God's Law [of the land], and who does it apply to.
"<u>I am the LORD your God, you shall have no other gods beside me</u>." Exod. 20:2–3; Deut. 5:6–7.

The "Law" of our Almighty God was given only to **Israel**, the white race of People, for we were formed from the dust of the earth, i.e., **Land**. Matthew 22:32 states: "**I am the God of Abraham, and the God of Isaac, and the God of Jacob**"; notice that He is not a God onto the other races, but **only that of Israel, the White Race, "Adam,"** for the Word of God was only given to Israel; "**He showed His word . . . His statutes and His judgments unto Israel. He hath not dealt so with any nation: and as for His judgments, they have not known them.**" Ps. 147:19–20. "**O children of Israel . . . You only have I known of all the families of the earth.**" Amos 3:1–2. "**. . . you shall be my own possession among all peoples; for all the earth is mine, and you shall be to me a Kingdom of Priests and a Holy Nation. These are the words which you shall speak to the children of Israel.**" Exodus 19:5–6.

Notes

1. Mark Pitcavage, "Every Man a King: The Rise and Fall of the Montana Freemen," http://www.militia-watchdog.org/freemen.htm (April 4, 1998).

2. I am grateful to Catherine Wessinger for letting me see a draft of a chapter on the Freemen from her forthcoming *When the Millennium Comes Violently* (Chappaqua, N.Y.: Seven Bridges Press). The text she showed me does not represent her final views on the subject.

3. Paul de Armond, "Christian Patriots at War with the State," http://nwcitizen.com/publicgood/reports/belief/ (October 8, 1998).

4. Burke Elder; Hale, personal communication, July 15, 1996.

5. There is an interesting tendency for these antigovernment movements to find their leaders among former military men (a word I use advisedly; women are scarce in the upper ranks of the militias). Timothy McVeigh was one, as was his coconspirator, Terry Nichols. According to a psychologist's report, McVeigh felt betrayed by the army. William Cooper, the Marcel Proust of the right wing—he writes endless memoirs detailing alleged treason by those in high places—claims to be a retired navy intelligence operative. In conspiratorialist circles, there is generally a special glamour attached to the renegade. Like other converts, he brings special fervor to his new calling, together with especially valuable knowledge of the "enemy." A conversion from the belly of the beast to the forces of light also lends special testimony to the power of the message. The value of renegades applies for the forces of the New World Order as well. It is reported that the FBI hesitated as long as it did before moving in on the Freemen because they had undercover operatives placed in the movement who supplied them with especially valu-

able data. See http://www.seattletimes.com/news/nation-world/html98/spyy_051298.html (October 5, 1998).

6. Michael Barkun, *Religion and the Racist Right: The Origins of the Christian Identity Movement* (Chapel Hill: University of North Carolina Press, 1996).

7. Paul de Armond, personal communication, October 11, 1998.

8. Jeffrey Kaplan, *Radical Religion in America: Millenarian Movements from the Far Right to the Children of Noah* (Syracuse, N.Y.: Syracuse University Press, 1997), 7.

9. Ibid., 173.

10. Joel Dyer, *Harvest of Rage: Why Oklahoma City Is Only the Beginning* (Boulder, Colo.: Westview Press, 1997), 170.

11. Pitcavage, "Every Man a King."

12. Quoted in ibid.

13. David Neiwert, "Patriot Spring: Showdown in Big Sky Country," Pacific Rim News Service, http://www.militia-watchdog.org/contrib.htm/neiwert1.htm (October 8, 1998).

14. Pitcavage, "Every Man a King."

15. They continued this behavior at their trial on charges leading to, and stemming form, the standoff. The first Freemen to go on trial were thrown out of court on the first day for cursing at the judge and everyone in the court. See CNN, "Disruptive Beginning to Freemen Trial," http://cnn.com/US/9803/16/freemen.trial/index.old.html#1 (April 6, 1998).

16. In a recent book, a couple who claim to have been undercover operatives at Justus Township report that the FBI delayed intervention because it did not want to lose the valuable intelligence they provided. See Dale Jakes et al., *False Prophets: The Firsthand Account of a Husband and Wife Working for the FBI and Living in Deepest Cover with the Montana Freemen* (Los Angeles: Dove Books, 1998).

17. Few observers seem to have noticed the possible Identity Christian implications of the name "Justus." Its implications appear when it is pronounced "Just Us," though it can equally well be taken as a pun on "justice." Perhaps both meanings apply.

18. SnetNews Mailing List (SNETNEWS@XBN.SHORE.NET), April 29, 1996.

19. See owner-fsnw-l@lists.primenet.com, May 20, 1996.

20. Tom Laceky, "FreeMen [*sic*] Verdict," Associated Press, March 31, 1998, http://209.67.114.212/forum/a159862.htm.

21. Bill Utterback (butterb@sagenet.net), May 27, 1996.

22. The best survey of cargo cults is still Peter Worsley's *The Trumpet Shall Sound: A Study of "Cargo" Cults in Melanesia* (New York: Schocken Books, 1968). More recent studies appear in Gary Trompf, ed., *Cargo Cults and Millenarian Movements: Transoceanic Comparisons of New Religious Movements* (Berlin and New York: Mouton de Gruyter, 1990).

23. The document comes via a tortuous chain of connections. I got it from Paul de

Armond, a close student of the American right wing, who got it from Jon Roland, founder of the Texas Constitutional Militia, who declares it simply "a Freemen document" and will provide no other information. De Armond reports that a number of experts vouch for its authenticity, and none question it.

24. Jon Roland, *Law and Antilaw* (San Antonio: Constitution Society, n.d.).

CHAPTER 12

COMET HALE-BOPP, PLANET NIBIRU, THE MASS LANDING, AND HEAVEN'S GATE

Recent years have seen a series of warnings that the earth faces a catastrophic collision with some wandering bit of space debris. This is always a possibility, but one wonders why these warnings arose so forcefully at the end of the millennium. After all, we have known about comets and asteroids for a century or so and have seen the craters their impacts leave, here and on the moon and other planets. We have had the potential power to deal with them for about thirty years, in long-range nuclear ballistic missiles. So why take alarm now? That the approach of the millennium could have an effect even on scientists gets little attention.

Astronomers remain mute on the subject, but there is some speculation that the threat of these galactic intruders might have a desirable effect on the budgets of NASA and its suppliers, to say nothing of the arms trade in general. All have suffered with the end of the Cold War. The alarm may also have arisen in response to the spectacular crash of Comet Shoemaker-Levy into Jupiter, as well as Comet Hyakutake's close approach to Earth.

These warnings died out for a while, but underwent something of a renaissance with the emergence of Comet Hale-Bopp. Its appearance was accompanied by news that brushes with comets appear to happen periodically, in reaction to "galactic tides" that bring increased activity every 30 million years or so.[1] We are now within a million years of the next close call, if not an actual collision. It seems that minuscule orbit changes add a disproportionate uncertainty to comets' courses, such that it would have been impossible to say for sure whether Hyakutake might have hit us more than a month in advance. But Hale-Bopp appeared to be something of a special case, at least where the Internet's millenarians are concerned.

The excitement began November 15, 1996, with a message posted on the Internet. "Flash!!! This Picture Just In!!! What on earth could that Saturn like image be to the right of the comet? This picture was taken November 14 at 6pm Houston time (CST)."[2] The message originated with a man named Chuck Shramek in Houston. He made the image with his own telescope and described it as showing something four times Earth's size, ringed like Saturn, emitting its own light at uniform brightness. Shramek claimed that the "object and event [were] verified by legitimate astronomers worldwide," but he also included the thoughts of some "remote viewers" in his Internet post.

These remote viewers were purported clairvoyants who work with or for an Emory University professor named Courtney Brown at something called the Farsight Institute (http://www.farsight.org). They assessed the object as artificial, made using "borrowed technology probably as old as Atlantis." While they could offer assurance that it was not a weapon, they could not tell what it was made of, though they were confident that it was formed of a combination of artificial and natural substances "within a matrix of thought." They were also confident that it was under its own intelligent guidance and would somehow "interact with human DNA."

By the clairvoyants' account, the object's aim was to "awaken" us in preparation for galactic evolution. It was something like the mysterious black object in the film *2001: A Space Odyssey.* The "Saturn-like object" (SLO), they declared, was alive, fully self-aware, and had telepathic abilities. There would be more of them headed our way. Its presence was the result of collaboration among many different races of space beings, including humans.

Many other watchers for signs of the times, from every spiritual persuasion, jumped onto Hale-Bopp's bandwagon.

Sheldon Nidle, who had for some time been proclaiming an imminent arrival of aliens to save us from the destruction of our civilization by an imaginary intergalactic body he called "the photon belt," quickly offered some "Mass Landings Information."[3] These "Mass Landings," in Nidle's prediction, would be the arrival of the Space Brothers to help us make the transition to the next evolutionary level, one of perfect spiritual being and unity.[4] There was a "window" available for this to happen, from November 10 until December 17, 1996, or "8 Cauca, 7 Xul, 5 Eb till 6 Cib, 4 Mol, 5

Eb," in Nidle's Mayan calendar reckoning.[5] The landing became a possibility, he explained, because American military forces finally accepted "Federation edicts."

The Hale-Bopp object, in this scenario, was not a ship, even though it carried some ten-thousand second-wave "colonists" in the mass landing. However, Nidle did not say just what it was, only that it was scheduled to arrive May 5, 1997, and set up its colony near the mystical site Ayers Rock in Australia. The newcomers would not take part in the planet's new government. Instead, they intended to be "quite interested observers." The landing he predicted would be a divine intervention heralding the arrival of a new golden age.

According to an unnamed source, "the rabbis" traditionally believe that a comet passing through Orion will signal the end of the world. There is indeed a Talmudic text to this effect.[6] *Tractate Berachot* 58b is among the "aggadic" Talmudic texts, that is, those that are today said to be subject to allegorical rather than literal interpretation. Hale-Bopp's trajectory carried it past Orion, and it reached its closest point on March 23, the very day of a "red moon" lunar eclipse that was visible in Jerusalem.[7]

John Leary of Rochester, New York, claimed Jesus Christ had informed him that the comet was going to change its course and plunge directly into earth. In Leary's account of Christ's words, warm clothes and blankets would see us through.[8]

Another Christian reading of the situation, "And The Stars Shall Fall From Heaven," relates Hale-Bopp to Revelation's Seventh Seal.[9] In particular, the book foretells the third angelic trump, when "there fell a great star from heaven, burning as it were a lamp." These interpreters insist this could only refer to the fall of a comet. According to Genesis, God planted the stars and other celestial bodies to be signs for us.

These Christians and others noted that the gospels and the prophets tell of great and fearful signs in the heavens during the last days. Earth will stumble in her orbit and the sun and stars will be darkened. Such displacements of the earth are almost common in Scripture; God uses these signs repeatedly to warn of His displeasure.

Another image of the comet showed it spewing out a jet of gaseous material indicating the presence of cyanide, leading immediately to the speculation that this was "a chemical weapons attack."[10]

While these conjectures were working their way across the Internet, there came another break in the story. Farsight's Courtney Brown and a colleague, a Ph.D. candidate named Prudence Calabrese, appeared on Art Bell's radio talk show with word of "hundreds" of photos made by an astrophysicist working at a "top-ten university" that supported Shramek's observations.[11] This anonymous astronomer was said to believe that the object was a hollow spheroid larger than our planet. According to Brown and Calabrese, he said it usually traveled behind the comet except for those times when it moved out for a little. They reported that it was giving off light and "intelligent" signals, which were picked up by a radio astronomer who was analyzing them at air time. No one said who either astronomer was, but the Internet, as usual, was buzzing with rumors.[12]

Then Whitley Streiber, another major player in UFO circles, appeared on Bell's show with Brown.[13] Bell, Brown, and Streiber all said they had the astronomer's photos. They were not to be released for a week, while the shy astronomer "talked to his family" to help them prepare for the enormous publicity orgy that would certainly follow the announcement he would make. The three said that if the photos were released at that point their quality would immediately reveal their source. The astronomer was, they said, internationally famous in his field as a pioneer of planetary astronomy, hence the perfect person to make the announcement.

According to these gurus, the astronomer entertained no doubt that the object was emitting light; one could see it reflecting off the debris around the comet. He had some doubt, though not much, that something was steering the object, because of its erratic movement. The gurus recounted the anonymous astronomer's report that a number of radio astronomers confirmed that the object was broadcasting, though they had not yet been able to decode its signals. There the matter rested for a while.

An e-mail said to be from Royal Greenwich Observatory in England confirmed that there was an anomaly, but it offered no speculation as to what or where it might be.[14] The Keck Observatory in Hawaii also acknowledged having observed "a number of anomalies" connected to Hale-Bopp, but none that would support this kind of speculation. The Keck astronomer replying also noted that there could be errors in their observations.

Someone at the Lick Observatory in California also confirmed the existence of the object, though the observatory would not officially confirm the confirmation. On December 5, the Royal Greenwich observatory denied that it had ever said the object was real, calling the e-mail mentioned above "a fiction of the Internet."[15]

There began to emerge predictable accusations of global government cover-up. The kindest said the scientists were acting out of "egocentric self-interest" and called for finding other sources of information to bolster what believers already knew. In the realm of conspiracy theory, contradiction of fantasy is disinformation, intended to keep the public in ignorance of the believers' startling repudiations of common sense.

When MSNBC posted a story about the controversy on its web site (http://www.msnbc.com/news/44673.asp), the believers found little glory in the mainstream media attention. One believer complained that "they" were ridiculing Shramek, the messenger, with quotes from "so-called 'authority' figures." This in itself made the story suspicious. Why mention the Hale-Bopp object if all you planned to do was debunk it? But what really gave the game away was that there were no new pictures on the site, no new evidence to discredit Shramek. In this way, the conspiracists said, NBC could "slow down" the story and give themselves credit for following it from the beginning.[16]

Nothing could deter the believers. One reported on his plans to watch the mass landings.[17] He took his patio lounge out of storage, added extra cushions, and set up a beach umbrella for protection from the elements. Of the latter, he said, "I can use [it] for shade or shelter should the need for either arise." It didn't seem to occur to him that no celestial events would be visible in rain or sunshine. Perhaps this was an ad hoc ritual of a kind, where the performance matters more than the result.

His ritual was not to be an ascetic one. He also provided two large coolers for food and drink and a long extension cord to power his coffeepot, hot plate, toaster oven, reading lamp, and refrigerator "equipped with an external tap for the 5 gal. Keg." With borrowed binoculars and telescope and a pair of sunglasses, he counted himself visually prepared. He took three days' vacation and warned his wife to leave him alone. His vigil was to be a solitary one. When he asked friends to join him, he got an unexpected response: "One individual laughed so hard he peed his pants."

The mysterious astronomer who provided the photo presented by Brown and Calabrese never revealed himself. He was almost forgotten in the excitements and diversions surrounding Hale-Bopp, until the announcement came in mid-March that the photo was clearly a fake. It was shown to be a not very cleverly manipulated version of a photo taken from the University of Hawaii web site. It was reversed and rotated to conceal its identity, then the companion object was added. Shramek's "object" was never in the image at all.

This tale of fraud and farce took an unexpected and quite tragic turn when, on March 26, 1997, the largest mass suicide in American history was discovered in San Diego. Thirty-nine members of a group that immediately came to be known as "Heaven's Gate" (HG) after a web site containing all their literature and a book by that name—their own name for themselves was "the Class" or "the Process"—had killed themselves with a mix of alcohol and sleeping pills, with plastic bags over their heads as insurance. In this case, unlike the Solar Temple deaths, there was no question of murder.

Much was made of the eerie neatness of the death scene. The bodies all wore uniforms of black pajamas and Nike running shoes. All the dead carried five-dollar bills in their pockets, and it was later discovered that the group had meticulously resolved all its debts before members killed themselves.[18] (They had lived by designing web sites and on the gifts members made to the organization: all they possessed, as is common with groups like these.)

HG members had killed themselves because their odd but not completely novel system of beliefs told them that they alone had sufficient purity to qualify for immediate transition to a place they called "the Level Above Human." They would make the trip via a spaceship that would arrive to take them there. It seemed to them that Hale-Bopp and the furor about it announced the time for their departure. They went to meet their destiny.

The Level Above Human, which they abbreviated as LAH or Telah, was, in effect, heaven, though in their system there was nothing supernatural about it. According to their teachings, dwellers in that realm have bodies, though they are not much like ours. For one thing, they are entirely sexless. The media's interest mounted even higher when it was discovered that some of the group's members had had themselves castrated in preparation for the transition. It was central to their beliefs that it was necessary for candidates for the passage to suppress and surpass their humanity. It was necessary to renounce all human attachments, including sex. The castration was explained the attempt of some members to remove temptation.

In some respects HG was typical, even stereotypical, of millenarian movements; in others, it was unique. For example, it is quite rare for a group that meets a violent end to leave such a large testimony behind. Usually whatever people in that position write is consumed in the same flames that destroy their bodies, but not only did this group leave a large and scrupulously detailed account of their beliefs and history, they ensured its worldwide dissemination. At one point, there were some six dozen mirrors of their web site available more or less complete.[19] Every conscious person in the world must at least have heard of what they did and why.

HG was perfectly typical in its leader's career, for the most part.[20] Marshall Herff Applewhite was the son of a nomadic Presbyterian minister who made his living setting up churches in small towns in Texas. He moved constantly, never settling into a church of his own. This pattern reappeared later in the workings of Heaven's Gate. Applewhite's friends described him as a normal, cheerful young man who took a stab at the ministry but dropped out of seminary in order to pursue a career in music.[21] He married and served in the military, apparently without incident. It was after he divorced that his life began to change.

Accounts of how this happened vary. According to his sister, Applewhite was hospitalized for heart problems and had a near-death experience that sent him the vision that changed his life, with the help of the lesser-known Bonnie Lu Trusdale Nettles, the nurse and part-time astrologer who would become his guru and, in this account, Delilah. Other accounts say that in 1970 Applewhite lost his teaching job because of homosexual liaisons with students, which, apparently, he did little to conceal.[22] In this version of the story, he checked himself into a psychiatric hospital seeking a "cure" for this condition, and it was there that he met Nettles, a practicing Theosophist and psychic later known as "Ti," while Applewhite became known as "Do."

So far the record is relatively typical of the prophet. He is steeped in his tradition, as Applewhite was raised and schooled in Christianity; he suffers a crisis of some sort—and both versions agree there was one—during which he receives his conversion and a calling to go and bring others to the same result. This, as we know, he also did.

The nature of this crisis and conversion raises an unusual aspect of Applewhite's career. Typically a person who has experienced a sudden and dramatic conversion, a removal of sin, is anything but reticent about it, because his conversion itself is his primary testament to the power and grace of God, or whatever agent is supposedly responsible. Applewhite acknowledges in his writings that his life was indeed in crisis, but all he ever wrote about meeting Nettles, which he calls the supreme high point of his life, was that they met when he was visiting a sick friend in the hospital. His reticence about his conversion raises questions about the depth of his conviction. How certain was he? Most of what he says in the Heaven's Gate book is closely hedged and always subject to change: "New information" was always coming from the Next Level.

Applewhite and Nettles ran an art center in Houston for a time, becoming ever closer in their chaste relationship and pursuing visions and dreams. They experienced contact with alien beings that instructed them to give up the things of this world. Their sense of mission grew, and in 1973 they left Houston and took to the road. A season in the wilderness grappling with God is an essential item on the prophet's résumé, and The Two had theirs: several months in isolation. In an Oregon campground they had the revelation that they were the two witnesses of Revelation 11, destined to die for their faith, revive, and be lifted to heaven in a cloud, which they took to be a spacecraft. This experience probably suggested the collective name they later took: The Two.

Applewhite, for all his solitary and nomadic ways, was a much more accessible figure than Nettles. In most outsider accounts, she is a vague figure. According to a 1976 *New York Times Magazine* piece, she and Applewhite shared an interest in astrology, and Applewhite had wanted his chart cast when they met.[23] Relatives were puzzled at the sudden turn in The Two's lives. Nettles's daughter was deeply hurt by her mother's abandonment, though she was nineteen at the time.[24] She blamed Applewhite for her mother's defection, or at least the coldness with which she carried it out, just as Applewhite's sister blamed Nettles for his change in direction. Nettles seems to have been the brains of the outfit, so to speak. Applewhite and the students spoke of her as the real Older Member, Do's "Father," in their genderless order of heaven. She died of cancer in 1985, but Do and the followers did not tell her daughter about it until some months later.

The Two set out to share their message with others. In one meeting among others they held in the early phase of their careers in Los Angeles they recruited twenty-four followers. After a number of false starts they finally settled on the highly disciplined lifestyle that would dominate the rest of the group's existence. It involved dividing the faithful up into pairs, called "check partners," whose task it was to monitor one another's every waking moment and to approve every decision the other made.[25] These pairs then were sent out on errands that replicated not only The Two's earlier wandering career but Do's boyhood as well. It became their job to find new recruits and start them in the "the Class."[26] Even in his new life Applewhite was still a teacher.

A telling reference to his past emerges when Do thoroughly condemns credit cards as tools of Satan.[27] Shortly after Do and Ti[28] took to the road, their first disciple gave them a gasoline credit card, apparently not knowing that her husband had reported it stolen. They used it, expecting the Lord to provide when the bill came due, though of course they would never get it. Do unilaterally extended the rental term on their Avis car, with the same blessed assurance.

These things only became a problem when they promised a newspaperman in Harlingen, Texas, the story of his career if he would meet them in a motel room. Since an important south Texas story was and probably still is drugs, the reporter brought some law officers with him to hear the story he assumed would be about that subject. When The Two saw the officers arrive, they panicked and ran, and the law, of course, pursued. Their tags came up as stolen, and Ti was held on the stolen credit cards, but then released. Do served six months in jail.

These events seem to have contributed to an increasing reclusiveness and secretiveness in the group's routine. They lived as far from ordinary social contact as possible. They lived in remote campgrounds until a member inherited enough money for the Class to buy houses, and even then they kept their blinds pulled and stayed indoors as much as possible. At one point, a couple of infiltrators were uncovered. Even though they only wanted to find a friend who had joined the group some time earlier, The Two decided they were targets of assassination and went into hiding, leaving the followers to fend for themselves. Do never lost the fear of assassination. In one of the group's last communiqués, he wrote:

> Another possibility is that, because of the position we take in our information, we could find so much disfavor with the powers that control this world that there could be attempts to incarcerate us or to subject us to some sort of psychological or physical torture (such as occurred at both Ruby Ridge and Waco).[29]

The fact was that the powers of the world seemed never to have heard of the Class.

Regardless of what the world thought, The Two (or at least Applewhite), like other prophets, saw the conversion of the world in their own terms. The world needed to experience their conversion. Like them, it had to give up sex. In fact, it had to give up humanity in order to move onward in its growth to the Next Level.

Neither Applewhite nor any of the students who published their notes was particularly clear about what the heavenly kingdom had to offer, except that humanity was definitely taboo. They are somewhat more definite about what is not in the heavenly kingdom. Bodies there have no sex organs, for one thing. Do said they rarely got "complete information" from the Next Level. Do never said much against the world, except that it is evil and is ruled by "Luciferians" (these, at least in the later doctrine, are "space aliens" who control the earth and establish its false value system). This is more or less taken for granted in his long talks, but he does not go into detail.

Most of his followers who left testaments despised the world. They found nothing in it that rewarded them. One talked of love as a fickle cheat; another spoke of the greed and ego that seemed to drive every achievement in this world. One remarked that even if The Two and all the students actually did share the same psychosis, it was far preferable to humanity. "I would gladly live this life of 'delusion' over the insanity of living your 'reality' full of ugliness, despair, and fruitlessness," she or he said.[30] (Members of Heaven's Gate adopted names like "Jmmody," partly in order to disguise their gender.)

This rejection of the world and all its attachments led to a slavish and highly personal attachment to The Two. Without exception, every testament refers to them in terms of deep particular devotion. It was not the least of this group's delusions that they had cast off humanity's attachments; in reality all they did was replace a set of frequently tenuous old ones with an intense singular attachment to Do. This is typical of charismatic millenarianism. In such movements there often occurs an intense breathless focus on the moment. Time is suspended and everything hangs in the balance. The leader is the source of holiness and life without him is unimaginable. In a poignant bit of irony, one testimony tells how "Do saved my life."[31]

Another interesting, and typical, aspect of Heaven's Gate is its attempt to recast traditional doctrine in contemporary terms. The Two managed, or at least attempted, to do this by putting the doctrine of the Second Coming and the incarnation in words that any fan of *Star Trek* would find comfortable, if not compelling. In the process, they dumped large portions of Christian doctrine. The Resurrection, for example, which was a subject of intense interest at the beginning of their mission in the 1970s, became irrelevant by 1992.[32]

In the early days of their mission, when they got their first round of national publicity, The Two announced plans for a "demonstration": They would be murdered, then resurrected three and a half days later.[33] Presumably they chose this schedule in accordance with their vision of the two witnesses in Revelation 11:3–11. The firestorm of media ridicule that greeted this and other announcements led them to declare themselves murdered in spirit by the media, as it were, and the continuation of their work, back in seclusion, the demonstration of their resurrection.[34] There may be a relationship between these events and the switch in doctrine.

HG had its own Gnostic form of theodicy, which handled the thorny problem of evil in an impressively neat way. Essentially, it said that the world was never intended to be good. It was created imperfect on purpose, to serve as a testing ground to prepare souls for life on the Next Level. This is made clear in the perception that it has failed and once again is due to for recycling.[35]

The essence of HG's belief and practice was a radical perfectionism. For them perfection was not only desirable, but necessary in order to escape the

hellishness of this life. And it could only be paid for with, literally, everything. Nothing human is good enough for heaven. Their discipline was to
shed all human attachments and ultimately humanity itself.

HG borrowed liberally from the school of UFOlogical thought that
constructs its own angelology and demonology around an epic struggle between any number of intergalactic races over the souls of humanity. "Space
aliens," according to Do and his information from the Next Level, are Luciferian spirits that inhabit near space in their inferior UFOs and prey on
humanity for recruits and to revitalize their degenerate stock.

HG put its doctrine into the language of *Star Trek* in an attempt to gain
a hearing among television-addicted potential converts. The Class as a
whole seems to have shared this addiction, for they had large-screen sets
and watched all the science fiction shows. In their "speaking in tongues,"
as they called it, God became the Admiral and Ti—the definitive "Older
Member" for Do and the group—the Captain.[36]

Their dogma was highly concrete and specific. Everything that comes
from the Next Level is simple common sense; it describes concrete realities.
The heavenly kingdom is a physical but inaccessible place, and its members inhabit tangible, if distinctly odd, bodies. Do had a definite aversion
to anything spiritual and hated religion as the greatest of Lucifer's lies. It is
not clear what category he would have put his own dogma in, but religion
was distinctly not it.

Much as Do hated established religion, he hated the New Age nearly as
much. Some journalists assumed that HG was a New Age group, but that
is inaccurate. New Age dogma generally advocates the belief that Godhead
is within anyone's easy reach, right here on earth. The Class believed the
opposite.

HG members expected to take their "vehicles" (their bodies) with them
to the Next Level. But they still considered it possible that someone, presumably the government, would attack them first. In that event, they were
prepared to kill themselves as the Zealots did at Masada, though they did
not anticipate that they would have to. Do explained succinctly the position of most millenarian movements in relation to the world:

> It is clear to all of us, that to the Anti-Christ—those propagators of sus-
> tained faithfulness to mammalian humanism—we are, and will be seen

as, their Anti-Christ. This is certainly to be expected, and it will not delay our return to our Father's Kingdom. It might even accelerate that return.[37]

Do's error here was typical. He attached much more importance to his movement and its actions than the world ever would, even after HG's final adieu. They were a nine-day media wonder, to be sure, but they never achieved the mass conversion they clearly kept hoping for.

HG had quite a different definition of suicide than ours: suicide is "to turn against the Next Level when it is being offered." So, from their point of view, it was the rest of us who killed ourselves by refusing to accept their offer of the Kingdom. This statement is an inversion of everyday logic, but again it is typical of believers in the millennium.[38] Elsewhere HG makes its position more clear: It is the rest of the world that has been "brainwashed" into rejecting their offer, not them into accepting it.[39]

A science-fiction "fanzine" called *Ansible* published a side note on the connection the Hale-Bopp hoax had with Heaven's Gate's departure. Gregory Frost, the author of "Cult Connections" discussed his own remote connection to the incident. Frost was a high school classmate of Chuck Schramek's. The pair used to concoct their own UFOs out of helium, dry-cleaner bags, and pie pans with flares attached. These were convincing enough, when launched at night, to get a mention in the local papers, when the pranksters called in their UFO reports to the local airport.

Schramek used his technological skills for other hoaxes as well. He would doctor his voice with electronic filters to sound like a B-movie alien and contact ham radio operators as a starry visitor. He managed to convince "a whole flock" of listeners that he was Venusian. He also dressed up as an alien (black clothes and a tinfoil head wrap) on at least one occasion to peer in the window of a believing neighbor. Frost then talked about what he'd seen in a broadcast, "proving" to the neighbor that he'd been visited from space.

When Frost heard of Schramek's "discovery" and its momentary notoriety, he concluded that his old friend was at it again. "After all, here was the only person I knew who'd ever tried smoking banana peels (it gave him a headache) pulling off a truly grandstand stunt." After Heaven's Gate made the comet the "marker" for their suicide, it didn't seem quite so funny, but Shramek, as he points out, wasn't really to blame, any more than any other "UFOzo."[40]

The document that follows is the last general publication issued by Heaven's Gate. As the title explains, it is a last call for interested seekers to join them. They never gave up talking to the wicked world, or at least that tiny fragment of it that could hear and respond to their message as they intended it, despite the intense rejection they got from everyone else. Rejection is always the world's response to the millennium's message, and that response has a lot to do with tragic outcomes like this one, though it does not seem to have been definitive in this case. Like the Order of the Solar Temple, Heaven's Gate declared its "joy" at its own closure. Hale-Bopp was the "marker" indicating that it was time for their departure. The Class was at the moment of "graduation." Even so, Heaven's Gate never ceased its evangelism. At the moment of death, they still offered books and tapes to seekers.[41]

• • •

CREW FROM THE EVOLUTIONARY LEVEL ABOVE HUMAN OFFERS—LAST CHANCE TO ADVANCE BEYOND HUMAN

The following statements could sound very presumptuous. However, these facts can come into focus or "prove" themselves if they are seriously explored a step at a time. They could also sound very "doomsdayish." Though, in truth, they may be the most joyous "sound of music" to the ears and eyes of those who have been waiting for them.

The Earth's present "civilization" is about to be recycled—"spaded under"—in order that the planet might be refurbished. The human "weeds" have taken over the garden and disturbed its usefulness beyond repair.

The human kingdom was designed (created) as a *stepping stone* between the animal kingdom and the Evolutionary Kingdom Level Above Human (the *true* Kingdom of God).

It is the *soul* that can progress from the human kingdom to the Kingdom Level Above Human. Both kingdom levels have their own unique physical "containers" (bodies) for the souls that reside in that kingdom level.

As the human goes out to "choose" servants from within the animal kingdom, from beasts of burden to seeing-eye dogs—if that animal grows to find pleasure only in serving its master, no longer identifies as an animal, but sees itself as a family member in that human family, and its behavior is pleasing to that human—the two become *bound* together. The human family then provides the body (a human infant) for that soul to enter, allowing it to move up into the human evolutionary kingdom. (This is not to suggest that all humans are containers for souls moving up from the animal kingdom, for most humans are containers for human kingdom *returnees* still bound to that family unit.)

In a more realistic way, periodically a Member of the Kingdom Level Above Human receives instruction to incarnate among humans to seek out the souls that have been "tagged" or given a "deposit" (an "implant") of knowledge concerning the TRUTH about the Evolutionary Level Above Human. That knowledge finds each *recipient* wanting to "separate from the pack," and prepares him to recognize the Teacher or Representatives sent from the Kingdom Level Above Human. When he/she connects with that Teacher—an "Older Member" in that Kingdom—he is then offered further instruction in knowledge and behavior that can open the door of service to him. If that human changes to the degree that he no longer desires any human behavior and he pleases that Member of the Kingdom Level Above Human, a *bond* is formed between them and a body belonging to that new Kingdom is provided for that soul to move up into.

Both the human kingdom and the Kingdom Level Above Human— the *true* Kingdom of God—are physical and biological. However, the human kingdom is made up of mammalian bodies—"seed-bearing" plants or "containers"—while the Kingdom Level Above Human is made up of *non*-mammalian, *non*-seed-bearing bodies or containers for souls. The Kingdom Level Above Human's "children," or young, are those who have graduated from the human kingdom under the tutorship (midwifing) of a Member of the *true* Kingdom of God who has been through that transition—bonded to *His* Father—at a previous time.

A "student" or prospective "child" of a Member of the Level Above Human can, with the help of his Older Member(s) from that Kingdom Level, overcome or rise out of *all* human-mammalian behavior—sexuality and gender consciousness—and all other addictions and ties of the human kingdom. Older Members, as experienced "clinicians," are necessary to take souls through this "weaning"—this difficult "withdrawal" from humanness and binding "misinformation" concepts. The student must complete this change to the point of abhorring human behavior before his soul can become a "match" with a biological body of the *true* Kingdom of God—for that new, genderless body is designed to function at a far more refined level.

The Evolutionary Level Above Human, the *true* Kingdom of God, the "Headquarters" of all that is, is a many-membered Kingdom which physically exists in the *highest,* most *distant* Heaven—a *non-temporal* place (*outside of time,* and therefore with *eternal* life). It is the only place from which *souls, life,* and all *creating* originates. Being non-temporal, it *was, is,* and *forever will be*—a concept that temporal creatures are not designed to comprehend. This "Next Level" Kingdom designed the "temporal" world outside its "borders" and designed temporal creatures for souls to inhabit while in the human "classroom." If the soul survives and moves forward through all its tests along the way—it can, with the help of a Member of the Level Above Human, lose its temporal characteristics and become a part of their non-perishable, non-corruptible world. However, *all other souls* who reach a certain degree of corruption (having of their own free will chosen to become totally separate from their Creator, whether knowingly or not) will engage a "self-destruct" mechanism at the Age's end.

The term TRUE Kingdom of God is used repeatedly because there are *many* space alien races that through the centuries of this civilization (and in civilizations prior) have represented themselves to humans as "Gods." We refer to them collectively as "space alien races in opposition to the Next Level," what historically have been referred to as "Luciferians," for their ancestors fell into disfavor with the Kingdom Level Above Human many thousands of years ago. They are not genderless—they still need to reproduce. They have become nothing more than technically advanced humans (clinging to human behavior) who retained some of what they learned while in the early training of Members of the Level Above Human, e.g., having limited: space-time travel, telepathic communication, advanced travel hardware (spacecrafts, etc.), increased longevity, advanced genetic engineering, and such skills as suspending holograms (as used in some so-called "religious miracles"). The Next Level—the *true* Kingdom of God—has the only truly advanced space-time travel vehicles, or spacecrafts, and is not interested in creating phenomena (signs) or impressive trickery.

These malevolent space races are the humans' GREATEST ENEMY. They hold humans in unknown slavery only to fulfill their own desires. They cannot "create," though they develop races and biological containers through genetic manipulation and hybridization. They even try to "make deals" with human governments to permit them (the space aliens) to engage in biological experimentation (through abductions) in exchange for such things as technically advanced modes of travel—though they seldom follow through, for they don't want the humans of this civilization to become another element of competition. They war among themselves over the spoils of this planet and use religion and increased sexual behavior to keep humans "drugged" and ignorant (in darkness) while thinking they are in "God's" keeping. They use the discarnate (spirit) world to keep humans preoccupied with their addictions. These negative space races see to it, through the human "social norm" (the largest Luciferian "cult" there is), that man continues to not avail himself of the possibility of advancing *beyond* human.

Just as the biological body is the "container" for the soul, the soul is the "container" for *Mind* ("Spirit"). *Mind* translates into the brain as *information* (knowledge). Information is available to humans from only two sources—the *mind* of the adversarial space races—or the *Mind* of the Kingdom Level Above Human. The *mind* of the adversarial space races yields misinformation (promoting the behavior and concepts of this corrupt world). The *Mind* from the *true* Kingdom of God yields *true* information (though the space races and their servants would reverse this interpretation). As we *change,* in the progression of overcoming humanness—the percentages change—of which *mind* occupies our soul— Truth *increases* as misinformation *decreases.* If one chooses to revert back to humanness, the process reverses—the Truth is aborted as the soul becomes more filled with mammalian *mind.* (The word "True" or "Truth" is defined as the most accurate perception available at any given level of understanding, changing at the level of the eye of the beholder.) That Next Level Truth can even be taken from us if we abuse it. When our "eye becomes single" or our soul is *filled* only with the *Mind* or "Spirit" from the *true* Kingdom of God, it becomes pure or "Holy" *Mind* ("Spirit").

The design of the *true* Kingdom of God permits the presence of an adversial element during a human civilization as the primary catalyst for growth. Without it, we would have no choices—our free will could not be exercised. Our *right* choices are what find us in alignment to receive a *"deposit" of recognition* when the Truth is offered.

Two thousand years ago, the Kingdom Level Above Human appointed an Older Member to send a Representative (His "Son"), along with some of their beginning students, to incarnate on this garden. (These students had brief periods of association with and guidance from Members of the Kingdom Level Above Human during the early generations of this civilization.) While on Earth as an "away team" with their "Captain," they were to work on their overcoming of humanness and tell the civilization they were visiting how the *true* Kingdom of God can be entered. The humans under the control of the adverserial space races killed the "Captain" and His crew, because of the "blasphemous" position they held, and quickly turned the teachings of the "Captain" (the Older Member's "Son") into watered-down *Country Club* religion—obscuring the remnants of the Truth.

Again an "away team" from the Level Above Human incarnated in the 1970's in the mature (adult) bodies that had been picked and prepped for this current mission. This time the "Admiral" (the Older Member, or "Father," incarnate in a female vehicle) came with the "Captain" and his crew. As the two Older Members put out a "statement" and held public meetings over about a 9-month period in 1975–76 to bring their crew together, the media tagged them the "UFO cult" because of their expectation of leaving aboard a spacecraft ("cloud of light") at the completion of their "overcoming." The two Older Members then went into seclusion with their crew (students), "lifting them out" of the world for almost 17 years (not accepting any new students), making Earth's surface their classroom. This isolation was absolutely necessary, for the *degree* of their *overcoming* of sexuality, addictions, and ties to the human environment has to be taken to the point of *matching* the minimum behavior and consciousness requirements of the Kingdom Level Above Human. Only then would their *new* "Next Level" bodies be *functional*. They resurfaced briefly for about a 3½-month period in 1992, allowing some of their "dropouts" to rejoin them.

This changeover (sufficient "overcoming" to inherit Next Level bodies) *is nearing completion,* and before this "away team" returns, representatives of the "Class" are instructed to put this information before the public. The Next Level will determine the future of *each individual soul* according to its response to this information and the Next Level's Representatives.

These space alien adversaries, for the most part, are about to be "recycled" as this human civilization is "spaded." They know that "rumor has it" that their days are numbered. They refuse to believe it and are desperate to recruit souls from the human kingdom into *their* "heavenly kingdom." There are many "counterfeit" heavens, and each "heaven" is at this time collecting "names in their book," forcing a stand of allegiance, polarizing each individual's commitment to his chosen "God."

When Members of the Level Above Human are physically present, the opposing forces work the hardest against them in order to support their own position. They do almost anything to keep humans from following the path toward the Evolutionary Level Above Human. They "turn up the heat" at this time in the area of mammalian behavior, primarily *sexuality* and *the family*. This has become such an overwhelming presence in the Earth's atmosphere that even some of the crew that came with us were lost to its temptation. Don't forget that when the adversaries were expelled, they had to condemn the *true* Kingdom of God in order to support their own desires, and see it simply as another path—inhumane and radically uncompromising.

When this present "away team" leaves (which will be very soon), the Truth will go with them. You cannot *preserve* the Truth in your religions. It is present only as long as a *Truth bearer* (Older Member from the true Kingdom of God) is present. It can only be your future if you have received the *gift of recognition* and you "reach out and grab" *further nour-ishment* while it is offered. The Truth can be retained (without signifi-cant dilution) only as one is physically connected with the Next Level, through an Older Member, and that relationship requires sustained, con-stantly upgraded perception and behavior.

Humans of this civilization have periodically been given laws by the Next Level to upgrade their behavior. For example, the laws given to Moses were elementary "commandments" designed to make order and to raise the standards of a very "young" (primitive, barbaric) society. Then some 2000 years later, the Level Above Human, through Jesus' teachings, brought major updates (far more demanding): the greatest command-ment is to *"Love the Lord thy God with all thy heart, with all thy soul, and with all thy mind"* (Matthew 22:37)— *"If anyone comes to Me and does not hate his father and mother and his wife and children and brothers and sisters—and even his own life also—he cannot be My disciple"* (Luke 14:26). Those wanting to go with Him had to *do* as He did. His teach-ings clearly spelled out the requirements (the actual *formula*) for making the literal and difficult transition from the human kingdom into the Kingdom Level Above Human.

When a soul which has previously received the *gift of life* is awakened by its Older Member(s) in a particular incarnation or "season" (well after adolescence), it is *picking up* in its lessons where it *left off* at the end of its previous time with an Older Member. What any individual partici-pates in prior to that "awakening" is of no real significance. If a soul had previously overcome such human characteristics as family ties and rela-tionships, then just prior to its *awakening,* or rejoining with its Older Member, he is seen by those around him as suddenly becoming unstable, for he is compelled to once again separate from those imposing ties and seek to connect with what he had previously sought or connected with.

Now, at the close of this Age, every significant soul of this civilization has returned (and is to some degree *in* or *attached to* a physical body) to reap its reward. Its *desires* and *attachments determine* which heaven it is going to (by what it chooses to *not overcome* or what it clings to, and which "God" it looks to—one that *increases* its humanness or one that offers a *way out* of its humanness). Most who *think* they are *for* the *true* Kingdom of God are in fact working for the opposing side—the counterfeit "gods"—and will want to condemn us.

Today's leaders in the "industrialized world," though claiming to be democratic, self-righteously *dictate* to the rest of the world their own ideas of what are acceptable practices and behavior.

Money RULES! The monetary systems, through *indebtedness, ownership,* and *insurance* (all against God's ethic for man), bind man to servitude. The powers behind the money have discovered man's most tempting addictions, and through advertisement, movies, television, radio, and publications, feed these addictions with the excitement of *sex, drugs* (legal and illegal), and all manner of *violence,* to ensure their continued monetary power. Under the guise of "the social norm," this same world also imposes its distorted religious concepts and values. Their selfish pursuits corrupt and pollute the physical environment of all their "subjects" as well.

The *pure* information brought by every Representative sent by the Level Above Human is the same—total renunciation of the human world and human ways is required for entry into the true Kingdom of God. However, all religions that were originally based upon the information these Representatives brought have been targeted by major misinformation campaigns by the adversarial space races to the point that only a trace of the pure information remains in any of these religions' teachings and practices.

The true "Jews"—God's chosen people (*the overcomers*)—can no longer be found in a genetic strain—a race—or a religion.

The true "Israel"—where God's chosen people (*the overcomers*) reside—cannot be found in a geographical location.

The true "Christians" cannot be found among the religious who put human *family values* on the ultimate pedestal. They claim to know Jesus (Yeshua) as their "Messiah" or "Savior"—even though He never had a wife or children, nor would He accept as His disciple any who would not leave all attachments and ties to this world in order to learn from Him. Any truly committed to *His* family or God's ways, are today seen as "cults" and a threat to all of the above social norms and systems.

When the Next Level sent a crew 2000 years ago, the world "cleansed" or "saved" *their* world from its "blasphemy" and merely got the crew their boarding passes back to the *true* Kingdom of God on the *true* "Enterprise" (spaceship or "cloud of light"). If you seek to cleanse the world of our "blasphemy" this time, you will simply be the instrument of *our* "days being shortened" while destroying *your* "last chance" in this civilization to *advance.*

Many say they live only for the "Harvest Time"—the "Last Days"—the "Second Coming." These have all arrived! There are souls—some of you, here now—who have received *a deposit of recognition,* and that knowledge finds you desirous of connecting and bonding with the Next Level. Those who have that deposit of *Life* will *believe* what we say, and *know* who we are. If they *continue* in that belief—sustain that *Life* (though the opposing space alien races will do anything to prevent them from nurturing that *gift*) they will be protected and "saved" from the approaching recycling and "spading under" of the civilization. They will have nothing to fear, nor will they know DEATH—even if they lose their human body. That continued *belief* will one day find them a member in the Level Above Human, in a physical body belonging to the true Kingdom of God—the Evolutionary Level Above Human—leaving behind this temporal and perishable world for one that is everlasting and non-corruptible.

—*Today's Next Level Crew* II

Notes

1. David L. Chandler, "Close Calls from Comets on the Rise," *Boston Globe,* November 10, 1996, A12.

2. Posted by Kent Steadman (phikent@ix.netcom.com) to iufo@world.std.com, Subject: Here comes Nibiru? Huge object suddenly appears next to Hale Bopp (November 15, 1996).

3. Posted by Wolf359 (Jabriol@cris.com) to Issues@catalina.org, Subject: Attention Lightworkers: Mass Landings Information (fwd), Excerpts from Sheldon Nidle Lecture Series #6 (November 15, 1996).

4. Space Brothers are a quasi-divine body of beings, similar in some respects to New Age Ascended Masters, who govern the cosmos from a central command post. They are de-

scribed as coming from all the cosmos's races, and are finally ready to make us aware of their benevolent rule.

5. Nidle follows the version of the Mayan calendar José Argüelles derived for the Planetary Convergence in 1987, when he expected the return of Quetzalcoatl, the feathered serpent founding hero of Mayan belief, whom they expect to return at the end of time. Argüelles proclaimed "the end of Armageddon" for the Convergence. (Quoted in Phillip C. Lucas, "The New Age Movement and the Pentecostal/Charismatic Revival," in *Perspectives on the New Age,* ed. James R. Lewis and J. Gordon Melton (Albany: State University of New York Press, 1992), 205.

6. Ohr Somayach, "Ask the Rabbi" no. 149, at http://www.virtual.co.il/education/education/ohr/ask/ask149.htm.

7. *Prophe-Zine,* no. 28, October 18, 1996.

8. Posted by Al warhead@feersum.demon.co.uk to mmlist-l@newciv.org (November 23, 1996).

9. Posted by Dave.Tilbury@UK.Sun.COM (David Tilbury—Sun UK) to iufo@world.std.com, mmlist-l@newciv.org, Subject: And The Stars Shall Fall From Heaven. The Church of Christ—1310 Broadway—Oak Grove—MO—64075—U.S.A. (November 20, 1996).

10. Posted by "Steve Wingate" to anomalous-images@world.std.com, Subject: Hale-Bopp Image Showing Second Object (November 17, 1996).

11. Bell's late-night show was broadcast live from a trailer in Pahrump, Nevada, and attracted a large following among those interested in contemporary occultism, conspiracy theory, UFOlogy, and weird science. It caused even a bigger stir when Bell resigned quite suddenly, claiming unspecified threats against his family. Listeners blamed Bill Clinton.

12. Posted by anomalous-images-approval@world.std.com to iufoworld.std.com Subject: (Fwd) Hale-Bopp object confirmed by leading astrophysicist (November 29, 1996).

13. Posted by "Steve Wingate" to iufo@world.std.com, Subject: (Fwd) Art Bell—BLOW OUT (November 29, 1996).

14. Sent by (deleted@ast.cam.ac.uk) to Joe LeSesne (raver187@m-net.arbornet.edu), Subject: Hale-Bopp anomalies (December 3, 1996).

15. "UFO News Story," at http://www.strieber.com/ufonews/bopp5.html.

16. "UFO News Story. The Hale-Bopp Enigma," posted by Allen Comstock to snet-news@world.std.com, Subject: Hale-Bopp & Shramek on NBC Web Page (Jan. 19, 1997).

17. Posted by "Name Withheld" to alt.alien.visitors, Subject: Waiting for Hale-Bopp—my plan (December 9, 1996).

18. According to a friend of the group, they invariably carried the bills after one of them was interrogated as a vagrant. Associated Press, "One-Time Cult Member Explains Mysteries of Castration, Bills," April 6, 1997, http://www.trancenet.org/heavensgate/news/402.shtml (October 9, 1998).

19. The *Washington Post* maintains a copy at their web site: http://www.washingtonpost.com/wp-srv/national/longterm/cult/timeline.htm.

20. The *Washington Post* has the best single source of historical information on Heaven's Gate, available on their web site at http://www.washingtonpost.com/wp-srv/national/longterm/cult/timeline.htm. Another concise and thoroughly cited source is Wendy Gale Robinson's "Heaven's Gate: The End?" http://jcmc.huji.ac.il/vol3/issue3/robinson.html.

21. It is an odd but probably insignificant coincidence that David Koresh also aspired to a career in music and failed. Judging by a recording someone found and posted on the web, he had a not-unpleasant tenor voice vaguely reminiscent of Bruce Springsteen's, but gave no signs of blazing talent in that area. It appears much more likely that a contemporary prophet will have abandoned a career in engineering than in most other fields, for reasons that elude me. Sun Myung Moon of the Unification Church used to be an engineer; so did Harold Camping, who predicted Jesus' return in his *1994?*, and Edgar Whisenant, who said the same about 1988.

22. David Daniel, "The Beginning of the Journey," *Time*, April 14, 1997, 36–37. Robert W. Balch is quite clear on this point: Applewhite was gay. See his "Waiting for the Ships: Disillusion and the Revitalization of Faith in Bo and Peep's UFO Cult," in *The Gods Have Landed: New Religions from Other Worlds*, ed. James R. Lewis (Albany: State University of New York Press, 1995), 141.

23. James S. Phelan, "Looking For: The Next World," *New York Times Magazine*, February 29, 1976.

24. Associated Press, "Children of Heaven's Gate Co-Founder Struggle for Answers," archived at http://www.nando.net/newsroom/nt/331sons.html.

25. The group's list of "Lesser Offenses" included "1. Taking any action without using my check partner. 2. Trusting my own judgment—or using my own mind." Major offenses were deceit, sensuality, and disobedience. See The Class, "Major and Lesser Offences," archived at http://www.washingtonpost.com/wp-srv/national/longterm/cult/timeline.htm.

26. The Class, "'88 Update—The UFO Two and Their Crew: A Brief Synopsis," archived at http://www.washingtonpost.com/wp-srv/national/longterm/cult/timeline.htm.

27. The Class, "Beyond Human—The Last Call—Session 5," archived at http://www.washingtonpost.com/wp-srv/national/longterm/cult/timeline.htm.

28. The Two had a number of aliases, including Bo and Peep at that early phase of their careers—they were looking for "sheep."

29. The Class, "Our Position on Suicide," archived at http://www.washingtonpost.com/wp-srv/national/longterm/cult/timeline.htm.

30. Glnody, "Warning: For Those Who Are Prone to Hasty Judgments," archived at http://www.washingtonpost.com/wp-srv/national/longterm/cult/timeline.htm.

31. Srrody, "Testament by Srrody," archived at http://www.washingtonpost.com/wp-srv/national/longterm/cult/timeline.htm.

32. The Class, "Beyond Human—The Last Call—Session 5," archived at http://www .washingtonpost.com/wp-srv/national/longterm/cult/timeline.htm.

33. "First Statement of Ti and Do, Sent out from Ojai, California March 1975," archived at http://www.washingtonpost.com/wp-srv/national/longterm/cult/timeline.htm.

34. The Class, "'88 Update—The Ufo Two and Their Crew: A Brief Synopsis," archived at http://www.washingtonpost.com/wp-srv/national/longterm/cult/timeline.htm.

35. Amid the general horror that greeted the suicides, a few voices proclaimed that The Class was really following an ancient Gnostic tradition in their rejection of the world and electing to leave it in the fashion they chose. There certainly are similarities in doctrine and practice between HG and, say, the Cathars of medieval France, but the comparison would be more persuasive if Do had left evidence that he had heard of either Gnosticism or Cathars. Since he did not, the connection seems spurious, especially in view of Do's repeated and vehement condemnation of every religious tradition as satanic deception. His own dogma, he said, was simple reality. There was nothing spiritual about it. Ideas reappear with no necessary relation to an earlier source.

36. The Class, "Overview of Present Mission," archived at http://www.washingtonpost .com/wp-srv/national/longterm/cult/timeline.htm.

37. The Class, "Do's Intro: Purpose—Belief. What Our Purpose Is—The Simple 'Bottom Line,'" archived at http://www.washingtonpost.com/wp-srv/national/longterm/cult/ timeline.htm.

38. The Class, "Our Position on Suicide," archived at http://www.washingtonpost.com/ wp-srv/national/longterm/cult/timeline.htm.

39. The Class, "Beyond Human—The Last Call—Session 4," archived at http://www .washingtonpost.com/wp-srv/national/longterm/cult/timeline.htm.

40. Gregory Frost, "Cult Connections," *Ansible* 117, http://www.dcs.gla.ac.uk/SF-Archives/ Ansible.

41. "Hale-Bopp Brings Closure to Heaven's Gate," archived at http://www.washingtonpost .com/wp-srv/national/longterm/cult/timeline.htm.

THE END

By the time he got to Jonestown, Jim Jones was a seriously impaired drug abuser. Mary Maaga makes a compelling case that when the Peoples Temple moved to Guyana, Jones was little more than a "mascot of cohesion" because the duties of organizing a pioneering life required expertise he did not have.[1] Management was now mostly up to his lieutenants. This coup and his drug-induced unreliability had faded his charisma to some extent. He was visibly incapacitated. Everyone knew it, though the rank and file probably did not acknowledge it among themselves at first. He told some followers that he had cancer, heart disease, a lung condition, and recurrent fever. All these claims proved to be untrue on autopsy, but it seems likely that his followers believed him and saw his ailments as he described them: stress-induced marks of his dedication to them. His grogginess and slurred speech were passed off as "low blood sugar," and "bad" members of the group were blamed for Jones's exhaustion and failure. He faked heart attacks and would "faint" when people challenged his authority.

The inner circle of the movement's staff, who had regular and close contact with Jones and ran the Peoples Temple in his incapacity, could not ignore his condition. They continued to affirm their faith in him and what he once stood for, because they had invested so much in the group and in him. However, Maaga argues that they had replaced Jones with the group itself and its message as the center of their lives.

They seem to have taken sending the message of the Peoples Temple as the last best action it could accomplish. It was their combined decision that led to the group's mass suicide in 1978; Jones was mentally incapable of planning and carrying it out himself, though he certainly served as a figurehead in its accomplishment.

The group was failing in every practical sense, and Congressman Leo Ryan's investigatory visit drove home the extent of the pressure mounting against it. The staff seems to have felt that suicide was the best and probably the only "positive" way to end the movement's career. They imagined that this death would have a degree of dignity surely lacking from the massacre they anticipated at the hands of the government. Maaga sums up in saying "it is possible that the timing of the suicides had to do with a combination of the Ryan visit, which threatened the integrity of the community from the outside, and Jones's behavior, which was threatening to undermine the community from the inside."[2] The leadership planned a "symbolic end . . . a message to the world." One of them wrote that "suicide . . . would go down better and might stir others to become socialists."[3]

Jones attempted to reassert his charisma, with some apparent success. During the suicide meeting at which the final decision was made, Jones said, "I'm going to tell you Christine [a follower], without me life has no meaning. I'm the best thing you'll *ever* have." He told his followers, "I've practically died every day to give you peace." He blamed one of the movement's highly placed defectors for their death, calling their suicide a "murder" resulting from his treachery, not only in defection, but in joining their opposition. The suicide, finally, would be victory: "We win when we go down," said Jones. He anticipated bloody reprisal—massacre and torture—for the attack on Ryan and his party.

During the suicide, which was taped, a believer speaks up to thank "Dad for giving us life, and also death." Both were a blessing. Jones appealed to the followers not to weep at death, but to die like socialists. "Lay down your life with dignity," he said. Suicide was an assertion of choice. In one of those millenarian theological twists on reality, Jones redefined their suicide as a revolutionary act.[4]

This pattern reemerges in many of the other groups that ended their efforts in this way. Suicide, an ultimate disgrace in nearly all other systems becomes something else here: a final expression of the group's message. It is a final political gesture, an ultimate refusal to surrender to the power of Babylon.

The Members of the Message, known to the world as the Branch Davidians, believed they would die at Armageddon sometime in 1993. They described how the frugal David Koresh (their living arrangements included no indoor toilets and limited electrical outlets; living in Mt. Carmel was like "camping indoors," as one member put it)[5] spent lavishly on boats and go-carts during the summer of 1992 because he was convinced they would face Babylon the following year in a final battle that they would lose—at least as the carnal world reckons these things.[6] Koresh's all-too-accurate prophecy proved his status beyond any doubt, for those who believed him already. Some of them predict his resurrection.

As Koresh lay bleeding from a stomach wound on the afternoon of April 19, 1993, there arose a plan. Since they fully expected Koresh to die, some of his followers decided they would carry his body out on a litter, under a flag of surrender. They would give the agents a tape recording of the final message he had prepared. As they handed Koresh's body over, the adult members of the Message would open fire on the FBI agents, ensuring their own deaths in return fire. At that moment, those unskilled with guns would blow themselves up with grenades on global live television. In this way, they would send the world their ultimate message of rejection of its ways.

It is not completely clear whose plan it was, and some survivors deny it existed at all, but trial testimony says it involved "translation," the members' euphemism for going to heaven, which did not necessarily involve dying.[7] Koresh seems to have believed he was about to die from his abdominal wound, and reports of his vital signs that nurses among the members phoned out to FBI negotiators support his assessment.[8] He called members to him to say goodbye, and they gathered afterward in an atmosphere of high emotion, praying and singing. A member came from where Koresh lay and asked them to be quiet because the messiah was talking to God.

The tape was delivered and aired; Dick Reavis, author of *The Ashes of Waco,* the best book on events there, describes it as incoherent, saying clearly only that Koresh thought he was supremely important.[9] Plans to leave Mt. Carmel developed. Koresh had promised to surrender, but at the last moment he retracted. God, he said, had told him to hang on.

Member Kathy Schroeder, testifying for the prosecution, described what happened in Mt. Carmel after the broadcast. The Davidians were told to gather in the house's cafeteria. The atmosphere, she said, was "joyful." "Everybody was ready to be translated" in the fulfillment of prophecy a final confrontation with Babylon would bring.[10] But Koresh—and God—disappointed them. The Members of the Message had sinned. As soon as the firing stopped they, or many of them, perhaps feeling that all bets were off, had violated the strict dietary rules the Davidians derived from their Seventh-Day Adventist roots. "People [had been] drinking liquor, smoking cigarettes, eating all kinds of junk food."[11] It was an orgy of sin in anticipation of defeat, perhaps. Koresh told the Members that if they had died at that point they would all have gone to hell.

The mainstreams of orthodoxy uniformly condemn suicide, in the ordinary sense. But for these extremists, death was desirable under these conditions. This is not an uncommon idea among devoted believers in a dualistic world and an afterlife. Both Heaven's Gate and Solar Temple followers proclaimed that they longed to depart. Both denied that their suicide was what it appeared to the carnal world; in fact, they said, our refusal of the salvation they offered was self-murder. Religions of much more moderate tone than those considered here have suggested, at least in metaphor, that death to the world is a desirable condition. Monasticism has long been considered a kind of self-destruction in worldly terms, even as it is said to be quite the opposite where God is concerned.

As with most of the ideas and actions we have met in this book, there is little new in the idea of religious suicide, even mass suicide. The Jewish Zealots who opposed Roman rule are a famous example. They had captured the fortress of Masada during a long revolt against Rome in which Jerusalem fell and the Temple was destroyed for the last (or most recent) time. The Zealots at Masada killed themselves in 73 C.E. rather than submit to pagan rule, and the site is something of a shrine to Israelis and others today. The Zealots are considered martyrs to their faith.

In Catholicism martyrdom has rather a different meaning. The church fathers wrote polemics against sectarians who were so eager to win a heavenly reward that they would volunteer for combat in the arena. Some were even said to have bullied passersby into killing them. Voluntary martyrdom has been considered simple suicide ever since, and its practice is heretical to Catholics.

The Order of the Solar Temple (OST) clearly considered themselves martyrs. But in its strict sense, the word means refusing to surrender one's faith on pain of death. That never happened to the OST. No one seemed much to care what they believed, certainly not to the extent of actual persecution. That indifference in itself may have been too much for them to bear.

The world's great crime against the OST that "drove" them to their sacrifice may have been that they were made to look ridiculous. The investigation into arms deals turned up nothing, but Luc Jouret's lectures were
losing popularity and there was talk of exposure both from within and
without. Antonio Dutoit, their stage manager, was threatening to reveal
the stagecraft behind their "miracles." What may have been decisive was
that their leader, Joseph DiMambro, was in failing health and for some
months had suffered a humiliating incontinence.[12] He told some followers
that he was dying of cancer. Whether or not this was true can not be established; his remains were too badly burned for an autopsy to reach a conclusion.

Koresh thought he was dying. Shoko Asahara had been telling his followers for some time that he was about to die from American gas and germ
warfare attacks. In his system failing health was a special mark of holiness.[13]
When he was arrested, first reports were that he was in the best of health,
but it later turned out that he was in fact sick. It seems that he may have
been among the very few casualties of the many germ attacks Aum
mounted on targets in Tokyo, including U.S. military bases.[14] All of them
went completely unnoticed at the time, with the exception of reports of a
"foul odor" following one of them.

Aum too had been ridiculed. Asahara and several of his disciples had lost
a parliamentary election in a particularly humiliating debacle, in which not
even all of Aum's own followers voted for them. The group had begun to
come under press criticism.[15] It was at this point that the kidnaping and
murder of an important opponent and his family was carried out. The opponent had evidence of Asahara's frauds, which the group had to cover up
in self-preservation. The group had become increasingly suspicious of and
hostile to the outside world and renounced its original plans to save all of
humanity from evil. The new goal was just to save Aum itself. It was also
apparent that plans to attract a large number of fully dedicated followers
would fail.

Whereas Asahara had proclaimed that the disasters he foretold could be
averted, he now began to preach that the world would be better off if they
ran their course. His own "divine" presence was still essential to the cause,
and it was clear that his paranoia was increasing. The group began stock-
piling weapons in defense against its powerful opponents. The 1994 sarin

attack in Matsumoto was specifically intended to silence a judge who was expected to rule against Aum in a land dispute.

The Kobe earthquake of January 17, 1995, convinced Asahara that his predictions were accurate: disaster was approaching the Land of the Rising Sun, as one of his book titles predicted. So the group began a campaign of terror that it expected would bring down Japan's government and, perhaps, bring the country to war with America. Asahara set out to fulfill his own prophecies.

But the group attempted no suicide. Unlike Heaven's Gate and the Solar Temple, Aum turned its violence outward.

Violence apparently turns inward when it appears that the center of the movement, its source of divine power, is about to fail. Marshall Applewhite, the leader of the Heaven's Gate group, also told at least one follower that he had cancer and would not live long. This was false, according to autopsy reports, but it seems to have swayed several believers.[16]

Narcissism is rarely absent from charismatic leaders. In fact, it may be a necessary component of the extravagant self-esteem that charisma is largely based on. We have seen Jones's own pronouncements of his divine worth, and one of Do's followers said, "Once he is gone, there is nothing left here on the face of the earth for me, no reason to stay a moment longer." Narcissism goes hand in glove with hypochondria. Sigmund Freud observed as much in his early writings on the subject, where he notes that libido seems to be bi-polar: the more of it one devotes to others, the less there is to spare for the self. He mentioned in this context "the paranoiac's phantasy (or self-perception) of 'the end of the world.'"[17] In Freud's terms, the narcissist's withdrawal into self drives him to perceive the thwarting of his desire as a personal illness, a physical crisis. Freud introduces here an interesting poetic take on the theodicy problem from which the millennium springs. In Heinrich Heine's *Schöpfungsleider* VII the poet imagines God getting sick and creating the universe in order to recover: Creative love is always the road to health, as Applewhite disastrously failed to discover.

The narcissistic and charismatic prophet may conflate external opposition with his own fantasies of destructive illness, creating a lethal fantasy of a doom that will finally save the world. The world will "get the message" from the prophet's own destruction, which it is all to easy to imagine as a the form of martyrdom. But this is martyrdom, not to oppressive forces striving to put an end to the movement's rebellious ideas, but to a world whose intransigence finally defeats the prophet. The world would not hear his message when he was alive to deliver it, so it will reflect in sorrow upon his death. In *Tom Sawyer,* Mark Twain has Tom imagine his own funeral. In a delicious orgy of self-pity, he imagines the mourners weeping their remorse for the injustices they paid him in life. In just this way does the prophet, perhaps, fantasize about the world's regret for his own death.

What humanity cannot be forgiven is its rejection of the message, the divine word of salvation. As DiMambro or one of his associates wrote:

> The Brotherhood has always influenced the major steps of Evolution because of its Presence, its radiance, and its actions. . . . Up to now they have sustained a proper balance between Shadow and Light, what alchemists call *Solve* and *Coagula.* Sadly, it is always and only after they are gone that we can realize, partially and in distorted form, the real meaning of their Message. Especially in this treacherous passage from the Age of Pisces to the Age of Aquarius has humanity rejected their radiant message.[18]

Not only that, humanity rejects the more mundane manifold gifts the movement offers, such as proper diet. The departure is a revenge on humanity's uncaringness. It cannot now escape the horrors of the apocalypse.

Do said precisely this about the world's rejection of his salvation. He had proclaimed his message publicly on three separate occasions, every time encountering typhoons of ridicule. The dramatic suicide was, at least in part, a calculated public relations ploy: The world, he fantasized, would have to attend to and accept his message once its seriousness was disclosed in this final way. He was certainly correct on one point: The world would hear of this extraordinary exit, but would condemn it as cultic excess.

Aum Shinri Kyo was in a similar plight. Having had everything its own way for years, apparently thriving on murder, kidnaping, bribery, and extortion, it was suddenly open to investigation by the government. Asahara had been proclaiming the imminent failure of his own health for some time. ("It's a miracle I'm still alive," he told his followers on at least one radio broadcast.) The leader's actual health is irrelevant, as long as his perceived charisma retains its power, as Asahara's did. His followers' perception of his health and of the strength of their opposition is what is crucial. When they perceive the group to be in extremis, they will rally to the cause.

The Montana Freemen threatened violence and were well equipped to carry it out, yet they conspicuously failed to do so, even in the evident failure of their leaders and extreme external pressure. Leroy Schweitzer, billed as the Freemen's main leader, was arrested even before the standoff began. The difference can be accounted for, I believe, by the absence of charisma. This was a purely political movement with radical but only partly religious millenarian aims. They claimed no divine impulse or sanction, and in fact seem to have been motivated as much by personal greed as any greater aim, despite their biblical rhetoric.[19]

It is possible that Jouret, Applewhite, DiMambro, Koresh, and Asahara were also motivated to some extent by greed, but there is little room to doubt the sincerity of their belief in their own divine election. They seemed totally convinced that they were chosen to serve their own gods and save humanity as neo-Noahs, enarked with their respective remnants on a voyage to paradise and eternal glory. At the very least, most of them made large sacrifices to their causes, none of them under extreme duress: they all could have surrendered. Their loss would doom the world, unless they could enlist the gods to intervene. Asahara, knowing his doom was fraud, could still turn and attack. Perhaps this was a desperate attempt to forestall the inevitable, as the police turned their belated attentions more and more his way; or perhaps he did fully believe in his own proclamations. He might have honestly thought that another disaster, met with as little competence as the Kobe earthquake a few months earlier, would cause the government to fail and bring on the Armageddon he expected. Or perhaps both motives were at work.

Ted Kaczynski, the Unabomber who for nearly twenty years evaded detection as he mailed bombs to his powerful opponents, the technocrats who despoil the planet in his Luddite vision, is perhaps a special case. A nearly total loner with no following, he had no one to convince (except the whole world), no one to support him, and no one aside from himself whose needs for glory he had to feed. Still, his cause exerted its demands. There was no possibility of betrayal except the self-betrayal inherent in his position. Had Kaczynski never published the manifesto that gave him away, he might have stayed at liberty, but his bombings would have been pointless. All terror must serve an explicit purpose, or else it is mere indulgence, like the butchery of serial killers. Silence is the terrorist's defeat, but so is isolation. Without friends, he has no place to hide. Kaczynski's millennium could not resolve this conflict with reality's chaos.

The millennium always strives to reconcile contradictions like this one. It always succeeds, until it must resolve its own defeat. When that is finally inevitable, the apocalypse turns back on itself like Uroboros, the snake of creation that forever swallows its own tail. Suicide or an attack on the world amounts to the same ultimate loss to the world's omnipotent chaos.

Notes

1. Mary McCormick Maaga,"Triple Erasure: Women and Power in Peoples Temple," Ph.D. dissertation, Drew University (Ann Arbor, Mich.: University Microfilms, 1996), 101.

2. Ibid., 132–33.

3. Ibid., 139.

4. Ibid., 166.

5. Dick J. Reavis, *The Ashes of Waco: An Investigation* (Syracuse, N.Y.: Syracuse University Press, 1995), 49.

6. U.S. District Court, Waco, Tex., *United States vs. Branch, et al.,* 1994, docket no. W93-406, p. 4315.

7. Ibid., 4479.

8. Reavis, *The Ashes of Waco,* 215.

9. Ibid., 219.

10. *U.S. vs. Branch,* 4484.

11. Ibid.

12. Massimo Introvigne, personal communication.

13. Asahara blessed Hideo Murai on the occasion of Murai's accession to sainthood within the order with these words: "[H]e did not give in to sleep. Napoleon slept for three hours and napped on his horse. But I have never seen Manjusrimitra [Murai] lie for more than three hours. Moreover, his pulse rate is 46 per minute-an unbelievable count for an ordinary person. It clearly indicates the extreme weakness of his body. Nevertheless, he is still alive. He sees, listens, and manipulates various phenomena repeatedly." From "The Ceremony of Mahayana Yoga Attainment," personal communication from Kohtaro Nishiyama (nishiyam@ucsu.Colorado.EDU), a member of Aum (July 1995).

14. William J. Broad, "How Japan Germ Terror Alerted World," *New York Times,* May 26, 1998, A1–A10.

15. Ian Reader, "Gas Clouds over Tokyo: Aum Shinri Kyo's Path to Violence," *NIAS Nytt: Nordic Newsletter of Asian Studies,* no. 2 (July 1995), archived at http://nias.ku.dk/Nytt/Regional/EastAsia/Articles/aum.html.

16. CNN, "Were Cult Members Misled?" March 30, 1997.

17. Sigmund Freud, "On Narcissism: An Introduction," in *Freud's "On Narcissism: An Introduction,"* ed. Joseph Sandler et al. (New Haven: Yale University Press, 1991), 6.

18. Order of the Solar Temple, "Transit pour le Futur," unpublished.

19. It seems to me particularly telling that this assessment comes from a champion of the Constitutionalist movement, former Colorado State Senator Charles Duke, who was one of the many unsuccessful negotiators during the Freemen standoff. Charles R. Duke, "A Truce to Save Lives." Independence Institute Op-Ed Syndicate, press release, May 29, 1996, archived at http://i2i.org/SuptDocs/OpEdArcv/Op052996.htm.

WORKS CITED

"About the Trilateral Commission." http://www.trilateral.org/MoreInfo/ABOUT.htm. June 27, 1998.

al-Ghazali. *The Remembrance of Death and the Afterlife*. Book 40 of *The Revival of the Religious Sciences*. Translated by T. J. Winter. Cambridge: Islamic Texts Society, 1989.

Amano, Jack. "Enter the Red Dragon: How Japanese Politicians Used Aum to Penetrate the Kremlin." *Archipelago*, http://www.pelago.com/0101/story2.html. July 1, 1996.

Ammerman, Nancy. "Waco, Federal Law Enforcement, and Scholars of Religion." In Stuart A. Wright, ed., *Armageddon in Waco: Critical Perspectives on the Branch Davidian Conflict*. Chicago: University of Chicago Press, 1996.

"And the Stars Shall Fall from Heaven." Posted by Dave.Tilbury@UK.Sun.COM (David Tilbury—Sun UK) to iufo@world.std.com, mmlist-l@newciv.org. Subject: The Church of Christ—1310 Broadway—Oak Grove—MO—64075—U.S.A. November 20, 1996.

Archipelago. http://www.pelago.com/Aumpedia/gospelofMatthew.html. April 25, 1996.

———. http://www.pelago.com/Aumpedia/susanSontag.html. April 25, 1996.

"Art Bell—BLOW OUT." Posted by "Steve Wingate" to iufo@world.std.com. November 29, 1996.

Asahara, Shoko. *Disaster Approaches the Land of the Rising Sun*. Shizuoka, Japan: Aum Publishing Co., 1995.

Ashlag, Yehuda, and Philip S. Berg. *An Entrance to the Tree of Life*. New York: Research Center of Kabbalah, 1977.

"Ask the Rabbi" no. 149. Ohr Somayach, Jerusalem. http://www.virtual.co.il/education/education/ohr/ask/ask149.htm.

"Attention Lightworkers: Mass Landings Information (fwd), Excerpts from Sheldon Nidle Lecture Series #6." Posted by Wolf359 (Jabriol@cris.com) to Issues@catalina.org. November 15, 1996.

Aum Shinri Kyo. "Buddhism Encompasses Christianity." http://www.aum-shinrikyo.com/english/index.htm/buddhism.htm. October 4, 1998.

———. "The Ceremony of Mahayana Yoga Attainment." Personal communication from Kohtaro Nishiyama (nishiyam@ucsu.Colorado.edu). July 1995. Unpublished.

———. "Guru Is Your Defense Lawyer at the Judgment after Death." http://www.aum-shinrikyo.com/english/index.htm/13-7.htm. October 4, 1998.

Aum Shinri Kyo. "How to Live during the Time of Radical Changes." http://www.aum-shinrikyo.com/english/index.htm/changes.htm. October 4, 1998.

———. "The Intrigue behind Information." http://www.aum-shinrikyo.com/english/index.htm/matter6.htm. October 4, 1998.

———. "Materialism—The Sermon of the Devil." http://www.aum-shinrikyo.com/english/index.htm/matter2.htm. October 4, 1998.

———. "Preparing for the Appearance of Christ at the End of the Century." http://www.aum-shinrikyo.com/english/index.htm/christ.htm. October 4, 1998.

———. "What Is Our Essence?" http://www.aum-shinrikyo.com/english/index.htm/11-2.htm. October 4, 1998.

———. "What Is Samadhi?" http://www.aum-shinrikyo.com/english/index.htm/11-20.htm. October 4, 1998.

———. "Where Do Extraterrestrial Come From?" http://www.aum-shinrikyo.com/english/index.htm/11-10.htm. October 4, 1998.

———. "World War III Is Coming Soon: The Control of Plasma." http://www.aum-shinrikyo.com/english/index.htm/plasma.htm. October 4, 1998

Avineri, Shlomo. *The Social and Political Thought of Karl Marx.* Cambridge: Cambridge University Press, 1996.

Balch, Robert, and David Taylor. "Seekers and Saucers: The Role of the Cultic Milieu in Joining a UFO Cult." *American Behavioral Scientist* 20, 6 (1977): 839–60.

Balch, Robert W. "Waiting for the Ships: Disillusion and the Revitalization of Faith in Bo and Peep's UFO Cult." In James R. Lewis, ed., *The Gods Have Landed: New Religions from Other Worlds.* Albany: State University of New York Press, 1995.

Barclay, Harold B. "Muslim 'Prophets' in the Modern Sudan." *Muslim World* 54 (1964): 250–55.

Barkun, Michael. *Religion and the Racist Right: The Origins of the Christian Identity Movement.* Chapel Hill: University of North Carolina Press, 1996.

Barnes, Douglas F. "Charisma and Religious Leadership: An Historical Analysis." *Journal for the Scientific Study of Religion* 17 (1978): 1–17.

"A Bavarian Illuminati Primer." http://www.bc-freemasonry.com/Writings/Illuminati.html. June 27, 1998.

"Bilderbergers Found Again: Meeting Scheduled in Eastern Canada." *The Spotlight* 22, no. 20 (May 20, 1996): 1.

Boyce, Mary. *Zoroastrians: Their Religious Beliefs and Practices.* London: Routledge and Kegan Paul, 1987.

Boyer, Paul. *When Time Shall Be No More: Prophecy Belief in Modern American Culture.* Cambridge: Belknap Press, 1992.

Broad, William J. "How Japan Germ Terror Alerted World." *New York Times,* May 26, 1998, A1–A10.

Broyles, Paul. "A Brief History of the Branch Davidian Seventh Day Adventist." http://www.geocities.com/CapitolHill/Senate/1400/koresh1.html. March 26, 1998.

The Bundahishn, or Knowledge from the Zand. Volume 5 of *Sacred Books of the East.* Translated by E. W. West. Oxford: Oxford University Press, 1897.

Campion, Nicholas. *The Great Year: Astrology, Millenarism, and History on the Western Tradition.* New York: Penguin, 1994.

Chandler, David L. "Close Calls from Comets on the Rise." *Boston Globe,* November 10, 1996, A12.

"Children of Heaven's Gate Co-Founder Struggle for Answers." http://www.nando.net/newsroom/nt/331sons.html. April 16, 1997.

Class, The. "Beyond Human—The Last Call—Session 4." http://www.washingtonpost.com/wp-srv/national/longterm/cult/timeline.htm.

———. "Beyond Human—The Last Call—Session 5." http://www.washingtonpost.com/wp-srv/national/longterm/cult/timeline.htm. April 8, 1998.

———. "'88 Update—The UFO Two and Their Crew: A Brief Synopsis." http://www.washingtonpost.com/wp-srv/national/longterm/cult/timeline.htm. July 18, 1998.

———. "First Statement of Ti and Do, Sent out from Ojai, California, March 1975." http://www.washingtonpost.com/wp-srv/national/longterm/cult/timeline.htm. July 18, 1998.

———. "Major and Lesser Offences." http://www.washingtonpost.com/wp-srv/national/longterm/cult/timeline.htm.

———. "Our Position against Suicide." July 18, 1998. http://www.washingtonpost.com/wp-srv/national/longterm/cult/timeline.htm. July 18, 1998.

———. "Overview of Present Mission." http://www.washingtonpost.com/wp-srv/national/longterm/cult/timeline.htm. July 18, 1998.

Cohn, Norman. *Cosmos, Chaos, and the World to Come.* New Haven: Yale University Press, 1993.

———. "Medieval Millenarianism: Its Bearing on the Comparative Study of Millenarian Movements." In Charles B. Strozier and Michael Flynn, eds., *The Year 2000: Essays on the End.* New York: New York University Press, 1997.

———. "Medieval Millenarism: Its Bearing on the Comparative Study of Millenarian Movements." In Sylvia L. Thrupp, ed., *Millennial Dreams in Action.* The Hague: Mouton, 1962.

Conze, Edward, ed. *Buddhist Scriptures.* New York: Penguin, 1959.

Crim, Kenneth, ed. *The Perennial Dictionary of World Religions.* San Francisco: Harper, 1981.

Dalrymple, James. "The Day Mighty Japan Lost Its Nerve." *Sunday Times Magazine* (London), August 13, 1995. Archived at irdial@irdialsys.win-uk.net.

Daniel, David. "The Beginning of the Journey." *Time,* April 14, 1997, 36–37.

De Armond, Paul. "Christian Patriots at War with the State." http://nwcitizen.com/publicgood/reports/belief/. October 8, 1998.

Do. "Do's Intro: Purpose—Belief. What Our Purpose Is—The Simple 'Bottom Line.'" http://www.washingtonpost.com/wp-srv/national/longterm/cult/timeline.htm. July 18, 1998.

Duke, Charles R. "A Truce to Save Lives." Independence Institute Op-Ed Syndicate, press release, May 29, 1996. Archived at http://i2i.org/SuptDocs/OpEdArcv/Op052996.htm, October 18, 1996.

Dyer, Joel. *Harvest of Rage: Why Oklahoma City Is Only the Beginning.* Boulder, Colo.: Westview Press, 1997.

Eliade, Mircea. *A History of Religious Ideas,* vol. 1, *From the Stone Age to the Eleusinian Mysteries.* Translated by Willard R. Trask. Chicago: University of Chicago Press, 1978.

———. *A History of Religious Ideas,* vol. 2, *From Gautama Buddha to the Triumph of Christianity.* Translated by Willard R. Trask. Chicago: University of Chicago Press, 1978.

"European History and Culture: The Great Age of Monarchy, 1648–1789: The Enlightenment" Britannica Online, at http://www.eb.com:180/cgi-bin/g?DocF=macro/5002/20/136.html. September 20, 1998.

"Exhibition Features Führer's World View." Associated Press, August 6, 1998.

Fest, Joachim. *Hitler.* San Diego: Harcourt Brace Jovanovich, 1974.

Foreman, Dave. *Confessions of an Eco-Warrior.* New York: Harmony, 1991.

Freud, Sigmund. "On Narcissism: An Introduction." In Joseph Sandler et al., eds., *Freud's "On Narcissism: An Introduction."* New Haven: Yale University Press, 1991.

Friedland, William H. "For a Sociological Concept of Charisma." *Social Forces* 43, no. 1 (1964): 23–24.

Friedrich, Otto. *The End of the World: A History.* New York: Fromm International, 1986.

Frost, Gregory. "Cult Connections." *Ansible* 117, http://www.dcs.gla.ac.uk/SF-Archives/Ansible/a117.htmlIIHale-Bopp. April 1997.

Glnody. "Warning: For Those Who Are Prone to Hasty Judgments." http://www.washingtonpost.com/wp-srv/national/longterm/cult/timeline.htm. July 18, 1998.

Griffin, Jasper. "New Heaven, New Earth." Review of *Cosmos, Chaos, and the World to Come* by Norman Cohn. *New York Review of Books,* December 22, 1994, 23–28.

"Hale-Bopp Anomalies." Posted by deleted@ast.cam.ac.uk to Joe LeSesne (raver187@m-net.arbornet.edu). December 3, 1996.

"Hale-Bopp Brings Closure to Heaven's Gate." http://www.washingtonpost.com/wp-srv/national/longterm/cult/timeline.htm. April 8, 1998.

"Hale-Bopp Image Showing Second Object." Posted by "Steve Wingate" to anomalous-images@world.std.com. November 17, 1996.

"Hale-Bopp Object Confirmed by Leading Astrophysicist." Forwarded by anomalous-images-approval@world.std.com. November 29, 1996.

Hall, John R., and Philip Schuyler. "The Mystical Apocalypse of the Solar Temple." In Thomas Robbins and Susan L. Palmer, eds., *Millennium, Messiahs, and Mayhem: Contemporary Apocalyptic Movements*. New York: Routledge, 1997.

Hannaford, Ivan. *Race: The History of an Idea in the West*. Washington, D.C., and Baltimore: Woodrow Wilson Center Press and Johns Hopkins University Press, 1996.

Hill, Michael Ortiz. *Dreaming the End of the World: Apocalypse as a Rite of Passage*. Dallas: Spring Publications, 1994.

Hitler, Adolf. *Mein Kampf*. Translated by Ralph Manheim. Boston: Houghton Mifflin, 1971.

———. *Sämtliche Aufzeichnungen 1905–1924*. Edited by Eberhard Jäckel. Translated by Richard S. Levy. Stuttgart: Deutsche Verlags-Anstalt 1980.

Hofstadter, Richard. *The Paranoid Style in American Politics and Other Essays*. Cambridge: Harvard University Press, 1965.

Hooker, Richard. "Imam." World Cultures Home Page, http://www.wsu.edu:8000/~dee/GLOSSARY/IMAM.htm. March 18, 1998.

"Huge Object Suddenly Appears Next to Hale Bopp." Posted by Kent Steadman (phikent@ix.netcom.com) to iufo@world.std.com. Subject: Here comes Nibiru? November 15, 1996.

Jakes, Dale, et al. *False Prophets: The Firsthand Account of a Husband and Wife Working for the FBI and Living in Deepest Cover with the Montana Freemen*. Los Angeles: Dove Books, 1998.

James, William. *The Varieties of Religious Experience: A Study in Human Nature*. New York: Collier, 1961.

Jameson, Frederic. "Metacommentary." In *The Ideology of Theory Essays, 1971–1986*. Minneapolis: University of Minnesota Press, 1988.

Johnson, Paul Doyle. "Dilemmas of Charismatic Leadership: The Case of the People's Temple." *Sociological Analysis* 40, no. 4 (1979): 315–23.

"Kala Jñana." http://www.wp.com/KalaJñana/. July 7, 1998.

Kamenka, Eugene. "Introduction." In Eugene Kamenka, ed., *The Portable Karl Marx*. New York: Penguin, 1983.

Kaplan, Jeffrey. *Radical Religion in America: Millenarian Movements from the Far Right to the Children of Noah*. Syracuse, N.Y.: Syracuse University Press, 1997.

Keller, Catherine. "The Breast, the Apocalypse, and the Colonial Journey." In Charles B. Strozier and Michael Flynn, eds., *The Year 2000: Essays on the End*. New York: New York University Press, 1997.

———. *Apocalypse Now and Then: A Feminist Guide to the End of the World*. Boston: Beacon Press, 1996.

Kendall, Henry. "Warning Issued on November 18, 1992." http://deoxy.org/sciwarn.htm. March 13, 1998.

Kinzer, Stephen. "'Love Letters' to Hitler, a Book and Play Shocking to Germans." *New York Times,* May 25, 1995, A6.

Lacayo, Richard. "Cults: In the Reign of Fire." *Time,* October 17, 1994. Archived at http://www.rickross.com/reference/S_Groups5.html.

Laceky, Tom. "FreeMen [*sic*] Verdict." Associated Press, March 31, 1998. Archived at http://209.67.114.212/forum/a159862.htm.

Lamont, William. *Godly Rule: Politics and Religion, 1603–60.* London: Macmillan 1969.

Lamy, Philip. "Secularizing the Millennium: Survivalists, Militias, and the New World Order." In Thomas Robbins and Susan J. Palmer, eds., *Millennium, Messiahs, and Mayhem: Contemporary Apocalyptic Movements.* New York: Routledge, 1997.

Landes, Richard. "The Apocalyptic Year 1000: Millennium Fever and the Origins of the Modern West." In Charles B. Strozier and Michael Flynn, eds., *The Year 2000: Essays on the End.* New York: New York University Press, 1997.

Lanternari, Vittorio. *The Religions of the Oppressed: A Study of Modern Messianic Movements.* New York: Alfred A. Knopf, 1963.

Lee, Martha F. *Earth First!: Environmental Apocalypse.* Syracuse, N.Y.: Syracuse University Press, 1995.

Library of Congress. "The Evolution of the Conservation Movement 1850–1920." http://lcweb2.loc.gov/ammem/amrvhtml/conshome.html. September 30, 1998.

Lifton, Robert Jay. "Reflections on Aum Shinrikyo." In Charles B. Strozier and Michael Flynn, eds., *The Year 2000: Essays on the End.* New York: New York University Press, 1997.

Long, Theodore E. "Prophecy, Charisma and Politics: Reinterpreting the Weberian Hypothesis." In Jeffrey K. Hadden and Anson D. Shupe, eds., *Prophetic Religions and Politics: Religion and the Political Order,* vol. 1. New York: Paragon House, 1986.

Lucas, Phillip C. "The New Age Movement and the Pentecostal/Charismatic Revival." In James R. Lewis and J. Gordon Melton, eds., *Perspectives on the New Age.* Albany: State University of New York Press, 1992.

Maaga, Mary McCormick. "Triple Erasure: Women and Power in Peoples Temple." Ph.D. dissertation, Drew University, 1996. Ann Arbor, Mich.: University Microfilms, 1996.

Mackey, Albert G. *Encyclopedia of Freemasonry.* Richmond, Va.: Macoy Publishing, 1966.

Marx, Karl. *The Communist Manifesto.* Edited by Frederic L. Bender. New York: W. W. Norton, 1988.

McGinn, Bernard. *Antichrist: Two Thousand Years of the Human Fascination with Evil.* San Francisco: Harper, 1994.

Miller, William Ian. *The Anatomy of Disgust.* Cambridge: Harvard University Press, 1997.

"Miraculous Rosary." Posted by Name@withheld.com to marian@mail.catholicity.com. July 19, 1998.

Mooney, James. *The Ghost-Dance Religion and the Sioux Outbreak of 1890.* Edited by A. F. C. Wallace. New York: Dover, 1973.

Muhyiddin Ibn 'Arabi. Translated by James Morris. In Michael Chodkiewicz, ed. *Les Illuminations de la Mecque/The Meccan Illuminations.* Paris, Sindbad, 1989.

Naess, Arne. "The Shallow and the Deep, Long-Range Ecology Movement: A Summary." *Inquiry* 16 (1973): 95.

Namgyal, Takpo Tashi. *Mahamudra: The Quintesssence of Mind and Meditation.* Translated by Lobsang P. Lhalungpa. Boston: Shambhala, 1986.

Negabahn, D. Josiah. "Muhammad al-Mahdi." World Cultures Home Page, http://www.wsu.edu:8000/~dee/GLOSSARY/IMAM.htm. March 18, 1998.

———. "Sh'i." *Encyclopedia of the Orient,* 1997, http://i-cias.com/e.o/. March 18, 1998.

Neiwert, David. "Patriot Spring: Showdown in Big Sky Country." Pacific Rim News Service, http://www.militia-watchdog.org/contrib.htm/neiwert1.htm. October 8, 1898.

Nomura, Yoshihiko. "Where AUM Shinrikyo Is Coming From." *Kansai Forum,* no. 20 (June–July 1995). Archived at http://www.notredame.ac.jp/POETS/IBH/KansaiForum/20/Aum.html.

Ohr Somayach, "Ask the Rabbi." No. 149, http://www.virtual.co.il/education/education/ohr/ask/ask149.htm.

O'Leary, Stephen. *Arguing the Apocalypse: A Theory of Millennial Rhetoric.* New York: Oxford University Press, 1994.

"One-Time Cult Member Explains Mysteries of Castration, Bills." Associated Press, April 6, 1997. Archived at http://www.trancenet.org/heavensgate/news/402.shtml.

Order of the Solar Temple. "Transit pour le Futur." Unpublished.

Pessar, Patricia R. "Millenarian Movements in Rural Brazil: Prophecy and Protest." *Religion* 12, 2 (1982): 187–213.

Phelan, James S. "Looking For: The Next World." *New York Times Magazine,* February 29, 1976.

Pitcavage, Mark. "Every Man a King: The Rise and Fall of the Montana Freemen." http://www.militia-watchdog.org/freemen.htm. April 4, 1998.

Pitts, William L., Jr. "Davidians and Branch Davidians 1929–1987." In Stuart A. Wright, ed., *Armageddon in Waco: Critical Perspectives on the Branch Davidian Conflict.* Chicago: University of Chicago Press, 1995.

"Press Release." http://www.ccnet.com/~suntzu75/pirn9735.htm. June 28, 1998.

Prophe-Zine, no. 28 (October 18, 1996).

Ravenscroft, Trevor. *Spear of Destiny.* New York: Samuel Weiser, 1987.

Reader, Ian. "Gas Clouds over Tokyo: Aum Shinri Kyo's Path to Violence." *NIAS Nytt: Nordic Newsletter of Asian Studies,* no. 2 (July 1995). Archived at http://nias.ku.dk/Nytt/Regional/EastAsia/Articles/aum.html.

Reavis, Dick J. *The Ashes of Waco: An Investigation.* Syracuse, N.Y.: Syracuse University Press, 1995.

Robinson, Wendy Gale. "Heaven's Gate: The End?" http://jcmc.huji.ac.il/vol3/issue3/robinson.html. April 10, 1998.

Roland, Jon. *Law and Antilaw,* San Antonio: Constitution Society, n.d.

Rudolph, Kurt. *Gnosis: The Nature and History of Gnosticism.* New York: Harper and Row, 1987.

Sachedina, Abdulazziz Abdulhussein. *Islamic Messanism.* Albany: State University of New York Press, 1981.

Sadra', Mulla (Sadr al-Din al-Shirazi). *The Wisdom of the Throne: An Introduction to the Philosophy of Mulla Sadra.* Translated by James Morris. Princeton: Princeton University Press, 1981.

Scholem, Gershom G. *The Messianic Idea in Judaism and Other Essays in Jewish Spirituality.* New York: Schocken, 1971.

———. *Zohar: The Book of Splendor—Basic Readings from the Kabbalah.* New York: Schocken, 1949.

Schwartz, Hillel. *Centuries' Ends: A Cultural History of the Fin de Siècle from the 990's through the 1990's.* New York: Doubleday, 1990.

Scott, James C. *Seeing Like a State: How Certain Schemes to Improve the Human Condition Have Failed.* New Haven: Yale University Press, 1998.

Shimatsu, Yoichi Clark. "Judea Cipher: Why Aum's Science Chief Had to Be Silenced." *Archipelago,* http://www.pelago.com/0102/story2.html. July 1, 1996.

———. "Starwars and the Final War: The Life, Death and Secret Weapons Research of Hideo Murai, Science and Technology Minister of Aum Shinrikyo." *Archipelago,* http://www.pelago.com/0102/story2.html. July 1, 1996.

Shipman, Pat. *The Evolution of Racism: Human Differences and the Use and Abuse of Science.* New York: Simon and Schuster, 1994.

Sontag, Susan. "The Imagination of Disaster." In *Against Interpretation,* New York: Farrar, Straus and Giroux, 1966.

Srrody. "Testament by Srrody." http://www.washingtonpost.com/wp-srv/national/longterm/cult/timeline.htm. July 18, 1998.

Staudenmaier, Peter. "Fascist Ideology: The Green Wing of the Nazi Party and Its Historical Antecedents." http://au.spunk.org/texts/places/germany/sp001630/peter.htm. May 6, 1998.

Strozier, Charles B. "Apocalyptic Violence and the Politics of Waco." In Charles B. Strozier and Michael Flynn, eds., *The Year 2000: Essays on the End.* New York: New York University Press, 1997.

———. "God, Lincoln, and the Civil War." In Charles B. Strozier and Michael Flynn, eds., *The Year 2000: Essays on the End.* New York: New York University Press, 1997.

Tabor, James D., and Eugene V. Gallagher. *Why Waco? Cults and the Battle for Religious Freedom in America.* Berkeley: University of California Press, 1995.

Talmon, Yonina. "Millenarianism." In *International Encyclopedia of the Social Sciences,* 10:349–62. New York: Macmillan/Free Press, 1968.

Trompf, Gary, ed. *Cargo Cults and Millenarian Movements: Transoceanic Comparisons of New Religious Movements.* Berlin and New York: Mouton de Gruyter, 1990.

"UFO News Story." http://www.strieber.com/ufonews/bopp5.html.

"UFO News Story. The Hale-Bopp Enigma." Posted by Allen Comstock to snetnews@world.std.com. Subject: Hale-Bopp & Shramek on NBC Web Page. December 4, 1996.

Theobald, Robin. "The Role of Charisma in the Development of Social Movements: Ellen White and the Emergence of Seventh-Day Adventism." *Archives des Sciences Sociales des Religions* 49, no. 1 (1980): 83–100.

Tucker, Robert C. "The Theory of Charismatic Leadership." *Daedalus* 97 (1968): 731–56.

United Sates District Court, Waco, Tex. *United States vs. Brad Eugene Branch, et al.* Docket no. W-93-CR-046. February 1994.

"Waiting for Hale-Bopp—My Plan." Posted by "Name Withheld" to alt.alien.visitors. December 9, 1996.

Wallace, Anthony F. C. "Mazeway Resynthesis: A Bio-Cultural Theory of Religious Inspiration." *Transactions of the New York Academy of Science,* 2d ser., 18, no. 2 (1956): 626–38.

Walzer, Michael. *The Revolution of the Saints: A Study in the Origins of Radical Politics.* Cambridge: Harvard University Press, 1965

Washington, Peter. *Madame Blavatsky's Baboon.* New York: Schocken Books, 1995.

Weishaupt, Adam. *An Improved System of the Illuminati.* Gotha, 1787.

Weiss, Raymond L., and Charles Butterworth, eds. *Ethical Writings of Maimonides.* New York: Dover Publications, 1975.

"Were Cult Members Misled?" CNN, March 30, 1997.

Wessinger, Catherine. *When the Millennium Comes Violently.* Forthcoming.

Wilder, Amos N. "The Rhetoric of Ancient and Modern Apocalypse." *Interpretations* 25 (1971): 436–53.

Worsley, Peter. *The Trumpet Shall Sound: A Study of "Cargo" Cults in Melanesia.* New York: Schocken, 1968.

Yates, Frances A. *Giordano Bruno and the Hermetic Tradition.* Chicago: University of Chicago Press, 1964.

INDEX

ABOUT THE AUTHOR

Ted Daniels is a folklorist and the author of *Millennialism: An International Bibliography* (New York, N.Y.: Garland Publishing, 1992). He is also the founder and director of the Millennium Watch Institute, a clearinghouse on ideas of global change and the people who promote them. The institute's collection of prophetic and predictive ephemera is housed at the University of Pennsylvania.